Virginia Woolf and the Literature of the English Renaissance

ALICE FOX

CLARENDON PRESS · OXFORD
1990

Oxford University Press, Walton Street, Oxford OX2 6DP

Oxford New York Toronto
Delhi Bombay Calcutta Madras Karachi
Petaling Jaya Singapore Hong Kong Tokyo
Nairobi Dar es Salaam Cape Town
Melbourne Auckland
and associated companies in
Berlin Ibadan

Oxford is a trade mark of Oxford University Press

Published in the United States
by Oxford University Press, New York

British Library Cataloguing in Publication Data
Fox, Alice
Virginia Woolf and the literature of the English Renaissance.
1. Fiction in English. Woolf, Virginia 1882-1941
I. Title 823'.912
ISBN 0-19-812988-2

Library of Congress Cataloging in Publication Data
Fox Alice, d. 1988.
Virginia Woolf and the literaure of the English Renaissance
Alice Fox.
p. cm. Bibliography: p. Includes index
1. Woolf, Virginia, 1882-1941—Knowledge—Literature. 2. English
literature—Early modern, 1500-1700—History and criticism.
3. Criticism—England—History—20th century. 4. Renaissance in Literature. I. Title.
PR6045.072Z643 1990
823'.912—dc20 89-8849
ISBN 0-19-812988-2

Typeset by Burns and Smith, Derby

Printed and bound in
Great Britain by Bookcraft Ltd.,
Midsomer Norton, Bath

VIRGINIA WOOLF
AND THE
LITERATURE OF THE
ENGLISH RENAISSANCE

Virginia Woolf, etching by Francis Dodd R.A.,
Private Collection.

To
Chris and Genevra

ACKNOWLEDGEMENTS

I WISH to thank Quentin Bell for permission to quote from the manuscripts and works of Virginia Woolf.

The following libraries have been most helpful: New York Public Library (Berg Collection), the University of Sussex Library, Cambridge University Library, the British Library, and the University of London Library.

I appreciate grants-in-aid from the Miami University Research Committee.

I wish also to thank the following people for various assistance: Margaret Barrier, Louise De Salvo, Anne Koehler, David Mann, Jane Marcus, Ruth and Alton Sanders, Brenda Silver, Lola Szladits, Constance and Heanon Wilkins.

To Frank Jordan and Josephine O'Brien Schaefer, who read the manuscripts and made valuable suggestions, I am most grateful.

A.F.

Regrettably, Professor Fox died during preparation of this book for the Press.

CONTENTS

ABBREVIATIONS

The following abbreviations of works by Virginia Woolf are used in the text. A full list of her works referred to in the text can be found in the bibliography.

'Anon.' ' "Anon" and "The Reader": Virginia Woolf's Last Essays', ed. Brenda Silver, *Twentieth Century Literature*, 25 (1979), 356–441.

AEFR Articles, essays, fiction, and reviews (Berg).

BA *Between the Acts* (New York: Harcourt-Harvest, 1941).

BA TS *Between the Acts*, typescript dated 2 Apr. 1938–30 July 1939.

B&P *Books and Portraits: Some Further Selections from the Literary and Biographical Writings of Virginia Woolf*, ed. Mary Lyon (London: Hogarth, 1977).

CE *Collected Essays*, ed. Leonard Woolf (4 vols.; New York: Harcourt, 1967).

CW *Contemporary Writers*, ed. Jean Guiguet (New York: Harcourt-Harvest, 1965).

D. *The Diary of Virginia Woolf*, ed. Anne Olivier Bell (5 vols.; New York: Harcourt, 1977–84).

'ELR' 'The Elizabethan Lumber Room' (1925), in *CE*.

EN Early Notebooks: various holograph notebooks, dated 1897 and later (Berg).

hol. Holograph drafts (all at Berg except *Mrs. D.* and *Orlando*).

I-XXVI Holograph reading notebooks (Berg).

HRN/*N&D* Holograph reading notes, Jan. 1909–Mar. 1911; at back of *Night and Day*, Chaps. 11–17, holograph draft.

JR *Jacob's Room* (New York: Harcourt-Harvest, 1923).

L. *The Letters of Virginia Woolf*, ed. Nigel Nicolson and Joanne Trautman (6 vols.; New York: Harcourt, 1975–80).

MB *Moments of Being: Unpublished Autobiographical Writings*, ed. Jeanne Schulkind (New York: Harcourt, 1976).

MHP Monk's House Papers (Sussex).

Mrs. D. *Mrs. Dalloway* (New York: Harcourt, 1925).

Mrs. D. Corr. *Mrs. Dalloway* (corrections). Holograph, in notebook dated 22 Nov., 1924 (Berg).

Mrs. D. Frag.	*Mrs. Dalloway.* Fragments (Berg).
MS 51,044	*Mrs. Dalloway* holograph, British Library Additional MS 51,044.
MS 51,046	*Mrs. Dalloway* holograph, British Library Additional MS 51,046.
N&D	*Night and Day* (New York: Harcourt-Harvest/HBJ, 1920).
Orl.	*Orlando: A Biography* (New York: Harcourt-Harvest/HBJ, 1928).
'Pargiters'	'The Pargiters' (8 vols.; holograph draft (Berg)).
Room	*A Room of One's Own* (New York: Harcourt, 1929).
'Sir T.B.'	'Sir Thomas Browne', *Times Literary Supplement*, 28 June 1923, 436.
3Gs	*Three Guineas* (New York: Harcourt, 1938).
TL	*To the Lighthouse* (New York: Harcourt, 1927).
VO	*The Voyage Out* (New York: Doran, 1920; New York: Harcourt-Harvest, 1948).
Waves	*The Waves* (New York: Harcourt-Harvest/HBJ, 1931).
Waves Hol.	*The Waves: The Two Holograph Drafts*, ed. J. W. Graham (Toronto: University of Toronto Press, 1976).
W&W	*Women and Writing*, ed. Michelle Barrett (New York: Harcourt-Harvest/HBJ, 1979).
Years	*The Years* (New York: Harcourt-Harvest/HBJ, 1937).

1

Introduction

BETWEEN 1907 and 1908 Virginia Stephen posed, book in hand, for the artist Francis Dodd. If her willingness to submit to having a likeness drawn was uncharacteristic, there is nothing out of the way in her holding a book. She was always reading—plays, novels, poetry, and a certain range of non-ficton. By the time she posed for the picture, she had become a professional reader: she was reviewing books for both the *Times Literary Supplement* and the *Cornhill Magazine* (once edited by her father, Sir Leslie Stephen). And she had begun her first novel, *The Voyage Out* (1915; American edition, 1920), a book that is among other things a record of her own reading. She ranged widely, but by the first decade of the century had 'gone through' Elizabethan literature especially 'with some thoroughness'; and throughout her life she returned to the classics with 'that absolute certainty of delight which breathes through us when we come back again to *Comus*, or *Lycidas*, *Urne Burial*, or *Antony and Cleopatra*'. In the great works of the Renaissance were qualities not found in contemporary literature, 'and there is a complete finality about them' (*CE* ii. 35, 39–40).

Woolf read the classics very often, sometimes with no thought whatever of writing about them, sometimes with a critical essay in view. She devoted two major essays to the early modern English period in her first collection, *The Common Reader*, 'The Elizabethan Lumber Room', and 'Notes on an Elizabethan Play'. Some of the general essays also contain important statements ('The Patron and the Crocus', for example). She continued throughout her life to write about the period in reviews of new editions that occasionally came her way, and in critical essays. The second *Common Reader* begins with three major studies, 'The Strange Elizabethans', 'Donne after Three Centuries', and 'The Countess of Pembroke's Arcadia'; and its concluding essay, 'How Should One Read a Book?', is heavy with English Renaissance writers. Towards the end of her life Woolf was writing a history of English literature, for which she read a large number of primary and

secondary sources on medieval and Elizabethan life and literature
(Silver 93); and she was drafting an essay on the Elizabethans at the
time of her death. Furthermore, every single one of her nine novels
treats the English Renaissance in some way, occasionally using the
period for setting, but more often in direct reference or allusion.

A special set of circumstances, some positive and some negative,
helped form the writer who thus harped on the early modern English
period. For, in addition to a basic attraction to the great age of English
literature that most readers feel, certain personal relationships and
circumstances also turned her towards the sixteenth and seventeenth
centuries. The most important of the circumstances was her sense of
inadequacy owing to her lack of a formal education. She had never been
to school; and her attempts to learn the classical languages and some
history lacked the continuity and rigour experienced by those who were
fortunate enough to proceed through the normal sequence of formal
education. The pose for the Dodd portrait, book in hand, suggests the
compensatory reading that she undertook. Since from her earliest years
and throughout her life Virginia Stephen and Virginia Woolf never felt
educated, she craved what could be learnt from books. She was already
set on a rigorous course of reading by the time of the first diary, when
she was fifteen. The sheer numbers are impressive, and the difficulty of
the works might have staggered readers years her senior (De Salvo in
Marcus, *Virginia* 78–108). She was not staggered; but neither was she
satisfied. She always seemed to feel that, although she might eventually
learn something, at the present moment she knew little, and more
reading was called for. She was a ship blocked by ice that only the heat
of her mind could melt (EN 7 Aug. 1899, 8), and she was not always
sanguine abouts its temperature (EN 30 June–1 Oct. 1903, 38–9). Often
when she tried to read a book she gave up because she felt that as a
woman she had no rights. The analysis of great literature, literature
written by men, was the prerogative of men, not women. Men were
properly educated, as they demonstrated by their ability to write
literary criticism. Ironically, the very man who had encouraged her in
her reading, Leslie Stephen, probably had inadvertently created an
atmosphere that she found too vexed to read in (39).

Virginia Stephen's father was one of the major men of letters of the
nineteenth century, with books on eighteenth-century thought and
literature, mountaineering, and biographies. He wrote hundreds of
articles for the *Dictionary of National Biography*, which he edited from
its inception until 1891. Among his many literary essays are pieces on

Shakespeare, Bacon, Donne, Sir Thomas Browne, Massinger, and Lord
Herbert of Cherbury. His essay entitled 'Did Shakespeare Write
Bacon?' (1901) is not only a clever spoof of the enormous Bacon
industry, but also a slight but pleasant consideration of the *Advancement
of Learning*. Of paramount importance is his authorship of five volumes
in the English Men of Letters series (on Pope, George Eliot, Hobbes,
Samuel Johnson, and Swift). His literary criticism came to seem, in the
years following his death, at least as important as his biographical and
historical writing; and now it is thought that, 'except for Matthew
Arnold, no other Victorian produced so large a body of distinguished
criticism' (Ullmann 11).

Stephen's was a standard that Woolf could aim for, and her father had
inculcated in her certain principles that would at least keep extraneous
matters from interfering with her judgement:

To read what one liked because one liked it, never to pretend to admire what one
did not—that was his only lesson in the art of reading. To write in the fewest
possible words, as clearly as possible, exactly what one meant—that was his
only lesson in the art of writing. (*CE* iv. 80)

Yet Woolf was ambivalent towards the man whose excellent advice she
accepted. From one point of view she knew that Leslie Stephen was an
excellent model as a critic, 'extremely truthful, serious, and aware of the
lasting side of life' (letter 3484a in Banks 199). She greatly admired 'his
love of books and literature' and 'the way in which he had guided her
first steps into the library'. But she could not help noticing that he often
failed to practise what he preached. Leonard Woolf reports that his wife
rather violently criticized 'the narrow Victorian morality which warped
[Stephen's] literary judgement of writers' (*Hours* 8). Woolf's tribute to
her father's injunctions to read what one likes and to write with
economy and clarity ends with the observation that 'All the rest must be
learnt for oneself'. The process, difficult in itself, was not made easier
by the haphazard informality of her education.

Julia Stephen had attempted to give her daughters the rudiments of
'Latin, history and French, while Leslie took the children in
mathematics . . .' (Bell i. 26). After Julia's death, when Virginia was
thirteen, her father tried to teach them.

The temperament of 'the hoop that must go at full speed or drop' is hardly that
of a judicious governess, and racing pace is not the pace for young minds.
Stephen . . . was grieved when he was told, as he had to be told, that his
anxious and self-sacrificing solicitude was doing harm. But, like the eminently

reasonable man that he was, he took the proffered advice, and then all went well. All went better every year. His daughters grew up, his sons went to public schools and then to Cambridge . . .

Stephen's friend and biographer, Frederic William Maitland, who wrote those words (477), clearly did not sense the irony in the sons being educated while their sisters remained at home, growing up. But Leslie Stephen simply did not believe in formal education for women, whereas he saw to it that his sons enjoyed the full benefits of 'the patriarchal machinery', public schooling followed by the university. 'Father laid enormous stress upon schoolmasters' reports, upon scholarships, triposes and fellowships' ('Sketch', *MB* 132). None of these was part of Virginia Stephen's own life, while they formed the minds of her brothers and their friends.

In the last year of her life Virginia Woolf looked back to the time when she herself had begun a career as a novelist and critic. All the men who had made names for themselves, with the exception of D. H. Lawrence, 'came of the middle class, and were educated at public schools and universities'. They were 'raised above the mass of people upon a tower of . . . gold—that is their expensive education'; and their education made possible their fine books (*CE* ii. 168). In contrast, Virgina Woolf's tower was 'a mere toadstool, about six inches high', consisting of the books she read (*L.* 3686, 2 Feb. 1941). Reading without training simply was not enough:

A boy brought up alone in a library turns into a bookworm; brought up alone in the fields he turns into an earthworm. To breed the kind of butterfly a writer is you must let him sun himself for three or four years at Oxford or Cambridge . . . he has to be taught his art . . . taught it by about eleven years of education—at private schools, public schools, and universities. (*CE* ii. 169)

Education had richly prepared the mind of every man of any importance to Virginia Woolf: Leslie, Adrian, and Thoby Stephen; Lytton Strachey; Clive Bell; E. M. Forster; and of course Leonard Woolf. Leonard contrasted his wife's approach to life with his own: she was a 'silly', he 'a born intellectual' (*Sowing* 56, 70). 'Sillies' were 'people who had extraordinarily little [facade], who seemed wonderfully direct, simple, spiritually unveiled. They may be highly intelligent and intellectual, but this nakedness of the soul gives them always a streak of the simpleton' (56). Leonard's education was not blameless, but he did develop skills that Virginia simply could not count on in herself. Under the tutelage of a Mr Floyd (the name of Jacob's tutor in *Jacob's Room*),

Leonard learned arithmetic so well that when he went to school he was 'quicker than most boys in manipulating figures . . .' (47). Virginia, on the other hand, learned what arithmetic she could from her irascible father, who frequently lost his temper. The result: 'Virginia continued throughout her life to count on her fingers' (Bell i. 26). Leonard's education at the 'Spartan' St Paul's School enabled him to translate both Greek and Latin at sight by the time he went to Cambridge (62). These were the two languages on which Virginia concentrated. She learnt enough to read both with enjoyment, although she appreciated having a translation by her side. Neither of the classical languages was 'part of the permanent furniture' of her mind as they were of Leonard's.

There is no need to document further the superiority of Leonard Woolf's education. He learnt at school, in addition to arithmetic, algebra and Euclidean geometry; in addition to Greek and Latin, French; and scripture; and history and geography (*Sowing* 51). And then there was Cambridge. Leonard's superior knowledge, Virginia's ignorance, were facts of their lives. Although sometimes she could joke about it, her ignorance of rather basic facts made for difficulties (as, for example, when Leonard had to explain the Equator—*D*. 1 May 1918—to the thirty-six-year-old Virginia).

Woolf's intellect was tested by two activities which she undertook in the first decade of the twentieth century—teaching and reviewing. In 1905 she taught history and literature one evening a week to working women at Morley College. It was immediately apparent that the teaching demanded no very high level of intellectual development. If the subject was literature, Woolf gave her impressions; if it was history, she simply read authorities and served up their conclusions as appetizingly as possible (EN Christmas 1904–31 May 1905). When she read for her lectures she was invariably bored, and skipped judiciously over huge chunks. Never having herself taken a written examination, for which she would have been trained to direct her energies towards a defined goal, she could hardly do so now. Nor was she paid for her teaching, and *noblesse oblige* is an undemanding tutor. At one point the authorities asked Virginia to teach literature instead of history, so little regard did she have for facts (Bell i. 106). The experience could not have boosted the teacher's ego.

Nor was reviewing any better. The books sent by the *Guardian*, the *Academy*, and the *TLS* were largely travel books and run-of-the-mill novels, the latter requiring little intellectual effort (EN 18 Mar. 1905). Furthermore, the editors wanted not sincere, carefully conceived analyses, but rather tactful and brief notices. The *TLS* expected a bit of plot summary, and a bit of commentary, a summing up in six hundred words. A novel that Woolf thought plodding, prolix, and mawkish (EN 23 Mar. 1905, 83) in the review became 'long, amiable, and pleasantly garrulous' (*TLS* 31 Mar. 1905, 106). Her deference to the real or assumed wishes of the editor would not have bolstered her belief in her own powers. And more devastating was the rejection of her review of a more substantive book, Edith Sichel's *Catherine de Medici*. Woolf had set to work in dead earnest, filling fifteen pages with notes and commentary, but the result would not do. When Bruce Richmond rejected the review as not academic enough (EN 25 Apr. 1905, 116), he confirmed Woolf's reluctance over doing it in the first place because 'I despair of my brains, which seem to be guttering like a tallow candle' (*L.* 221, 11? Mar. 1905).

Even when she wrote an informal essay, she severely criticized herself: if it was upon music, she saw her cleverness concealing a woeful lack of information, if upon Greek, even a week's work could not erase inaccuracies (EN 30 Jan. 1905, 30; 9 Feb. 1905, 40). She audaciously sent 'Magic Greek' to the *Academy*—the rejection arrived when she was teaching Greek history at Morley College (25 Mar. 1905, 95).

In 1905, the year of self-questioning prompted by teaching and reviewing, Woolf also came to know the Cambridge intellectuals through Thoby Stephen's 'Thursday Evenings' at Gordon Square. Later she would write to Lytton Strachey, with defensive jocularity, that she was terrified by his friends' 'congregation of intellect', that her 'reverence for clever young men [affected her] with a kind of mental palsy' (*L.* 409, 28 Apr. 1908). In fact, in 1905 she had her chance to talk to quite a congregation of clever young men. Clive Bell, Saxon Sydney-Turner, Lytton Strachey, and many others enlivened those Thursday Evenings, providing the sort of conversation Woolf had once thought available only at the university (she had envied Thoby's chances to build on his education with talk—see *L.* 81, May 1903).

The talk was on a wide variety of topics. At least two of the men present on Thursdays, Thoby Stephen and Lytton Strachey, 'adored' Elizabethan literature. When Thoby was still at Cambridge some three years earlier, his sister had written to him about the first of Shakespeare's plays to catch her interest—*Cymbeline*. Virginia had wondered if her difficulties with Shakespeare's characterizations might be attributed to her 'feminine weakness in the upper region' (*L.* 39, 5 Nov. 1901). Both the sentiment and the fact that she turned to her brother were typical of the teenage Virginia Stephen. In letters she had sought his advice on Latin and Greek, and his holidays were her big opportunities for 'endless arguments—about literature' (*L*. 2, 9, 36, 75 [1896–1903]). Now, with Thoby living in London and inviting his Cambridge friends to their home, Virginia was immersed in an atmosphere thick with the literature of Greece and of Elizabethan England.

These two areas were initially associated with Thoby, and *Jacob's Room*, Woolf's elegy for her brother, stresses them both. Among Jacob's books at Cambridge are the *Faerie Queene* and 'all the Elizabethans' (39); he writes an essay on Marlowe, and he admires Donne. At one time in his life Jacob sees no point in reading anyone but Marlowe and Shakespeare. Of all the Elizabethans, it is Shakespeare with whom in Woolf's imagination Thoby was most closely linked, and that from a very early age:

He had consumed Shakespeare, somehow or other, by himself. He had possessed himself of it, in his large clumsy way, and our first arguments—about books, that is—were heated; because out he would come with his sweeping assertion that everything was in Shakespeare: somehow I felt he had it all in his grasp . . .

Years after Thoby's death Woolf felt convinced that Shakespeare was 'the place where he got the measure of his daily world: where he took his bearings . . .'. He could look on sordid scenes with great calm for, Woolf imagined, Shakespeare's characters gave him some perspective; he had the 'look of one equipped, unperturbed, knowing his place, relishing his inheritance . . . proud of being a man and playing his part among Shakespeare's men' ('Sketch', *MB* 119).

Just as Woolf may have felt 'that the Greeks belonged to Thoby in a way that they didn't belong to her, that they formed a part of the great male province of education' (Bell i. 27), so did she view Elizabethan literature. Thoby was so thoroughly familiar with Shakespeare, for example, that it seemed to Woolf he felt the sort of pride in Shakespeare one might feel for a friend. When Shakespeare 'shuffled Falstaff off without a sign of sympathy', Thoby approved 'that large impartial sweep' ('Sketch', *MB* 119; *CE* ii. 31); and Woolf in her turn approved of her brother's easy way with Shakespeare and his contemporaries. With the example of Thoby and his friends in mind, she was to assert, towards the end of her life, that in order to prove the 'nobility' of our minds, we 'quote the Elizabethans' ('Anon.' 386). Emulation of Thoby and his Cambridge friends would have reinforced the thoroughgoing enjoyment Woolf naturally felt in reading English Renaissance literature.

The Elizabethans were especially associated with Thoby's friend Lytton Strachey, who became one of Virginia Woolf's friends. Dissimilar though they were in personality (*L*. 446, 30 Aug. 1908), Strachey, like Thoby, knew the Greeks and the Elizabethans, and 'his resources [were] infinite' (*L*. 429, 9 Aug. 1908). Yet this clever man was comparatively easy for Woolf to get to know. Their mutual 'passion for the Elizabethans' (James Strachey 10) was one of the things that made their conversations more satisfying than Woolf's literary talk with others. They had 'tastes in common'; and she found him 'in some respects the most sympathetic & understanding friend to talk to' (*D*. 12 Dec. 1917; also 5 Apr. 1918, 22 Jan. 1919). Both were beginning in 1904 to write for religious publications, and both resented the restrictions that that entailed (James Strachey 9; *L*. 194, 26 Nov. 1904). They would have had a lot of 'reviewers' shop' and other talk about literature, and Lytton had only to mention a forthcoming review for Virginia to get the publication (*Woolf–Strachey Letters* 27 Sept. and 4 Oct. 1908, 17, 19). In fact, she seems to have read most of his essays when they originally appeared, as well as when he personally gathered some together, and when they were reprinted in collections (*L*. 685, 687, 688). Indeed, in the case of *Books and Characters*, she asked him to send her the proofs (*L*. 1212, 1 Feb. 1922). The final collection made during Strachey's life, *Portraits in Miniature*, Woolf read as soon as it came out, and found 'rather masterly in technique' (*L*. 2375, 23 May 1931). Even after Lytton's death she continued to read and analyse his work. She admired the craftsmanship of an early essay on 'English Letter Writers' reprinted posthumously (*L*. 2628, 6 Sept. 1932), the first section of which was devoted to a wide range of Elizabethans, including some out-of-the-way examples. In the early years of their friendship she read his essays on Lyly, Sir Thomas Browne, Marvell, the Elizabethan pastoral, Spenser, Wotton, the Elizabethan drama, Bacon, the Shakespeare apocrypha, and, over a dozen times, Shakespeare. Over the years the production continued. And of course Lytton was the author of *Elizabeth and Essex*. He returned to Shakespeare and his contemporaries because they possessed 'an extraordinary capacity for expressing with immense vigour and endless variety the breadth and depth of human life' ('A Poet on Poets' 502).

Yet, despite their shared enthusiasm for English classical literature, and despite Woolf's continuing interest in Strachey's writing, she was not uncritical. His 'metallic & conventionally brilliant style' masked deficiences in substance. His 'superbly brilliant journalism', the very quality that so enlivened conversatons, vitiated his prose (*D.* 24 Jan. 1919). When he called her 'the best reviewer alive', and the 'inventor of a new prose style', she could not return the compliments (*D.* 25 May 1919, 29 Apr. 1921). Perhaps generosity was easier for Strachey than for Woolf, in that she needed to earn the reputation for authority which he had long since won at Cambridge and supported thereafter in a series of essays on Renaissance literature. Not a single one of the twenty-four books she was sent in her first year of reviewing even touched on it and most were decidedly ephemeral. The situation gradually improved, but in eighteen years of reviewing she in fact was given only ten volumes of or about English classical literature. The remedy came with Woolf's decision to collect her essays, much as Strachey had done.

The first volume of essays she called *The Common Reader* (1925), followed by *The Common Reader: Second Series* (1932). Both included, in addition to reviews, original critical essays, five of which were devoted exclusively to literature of the English Renaissance. Each is substantial, calling for thorough reading of primary sources and the hard work of assembling an array of particularly telling quotations. But the *Common Readers* were well worth the time, for in addition to their intrinsic merit they served an important personal purpose: of the second collection she said, '. . . I must go on with the C. Reader—for one thing, by way of proving my credentials' (*D.* 16 Feb. 1932). Without any but the most casual education, Virginia Woolf none the less wanted the respect of educated people in the area where a trained intellect most mattered. Never mind that by 1925 she had published *The Voyage Out*, *Night and Day*, *Jacob's Room*, and two collections of short stories; that she was preparing *Mrs. Dalloway* for publication in that year, or that *Jacob's Room* was a critical success. As she said in 'Women and Fiction' (1929), writing novels was unlike 'the practice of the sophisticated arts, hitherto so little practised by women . . . the writing of essays and criticism . . . (*CE* ii. 148).

Thus Virginia Woolf the successful novelist still had to 'prove her credentials' as an intellectual by publishing the first *Common Reader*. Significantly, she dedicated it to Lytton Strachey, who 'said the C.R. was divine, a classic . . .' (*D.* 18 June and 9 May 1925). This, coming from a man whose 'superior education' she had always envied, had to be enormously satisfying, especially given Woolf's memory of his

contention that she was 'not a good ratiocinator' (Holroyd 1967, i. 403).
By the time she brought out the second *Common Reader*, in 1932, she
was considered a major English novelist. *Mrs. Dalloway*, *To the
Lighthouse*, *Orlando*, and *The Waves* were all behind her. But the usual
love of reading, and the usual need to prove to the world that she was a
good thinker, combined to keep her at work on critical essays. Strachey
died on 21 January 1932, when she was revising the Elizabethan essays
she would include in the second *Common Reader*.

Why did I ever say I would produce another volume of Common Reader? It
will take me week after week, month after month . . . These remarks are jotted
down at the end of a long mornings work on Donne, which will have to be done
again, & is it worth the doing? I wake in the night with the sense of being in an
empty hall . . . What is the point of it . . . Lytton is dead . . . (*D.* 8 Feb. 1932)

It was a wrenching personal loss, a jarring professional loss. But by then
all that Lytton had represented to her was internalized, just as the
values of Leslie and Thoby Stephen had been, and of course Woolf did
go on to complete the second *Common Reader*. The 'empty hall' was
only a momentary illusion.

At twenty-one Virginia Stephen had wondered how she, a woman,
dared to write about male literature. By the time she was fifty, her
Common Readers had established Viriginia Woolf's claims to intellectual
respectability. The transition was facilitated by her decision not to
sound like a woman. Woolf's reading notes for an essay on Spenser's
Faerie Queene published posthumously by Leonard Woolf, and for one
on Sidney's *Arcadia* published in the second *Common Reader*, provide
some perspective on the relationship between the masculine critical
heritage as Woolf perceived it and her own published criticism. It
becomes clear as one examines Woolf's inclusions and exclusions of
material in the finished essays that she chose to approach English
Renaissance literature from a gender-neutral viewpoint.

Woolf's work on Sidney's *Arcadia* and Spenser's *Faerie Queene* took
place during what might be called her feminist decade, from the late
1920s to the late 1930s. She published *Orlando* in 1928, *A Room of
One's Own* in 1929; she read Sidney's *Arcadia* in 1931, and published
her essay on it in 1932; she was revising *The Years* in 1935, in the very
months when she read the *Faerie Queene*; and she did research for *Three
Guineas* (published finally in 1938) as she drafted her essay on Spenser's
poem. Yet if one were to read only the essays on Sidney and Spenser,
one would never suspect that Woolf was a feminist. Her holograph

notes show that she was reading both books from a feminist perspective.

In *A Room of One's Own* Woolf suggested that a book was needed on the 'profoundly interesting subject, the value that men set upon women's chastity . . .' (110). That very idea surfaced again when she was reading the *Arcadia* in preparation for her essay in the second *Common Reader*. She had begun reading with great pleasure, for she thought that Sidney was 'in favour of women' (MHP/B2f, 7) when a narrator states that women 'are framed of nature with the same parts of the minde for the exercise of virtue, as wee are'. But after 120 more pages of the *Arcadia* she became convinced that Sidney was after all bound by conventional notions and gave 'the man's idea' of woman's chastity.

In Sidney's narrative, the princess Philoclea lives with her family apart from their former court and its dangers. At first the father's attempt to ensure his daughter's purity works, and Philoclea vows chastity, 'the chief of heavenly lights, | Which mak'st us most immortal shape to wear'. The first real test of this vow comes when she learns that the Amazon 'Zelmane' is in fact a man, Pyrocles. Although her relief is immense, she is overcome by fear and guilt, and flagellates herself at length for 'staining' the pureness of her 'virgin-mind'. She finally tells Pyrocles, 'Thy virtue won me: with virtue preserve me. Dost thou love me? Keep me then still worthy to be beloved.' Woolf saw in these words Sidney's own masculine conception of woman's chastity (16). I take it she meant that a male writer would want to pin a woman's worth on her negation of her own desire, and yet at the same time would boost the male ego by depicting its intensity.

Another episode exemplifying this same male bias involves the amorous Andromana, a married woman with a taste for young men. This sexually active female courts both Pyrocles and his cousin Musidorus when she has them in prison, but they object to the 'faultiness of her minde' and her 'shamelessness'. As Woolf did on her note about Philoclea's virtue, she encircled the page reference to this passage—something she rarely did—to remind herself of a useful focus for the essay she was about to write.

Neither passage, however, appears in the published essay—and Woolf's comments on the Elizabethan work are not feminist, but rather remain within the traditional bounds of criticism. The essay, 'The Countess of Pembroke's Arcadia' (*CE* i. 19–27), finds fault with the *Arcadia* for following the pattern of Romance, a series of unrealistic tales told by aristocrats. But the reading notes show that Woolf read and enjoyed a tale told by a middle-aged peasant woman, Miso, who remembers how when she was young and beautiful she learned the nature of love from an older woman. Because Cupid is 'a foul fiend', she was told, 'do what thou list with all those fellows one after another, and it recks not much what they do to thee, so it be in secret; but upon my charge, never love none of them'. The situation of an older woman instructing a younger would have exerted a strong fascination on Woolf, and the modernity of the message is unmistakable. She thought Miso's tale 'much the best: racy & simple' (16), a welcome antidote to Sidney's more usual emphasis on female chastity.

Putting together, then, Woolf's statements in the reading notes with those in the published essay, it is possible to discern the gist of her feminist reading of the *Arcadia*, one which would fault Sidney for not upholding his early proclaimed favouring of women, but rather denying them sexual freedom except in a humorously intended fabliau. Sidney exemplified for Woolf the age-old conspiracy of men to set high value on woman's chastity.

But when, some three years later, she came to read the *Faerie Queen*, she discovered in Spenser a rather different orientation to the subject of chastity. She was pleased to find him referring to his *own* chastity when he refrains from describing the genitalia of a female character. Woolf applauded the reticence, praising Spenser's 'sensitive heart', his 'natural chastity, so that some things are judged unfit for the pen' (*CE* i. 16). Nor was it sexual squeamishness on Spenser's part, for Woolf went on in the reading notes to admire his handling of a sexually explicit scene. When a jealous husband observes his wife *in flagrante delicto* with a satyr ('Nine times he heard him come aloft ere day'), Woolf amusingly enough commented, 'the love making of the satyrs— very realistic' (MHP/B2m, 16).

It is not that Spenser always portrays sexually active women, for indeed he frequently depicts utterly chaste females. But his manner of presenting them distinguishes them from, say, Sidney's Philoclea. Belphoebe, for example, is not simpy chaste; she *is* chastity. She does not desire any man whatsoever, and thus does not embody male ego-gratification. She is simply a woman of great integrity, and is portrayed as such. Woolf recorded Spenser's tribute to Belphoebe: 'she standeth on the highest stair of honorable womanhood' (16). To take one further case, Woolf enjoyed Spenser's initial handling of a timorous young woman named Florimell, who is pursued by a ne'er-do-well, whose 'brutish lust' burns his bowels. Her escape, his pursuit, and then the pursuit by a hyena-like beast 'that feeds on wemens flesh', all made, said Woolf, a 'very good' story (16). Here Spenser is dealing with another compelling side of chastity—a young girl's horror at the bestial in desire.

Spenser refuses to oversimplify the question of chastity, and in fact devotes an entire book of the *Faerie Queene* to that subject. In making the 'hero' of Book Three a female knight, Britomart, the poet creates an opportunity for exploring a further question, the relationship between aggressiveness and gender, an issue much in Woolf's mind at the time that she was reading the poem. The knight of chastity sees in a crystal ball a vision of the man most 'fit for love', Sir Artegall, who seemed 'wise, warlike, personable, courteous, and kind'. Spenser's male knight, though warlike, possesses womanly traits as well; the female knight, though womanly, is one of the best fighters in the poem. The two characters approach androgyny, Artegall ultimately man–womanly, Britomart woman–manly. Aggressiveness is thus to be found in both sexes.

Woolf also approved of Spenser's discussion of the pacifism of women in literature. He contends that women had once been noted for their victories in battle, but that 'envious men' curbed women's liberty to fight because they feared a usurpation of their sovereignty. Here was an Elizabethan writer capable of analysing the restrictions against women much as Woolf had in *Orlando* (158). She triumphantly headed her notes on this passage of the *Faerie Queene* 'Spenser as a feminist', as she did again when he went on to attribute the suppression by male writers of women's 'brave atchievements' with 'shield and speare' to the writers' weak egos.

The *Arcadia* essay published in the second *Common Reader* did not include the material on Sidney's handling of chastity; nor did the draft-essay on the *Faerie Queene* include either what Woolf took to be Spenser's much more satisfactory treatment of the same subject, or his development of the issues of aggressiveness and pacifism as they relate to gender. Her decision not to use these materials that she had gathered while reading must be attributed to the reticence she always felt when preparing essays for the *Common Reader*, for they were her claim to a place in the critical establishment. It was perfectly possible for her to be more forthright in other contexts, and in *Three Guineas* she frankly discussed the two feminist issues that had greatly interested her in her reading of the *Arcadia* and the *Faerie Queene*, the so-called 'man's' idea of womanly chastity, and the relationship between aggressiveness and gender. In *Three Guineas* she could state outright her relegation of the concept of bodily chastity to the dustbin, and insist instead on an inviolable chastity of the mind (125). She could take a Spenserian position on the question of gender and aggressiveness: 'the fighting instinct' in women, she said, could be either developed or destroyed; with Spenser too she could call for women's 'liberty of choice' on whether to fight or not (163, 269 n).

Readers have become accustomed to Woolf's outspoken feminism in *A Room of One's Own* and *Three Guineas*; but without the reading notes we would not know that in the decade between the publication of those two books Woolf was reading Elizabethan literature from the same feminist perspective. Neither essay falsified Woolf's basic responses to Sidney and Spenser; but, in spite of the enormous amount she did manage to say, she also suppressed much. The contrast between the essays on Sidney and Spenser, and the reading notes, suggests that the spectre of Thoby Stephen and Leslie Stephen and Lytton Strachey still exerted much force. For the purpose of speaking authoritatively, Woolf chose to omit in her criticism of English Renaissance literature the feminism which otherwise occupied her thinking at the time and which is everywhere manifest in her ficton.[1]

There is firm evidence that Woolf made a conscious decision to eschew a feminist response when writing criticism. In 1921 she decided to write a book called 'Reading' (and in 1925 she published a related but different book, under the title of *The Common Reader*). By 1922 she had made plans for chapters on the *Paston Letters*, the *Odyssey*, Shakespeare and other Elizabethans, and some later writers; and she had drafted an introductory essay entitled 'Byron and Mr. Briggs', an extremely important document that develops at some length the critical stance which is briefly adumbrated in the preface to *The Common Reader* (Hungerford 322). Woolf gives the common reader a name (Mr Briggs), a century (the nineteenth), and descendants (reviewers). A 'grandchild of Briggs' then offers a discussion of Byron's letters, complete with comparisons with Wordsworth and Shelley. The 'grandchild of Briggs', says Woolf, mentions love, and so proportions the criticism that it is clear that 'he is a woman'. None the less Woolf concludes that 'the writer's sex is not of interest; nor need we dwell upon

---

[1] Zwerdling (218–19) finds fiction far better suited than non-fiction for the feminist exploration of 'the psychological imperatives at work in the relation between the sexes'. I will discuss in Chs. 2 and 4 especially Woolf's use of Elizabethan materials to further that exploration in her fiction. See also the two collections of feminist essays edited by Marcus.

the peculiarities of temperament which make one pe₁
Byron's letters different from another's. It is the quality
in common that is interesting . . .' Regardless of how con
was that her perception of literature frequently differed ₁
men because she was a woman, she finally made common ₁
them: Woolf the 'common reader' would not be idiosyn   ₁cally
feminist.

Woolf became part of the critical establishment in her lifetime and is
as frequently quoted today as many of the critics with whom she is
thought to have some kinship. At one time or another she has been
likened—in style, method, or ideas—to Hazlitt, Lamb, Pater, Samuel
Butler, T. S. Eliot, Henry James, Leslie Stephen, and Lytton Strachey.[2]
Each suggested 'influence' or similarity has much to recommend it,
even when two scholars attribute a passage or larger idea in Woolf's
criticism to two different 'fathers', as Meisel (73–103) and Farwell (450)
do with 'Incandescence', a concept and metaphor taken directly from
Pater, but also influenced by Eliot's 'unified sensibility'. Indeed, with
very little effort one could extend the list of Woolf's critical ancestors.
The point is that she does sound and proceed like some of the best
critics of the nineteenth and early twentieth centuries; and it would be
peculiar if she did not. She read them, she wanted to be of their
number, and she learned 'a few tricks' of style by studying their essays
(Fox 152–4). In *A Room of One's Own* (132) she mentions in this
connection Lamb, Browne, Thackeray, Newman, Sterne, Dickens, and
De Quincey. As this list makes clear, when it came to models Woolf
preferred older to more current writers, and literary men to academics.
Once again it was a conscious choice, as is clear in her commentary on
the sample piece of criticism which she herself wrote and then subjected
to analysis in 'Byron and Mr. Briggs': '. . . no Byron expert and no
scholar could write so carelessly'; nor would the scholar pay so much
attention to personality, or demote 'aesthetic problems' to a secondary
position. When she called herself a 'common reader' she specifically
eschewed the approach of 'scholars and critics', who 'read differently,
in a way of their own' (333).

When Woolf made common cause, then, with men, it was with the
educated men of the nineteenth-century essay tradition, rather than

---

[2] See Pacey 242–4 (Hazlitt); Goldman 278 (Eliot) and 281 (Henry James); Wellek 423
(Lamb, Hazlitt, Pater); McLaurin (Butler); Meisel (Pater); Hyman (Stephen); Hill
(Stephen); Rosenbaum (Stephen); and Gordon 71–2 (Stephen).

with scholars and academic critics. True, she admitted in 'Byron and Mr. Briggs' that she still might find the latter useful (349), but their concerns and methods were antithetical to her own. Today we are well aware of Woolf's animosity to academics. It was really, however, only after she attempted in the 1922 essay to articulate her critical principles that the issue became clear in her own mind. At the beginning of her career as a reviewer she appreciated the difficulties that academics met—in editing texts for example—and was pleased that they took the trouble ('Philip Sidney' 174). And in her first novel academics are rather harmless drudges whose devotion to the restoration of classical texts might make them egoistic and unsociable, but not ludicrous and certainly not corrupt. In the early 1920s, however, Woolf became a bit more critical. Around the same time that she wrote 'Byron and Mr. Briggs' she portrayed in *Jacob's Room* several Cambridge dons, all learned, but failing to conform in their personal lives to the ideals of the literature they study. Erasmus Cowan, for example, though a Virgil scholar, does not care for 'arms, bees, or even the plough', as Woolf quite unreasonably, if humorously, thinks he should. But the criticism is muted and obviously far from Woolf's well-known virulent attack four years later on Professor Walter Raleigh.

In 1906 Raleigh was 'one of the few writers from whom we can bear illumination', said Woolf, 'and of whom we can say that although he orders [the world of Hakluyt], he rather increases than impoverishes its beauty' ('Trafficks and Discoveries' 440–1). In 1917 Woolf praised Raleigh to the skies for discarding labels and '[touching] his subject with life'—'Like all scholars who know what there is to be known and mix their learning with love . . .' ('Romance'). But she discovered in 1926 that Raleigh failed to think about literature in his spare time. Instantly his books, 'readable, just, acute, stimulating' as they might be, were after all 'rather tight, highly academic books' (*CE* i. 315–16). Although 'Walter Raleigh was one of the best Professors of Literature in our time', Woolf sneered that 'he did brilliantly whatever it is that Professors are supposed to do' (315).

If one academic book was harmful, two more than doubled the problem, for the critics and scholars employed such different criteria and methods as to confuse anyone going to them for help. Woolf once demonstrated the point by pitting Saintsbury, who subjected poetry to metrical analysis, against Raleigh, who represented, she said, 'the school that bids one not criticize but cry' (*CE* iv. 57–8). Nor did Woolf confine her criticism of academics to her own century. Richard Bentley, the great eighteenth-century classicist, was 'the most quarrelsome of mankind' and incapable besides of appreciating Milton; thus his judgements on Horace and Homer were not to be trusted (107, 111). Having discovered what she apparently took to be a universal failing of academics, Woolf could no longer countenance their untrustworthy pronouncements. Petty, vain, and arrogant, they represented an authoritarian tradition that was inimical to the values Woolf herself saw in literature. Thus she concluded that 'to admit authorities, however heavily furred and gowned, into our libraries and let them tell us how to read, what to read, what value to place upon what we read, is to destroy the spirit of freedom which is the breath of those sanctuaries' (*CE* ii. 1).

Woolf found it best for her purposes as a literary critic to steer clear of the opinions of other critics, and urged readers to embrace the same independence, for 'nothing is more disastrous than to crush one's foot into another person's shoe',[3] no matter how beautifully shaped and polished that shoe might be. She advised people first to read a work on their own, and to mull over their reactions; then to make comparisons with other works; then to try to ascertain the book's 'absolute value'; and only then to go to the critics, 'to the very rare writers who are able to enlighten us upon literature as an art. Coleridge and Dryden and Johnson, in their considered criticism, the poets and novelists themselves in their considered sayings, are often surprisingly relevant . . .' (*CE* ii. 10).

Such an attitude, incidentally, justifies Woolf's publishing two volumes of criticism. I do not of course mean to suggest that she claimed for herself the sagacity of her great predecessors of the eighteenth and nineteenth centuries. But I think that in her more confident moments she hoped for a place just below them, such a place as Hazlitt then occupied.

Woolf wrote a major essay on Hazlitt in 1930, on the hundredth anniversary of his death, for which she read the complete works over an eight-month period. Her evaluation of Hazlitt's criticism, as Wellek has pointed out (437), commends those qualities which she herself exhibits in her best essays. She praises Hazlitt's 'faculty for seizing on the important and indicating the main outline' of a work of literature. This outline, she says, 'learned critics often lose and timid critics never acquire' (*CE* i. 162). Hazlitt has a clear vision of 'the hard and lasting in

---

[3] 'How Should One Read a Book?' 43. This is the first version of the essay revised in 1932 for inclusion in the second *Common Reader* (and now in *CE*). It incorporates some material from the unpublished 'Byron and Mr. Briggs'.

literature, of what a book means and where it should be placed . . . He singles out the peculiar quality of his author and stamps it vigorously' (163). Clearly Woolf approves of such a goal, and herself worked hard to achieve it. She took voluminous notes so as not to miss something that would emerge as a salient feature of a single writer or a group, and she allowed herself time to mull over her ideas until she felt certain that she had 'seized on the important'. Drafts of her essays reflect her constant effort to pare away the unessential and to communicate her thoughts with the greatest possible clarity. When she published an essay a second time, she almost always used the opportunity to rethink, or at the very least rephrase, some of its points. The essay on Hazlitt is typical. She had written one version for an American newspaper, but subjected it to further revision for its appearance in the *TLS*. Even then, however, she had her doubts: '. . . I am not sure that I have speared that little eel in the middle—that marrow—which is one's object in criticism' (*D*. 8 Sept. 1930).

To 'spear that little eel in the middle' vividly conveys Woolf's sense of the immense difficulty in achieving her goal in criticism, and does so characteristically, with a metaphor, as Hazlitt himself did. She thought in metaphors and in the essays used the images in them as 'the fastest, most concrete, and effective means of explanation . . .' (Bell and Ohmann 365). With none of the essays was the need as pressing as with those Woolf wrote on the English classics: she contended that 'with our natural reverence and inevitable servility, we seldom make our position, as modern readers of old writers, plain' (*CE* ii. 31). The figurative language that she employs in these essays makes her position plain, makes it attractive, and is at once accessible and elegant.

Let me give a few examples. In Donne's Holy Sonnets Woolf hears 'incongruous clamours and solemnities, as if the church door opened on the uproar of the street'. No sooner does one read the *Faerie Queene* than 'the eye of the mind opens'. As for prose, Hakluyt's *Voyages* is a 'lumber room'; in the *Defence of Poesie* Sidney 'freely and naturally reaches his hand for a metaphor'; in his *Arcadia*, 'as in some luminous globe, all the seeds of English fiction lie latent'. The perfection of English prose came with 'that jungle, forest, and wilderness which is the Elizabethan drama': 'the stage was the nursery where prose learnt to find its feet.' With the exception of the 'luminous globe' (itself not difficult to envisage), the images are drawn from everyday life, often at its most prosaic. Yet there is nothing prosaic about the metaphors and similes Woolf creates out of the images. The figures of speech are alive on the page, drawing vigour from Woolf's ongoing sense of dis

And that is what the literature of the English Renaissance prov
Woolf. There was not a genre that she failed to touch upon, not a major
figure that she omitted over the years. Poetry, prose, and drama she
read with some thoroughness, nor was she afraid of lesser-known figures
and works. Even the occasional experience of frustration in the face of
an uncongenial or obscure work could not diminish her natural taste for
the great works of the past, reinforced as it was by her conviction that in
the appreciation of such literature one's intellect and nobility were
measured.

At a time when she was reading Elizabethan writers, seriously, 'with
pen & notebook', she predicted that her *Common Reader* would be 'a
rough, but vigorous statue testifying before I die to the great fun &
pleasure my habit of reading has given me' (*D.* 28 July 1923). Not only
do the two *Common Readers* do just that, but so does every one of the
novels, testifying to her pleasure in the English Renaissance more than
in any other period. Shakespeare is a constant presence in the essays, the
letters, and the diaries, and he appears in one way or another in all of
the novels. The evidence of the reading notes is also impressive, for
these cover over twenty of Shakespeare's plays, a few times recording
two separate readings; and it is clear that notes on other readings once
existed. There is no question of the centrality of Shakespeare in Woolf's
imagination. But the writer who inaugurated the Renaissance reading
spree that lasted a lifetime was not the best or most famous of the
writers of that time. He was Richard Hakluyt, a collector of accounts of
travel written in the heyday of British exploration. His *Voyages,
Travels, and Discoveries of the English Nation* first struck a chord in the
young Virginia Stephen. Virginia Woolf would devote several essays to
Hakluyt's collection, and it would also figure in her novels. It is time,
then, to turn to the story of Woolf and Hakluyt.

2

Hakluyt's *Voyages*

It was the Elizabethan prose writers I loved first & most wildly, stirred by Hakluyt, which father lugged home for me—I think of it with some sentiment—father tramping over the [London] Library with his little girl sitting at HPG [Hyde Park Gate] in mind. He must have been 65; I 15 or 16, then; & why I dont know, but I became enraptured, though not exactly interested, but the sight of the large yellow page entranced me. I used to read it & dream of those obscure adventurers, & no doubt practised their style in my copy books.

THAT is the way Virginia Woolf remembered her first reading of Hakluyt's *Voyages, Travels, and Discoveries of the English Nation* (D. 8 Dec. 1929), the monumental compendium of British voyages of exploration published at the end of the sixteenth century. The thousands of pages cannot be read without an awareness of their repetitiveness, and many of the documents go on at length listing latitudes, ships' personnel, the commodities of foreign lands, and so on. Yet it is to the credit of the voyagers, and of the assiduous compiler of their documents, that the teenage Virginia Stephen could read with rapture. She told Winifred Holtby that she 'devoured Hakluyt's *Voyages* with nothing less than passion' (15), and it was the subject of the first (and only) essay she ever showed to her father ('Sketch', *MB* 118). Her first extant remarks are in the review she wrote for the *Speaker* of Professor Walter Raleigh's *English Voyages of the Sixteenth Century*, a critical study of Hakluyt to accompany MacLehose's 1906 reissue of the *Voyages*. By this time she appears to have bought her own copy of the edition that her father had lugged home for her, 'those five cumbrous volumes in which the printers of 1811 thought good to entomb' Hakluyt.[1] She confessed that in earlier readings her head had been

so gloriously confused with the medley of rich names and places, of spices and

---

[1] Personal letter of 9 Dec. 1981 from Olivier Bell (Mrs Quentin Bell) that the Evans edition is now in their library. Its heraldic bookplate of AVS probably suggest acquisition 'a good long time' before marriage.

precious stones, of strange lands and monsters, of regal charters and proclamations that the hard outlines of the earth swam and melted in a gorgeous mist. The reader could never detach [herself] sufficiently from the yellow page with its decorative spelling, to supply the spectators comment, and see the whole pageant in its proper proportions.

Thanks to the work of Professor Raleigh, Woolf discovered that Hakluyt's world 'was all founded on hard truth, that the voyagers were substantial Elizabethan seamen, and that the whole makes a consecutive chapter of English history' ('Trafficks and Discoveries' 440–1). Not only was her enthusiasm more firmly based than in earlier years, but she was actually inspired to read Hakluyt again. Raleigh paraphrased and otherwise referred to Drake's circumnavigation (1577) and Raleigh's discovery of Guiana (1595), but he did not quote from them. In her review Woolf quotes from both Elizabethans directly. When, for example, she notes that Professor Raleigh calls Drake's progress 'a carnival of plunder', she illustrates the point in this way:

Silver and gold in wedges and bars 'of the fashion and bigness of a brickbat,' silk and fine linen, china ware and precious stones, crucifixes set with 'goodly great emeralds,' poured into the ships in a continuous stream. Great Spanish vessels waited them, laden from the kingdom of Peru, lying innocently at anchor without guard or suspicion. (441)

Woolf's description, taken directly from Hakluyt's account (iv. 238) of how Drake rifled first three Spanish 'barkes' at the port of Arica on the northern tip of Chile, and then several other ships, supports her point that the southern voyages always promised riches of one sort or another, riches realized finally in Drake's voyage. The quotation she uses is obviously apt, and in its vividness became part of her imagination. She would make further use of it in her first novel.

Another voyage which appealed to Woolf at the time, and which she would also use again, is Raleigh's discovery of Guiana. Raleigh recounts the story of a trek he and his men undertook while exploring one of the tributaries of the Orinoco. Making for a magnificent waterfall seen in the distance, its 'strange thunder of waters' luring them on, they came upon a lovely valley:

I never saw a more beautifull countrey, nor more lively prospects, hils so raised here and there over the valleys, the river winding into divers branches, the plaines adjoyning without bush or stubble, all faire greene grasse, the ground of hard sand easie to march on, either for horse or foote, the deere crossing in every path, the birdes towards the evening singing on every tree with a thousand severall tunes, cranes and herons of white, crimson, and carnation pearching in the rivers side, the aire fresh with a gentle Easterly winde, and every stone that we stouped to take up, promised either golde or silver by his complexion.

It is small wonder that Woolf was impressed. Such 'little landscapes' seemed the more romantic, she said, because they were to be found in the midst of totally sober accounts of the 'commodities' of the region, 'observed with the same sober and veracious eye and inscribed with the same stiff pen'.

Throughout the review one can sense Woolf's attempts to 'place' the writers of Hakluyt's *Voyages*, who were adventurers first and generally took up their pens with little thought beyond conveying the information that would inspire others to finance expeditions, grant charters, or themselves join subsequent voyages of exploration, in service to the crown, the church, or their own pockets. Woolf was none the less struck by 'the largeness of their imaginations'. She came across passages of great lyric beauty that supplemented Professor Raleigh's briefer quotations, and she concluded that the voyagers' 'laborious pens, dipping into the stately vocabulary which was common to seaman and poet, build up such a noble structure of words in the end that the effect is as rich and more authentic than that got by more artistic processes' (440).

Woolf's early admiration for Hakluyt's *Voyages* was thus confirmed and even strengthened by the re-reading of 1906. She returned to the collection throughout her life frequently enough for its subject-matter and its style to exert a continuing influence on her creative imagination. But the 1906 reading was to have a dramatic effect immediately on Woolf's writing.

The Voyage Out (1915; American edition, 1920), Woolf's first novel, depicts its heroine's adventures at sea and in South America, a place that Woolf had never seen. But she knew something about it from her reading of Hakluyt's *Voyages*, which suggested precisely the ambience needed for the adventures of her heroine. The successive drafts of the novel written over a five-year period reveal the author's developing awareness of how best to use Hakluyt's *Voyages* and the Elizabethan world from which it sprang and to which it contributed.

The very plot of the novel resembles countless narratives in Hakluyt: Rachel Vinrace journeys to South America on her father's ship, has a number of new experiences, and dies of a mysterious disease apparently contracted while exploring. But it is not simply a matter of plot. At least as early as the so-called Extant Draft A (De Salvo 'Sorting'), written during the summer and early autumn of 1908, Woolf envisaged her early twentieth-century scene as having other connections with Hakluyt's sixteenth-century world. She likened Helen Ambrose and the heroine, here called Cynthia (Rachel), to credulous Elizabethans 'who had never left the shore' listening to tales of 'the huge monsters and the rocks of diamond which were to be found in that land across the [Bristol] channel'.

By the time of the first substantial draft, B, written March 1909–March 1910, and revised some two years later (De Salvo, 'Sorting' 282), Woolf had established an extensive Elizabethan milieu. As soon as the *Euphrosyne* reaches South America, where Rachel's development is to take place, Woolf insists at length on a parallel with the age of Elizabeth. The scholarly Mr Pepper thinks back three hundred years, just as he does in the novel, to the arrival of five Elizabethan barques at the very spot where the modern ship docks:

Half-drawn up upon the beach lay an equal number of Spanish galleons, unmanned, for the country was still a virgin land behind a veil. Slipping across the water, the English sailors bore away bars of silver, bales of linen, timbers of cedar wood, golden crucifixes knobbed with emeralds. When the Spaniards came down from their drinking, a fight ensued, the two parties churning up the sand, and driving each other into the surf. The Spaniards, bloated with fine living upon the fruits of the miraculous land, fell in heaps; but the hardy Englishmen, tawny with sea-voyaging, hairy for lack of razors, with muscles like wire, fangs greedy for flesh, and fingers itching for gold, despatched the wounded, drove the dying into the sea, and soon reduced the natives to a state of superstitious wonderment. (88–9)

Woolf's source is Drake's circumnavigation of the globe. Drake set out from England in 1577 'with a fleete of five ships and barkes' (Hakluyt iv. 232). At various ports the Englishmen rifled 'many boords of Cedar-wood', '13. barres of silver', and 'wedges of silver' from unmanned ships. And so the narrative in Hakluyt continues, with an account of Drake's finding plate, silks, and linen, and even 'a crucifixe of gold with goodly Emerauds set in it' (238–9). At Nova Albion the natives thought Drake and his men gods, and went on to crown him their king (240–1). Here, then, in ten pages of Hakluyt, one finds Woolf's five Elizabethan barques; the unmanned Spanish ships, their crew in town; the superstitious wonderment of the natives; and the precise spoils of 'bars of silver, bales of linen, timbers of cedar wood, golden crucifixes knobbed with emeralds'.

Having established the parallel between the modern seaport and South American ports visited by Drake at the end of the sixteenth century, Woolf went on to characterize the place she eventually was to name Santa Marina: 'In arts and industries', she said, the town was 'where it was in Elizabethan days' (Draft B, L8/6). In the ascent of Monte Rosa, where Rachel comes into contact with Terence Hewet, the young man to whom she eventually becomes engaged, Woolf is again careful to stress connections between the present and the Elizabethan past, this time by having the company see an Elizabethan watch-tower. Her presentation of the material in the successive drafts suggests Woolf's growing concern that the connection be strengthened and, in a sense, legitimized. In the first version, a minor and rather negative character discusses the watch-tower; in the final version the Elizabethan connection seems more authoritative since it is assigned to the trustworthy narrator's voice.

The book becomes more Elizabethan through these references to the watch-tower and to barques arriving centuries earlier where the *Euphrosyne* now docks. It is further appropriate that this ship be not a pleasure craft, but rather a British mercantile vessel, and thus a reminder of the opening of trade during the reign of Elizabeth. Several additions that Woolf made in manuscript also suggest a kinship between the excursions of the major characters and the voyages of the Elizabethans. At the end of 1912 she was revising the scene in which Rachel looks down at the sea with Terence Hewet from the top of a cliff: 'The water was very calm [as] it had been at the birth of the world, and so it had remained ever since. Probably no human being had ever broken that water with boat or with body' (210–11). The scene recalls Drake's first view of the Pacific Ocean. Similarly, Woolf seems to have worked to make another scene tally with accounts of the explorers in South America: when the other men have fallen asleep and Hewet remains awake, in one version he is simply aware of leaving the familiar; in the next, he moves towards 'some experience which he could only suspect'; but finally he experiences something that could come out of Hakluyt, a sensation of 'slipping over barriers and past landmarks into unknown waters . . . (266). This sharpening of allusiveness is evident in Woolf's revisions of other material surrounding the journey up the river. Her description of the river itself varies with changes in her concept of the heroine. In an early draft, by stressing the unexplored terrain of the river's source (Draft B, E19/1), Woolf addresses the important issue of Rachel's virginity from the point of view of a young woman's psychology. In her next draft Woolf substituted the relatively

unimpassioned description that appears in the novel. But son
else was needed. There is a long passage in the novel beginning `
the time of Elizabeth very few people had seen the river, and not
had been done to change its appearance from what it was to the eyes of
the Elizabethan voyagers . . .'—this passage Woolf added at a late date,
thereby drawing together the other allusions to Elizabethan voyages
scattered throughout the novel, and making of *The Voyage Out* an
Elizabethan voyage.

The parallel might suggest that Rachel's voyage could, like the earlier
ones, yield treasure and discovery, or disappointment, or even death.
But the expectations of a woman about to become engaged and married
depend in large part on society, for the treatment of women at any
particular time in history obviously can encourage, or thwart,
achievement. Rachel's milieu is depicted as Elizabethan, and only the
naïve Evelyn Murgatroyd would see that as propitious:

> It must have been so much easier for the Elizabethans! I thought the other day
> on that mountain how I'd have liked to be one of those colonists, to cut down
> trees and make laws and all that, instead of fooling about with all these people
> who think one's just a pretty young lady. (192)

Woolf's later portrait of Judith Shakespeare in *A Room of One's Own*
puts the lie to Evelyn Murgatroyd's romanticizing. Woolf well knew
that life was not 'so much easier for the Elizabethans'. In making
Rachel Vinrace's society 'Elizabethan', then, Woolf shows the barriers
to achievement the young woman would have to face, and suggests
moreover the restrictions still operative in the twentieth century upon
the seemingly more open relationships between men and women.

To body forth a world fraught with these barriers and restrictions,
Woolf employs allusions to *The Tempest*: Mr Grice recites 'Full fathom
five thy father lies' (54), Ariel's song; and Hewet tells Rachel that when
he first saw her 'I thought you were like a creature who'd lived all its life
among pearls and old bones' (293), another allusion to the same song. In
Draft B Rachel tells Hewet that she thinks about 'images and spirits and
the sea' (L16/2). These allusions to *The Tempest* set up an analogue
between the heroine of that play, Miranda, and Rachel Vinrace. The
analogue is justified in several respects. Like Miranda, Rachel has lost
her mother; like Miranda, Rachel remembers women about her; like
Miranda, Rachel fears and loathes the bestial; like Miranda, Rachel is
fond of her father; and like Miranda, Rachel transfers her affections
from her father to a young man.

But Miranda is going home, Rachel to a figurative exile. Miranda will become a queen, and a queen with some knowledge of the unscrupulousness of the political scene. Her father is quick to warn her that the 'brave new world' seems so only to the inexperienced. Rachel's father, on the other hand, has kept her ignorant (80). On the 'lonely little island' of the ship (87–8) Rachel is shocked by the amatory advances of Richard Dalloway and later has a nightmare in which she is 'alone with a little deformed man who squatted on the floor gibbering, with long nails. His face was pitted and like the face of an animal' (77). The scene, suggestive of Caliban's attempted rape of Miranda, cannot be blotted out, as Miranda's experience is, by the arrival of Rachel's 'Ferdinand', Terence Hewet. And that is precisely where the analogue to *The Tempest* points up the irony of Rachel's position. Although Prospero's tuition has prepared Miranda for life as an Elizabethan queen, Willoughby Vinrace's benign neglect, based on a 'good-humoured . . . but contemptuous' attitude towards women, has prepared his daughter for nothing at all, not for a career, not for marriage. Death, rather than a new life, ends her voyage.

References to Shakespeare and other writers of the Elizabethan period are scattered through the drafts of *The Voyage Out* and in the novel itself. As is true of much else in the slow development of her first novel, Woolf groped towards a coherent statement to be made by these literary associations. She differentiated more and more clearly between her male and female characters, both as readers and as voyagers. As might be expected given Woolf's belief that Elizabethan literature was a male preserve, the women were consistently less associated with it in successive drafts. For example, at an early stage Helen Ambrose is said to have read at least *Hamlet* (Draft B, E2/16), but her modest accomplishment in Elizabethan literature disappears from subsequent drafts, to be replaced by familiarity with 'Defoe, Maupassant, or some spacious chronicle of family life' (124). The colourless Susan Warrington fades rapidly in the successive drafts of the novel. In the scene of Mr Bax's sermon, Susan follows the words of a psalm 'with respectful courtesy, as she followed the somewhat distraught exclamations of characters in Shakespeare' (Draft B, E17/4)—not, on the face of it, reprehensible. But in the more satiric next draft she follows 'mechanically & with respect' exclamations of characters now dubbed 'violent' (Draft C, H1/29). Immediately after this version, Woolf achieved the specificity that leaves no doubt about Susan Warrington: 'she followed them with the same kind of mechanical

respect with which she heard many of Lear's speeches read aloud'
(Draft C, L17/13; and *VO* 227). Needless to say, Woolf's reaction to
King Lear (when in fact writing *The Voyage Out*) was of a different sort:
'the greatness of all the characters strikes me' (HRN/*N&D* 8).

A telling instance of de-Elizabethanizing the women of the novel is
the case of Mrs Flushing. In Draft B the positive associations of
Hakluyt's voyagers cling to the woman as she stands 'upright and
defiant' in the bow of the boat on the trip up the river, like 'an heroic
figurehead to some Elizabethan barque . . .' (E20/1). In the next
version, stripped of the glamorous association, she merely stands in the
bow 'declaiming, with sudden bursts of laughter' (Draft C, H2, ch.
23/59), and finally is removed from the bow altogether.

Interestingly enough, something else in the development of the
novel undergoes the same transformation, an inanimate object, the
Euphrosyne. Woolf experimented only briefly with an Elizabethan
association for the ship:

. . . when the sun shone, and the long still days were blue, her state was far
more wondrous than the state of England. She was a bride going forth to her
husband unattended.

> 'Loe! where she comes along with portly pace,
> Like Phoebe, from her Chamber of the East.'

(L2/1)

The quotation from Spenser's 'Epithalamion', describing his bride on
her way to the wedding, was of course appropriate to the *Euphrosyne,*
which carried the virgin Rachel towards her engagement. But Woolf
none the less revised the passage immediately, substituting the words
found in the novel, 'She was a bride going forth to her husband,
unattended, a virgin unknown of men' (L1/12), and later added the limp
'in her vigour and purity she might be likened to all beautiful
things . . .' (32). Schlack rightly sees the change as evidence that Woolf
wanted 'to invest greater significance in the *Euphrosyne* in these early
drafts than emerges in the final text' ('The Novelist's Voyage' 322). To
extend her argument, one might notice that the ship, grammatically
feminine, suffers the same fate as those whose natural gender is
feminine. Woolf consistently divested females of the patina conferred
by rich associations with Elizabethan literature.

What the women lose, the men gain. The most important males of the
book, all writers (Ridley Ambrose a scholar, St John Hirst a poet,
Terence Hewet a novelist), all show more and more interest in

Elizabethan literature in the successive versions of the novel. Ambrose, a Greek scholar, is amused, in Draft B, at Rachel's request for Gibbon because 'it might be interesting': ' "Books can be very interesting" he remarked ironically. "Homer, Shakespeare, Boswell" ' (E13/1). In the next draft he is voluble in his advice, rattling off a good many names, suggesting a method, and wondering if Rachel would prefer beginning with the Lake poets or the Elizabethans (Marlowe happens to be on the shelves (L14/3-4)).

Nor is Ridley alone in recommending to Rachel the reading of Elizabethan literature. Although in an earlier draft St John Hirst suggests Ibsen, Butler, and Shaw (B, E16/3), a later draft (C, L14/7) and the novel itself (172) have him urging, along with Gibbon and Wedekind, Donne, Webster, 'and all that set'. Hirst adds, 'I envy you reading them for the first time,' so far past that stage is he. In the same way Terence Hewet knows by heart the poetry which Rachel has never even read. It is Hewet, furthermore, who makes an allusion to *The Tempest* mentioned above, who wants to take a copy of Donne along on an expedition, and who plans to write a 'Stuart tragedy'.[2] In the context of Elizabethan literature, moreover, Hewet's reactions to the forest through which they glide up the river are of special interest. He says in the novel, ' "That's where the Elizabethans got their style," . . . staring into the profusion of leaves and blossoms and prodigious fruits' (268). The comment, because it aptly characterizes lush Elizabethan style, shows not only Hewet's easy familiarity with that literature, but also his ability to deal with it somewhat critically.

Some passages in the holograph of Draft C reveal how Hewet came by that critical ability. In the first, Hirst says, 'I feel just like the late Sir Walter Raleigh . . . I see now where the Elizabethans got their style.' Next Hewet muses that 'The Elizabethans probably got their style from this sort of thing,' and goes on, in an immediately deleted passage, to say, 'Sir Walter Raleigh—now was this the river they discovered when they came to South America?' (H2, ch. 23/54). In the heat of composition Woolf was obviously confusing the explorer of 'Guiana', who died in 1618, with her own contemporary, Professor Walter Raleigh, still very much alive in 1912 when she wrote the passage. It was in the professor's book that Woolf had read in 1906 that 'without the Voyagers Marlowe is inconceivable': 'That marvellous summer time of the

---

[2] In the Hogarth Press edn. (1915), 264. Ultimately Woolf deleted the idea in the American edn. (1920). De Salvo, 'Revisions' 363.

imagination, the Elizabethan age, with all its wealth of flowers and fruit, was the gift to England of the sun that bronzed the faces of the voyagers and of the winds that carried them to the four quarters of the world' (168, 151–2). I suspect that the bookishness and ambiguity of Woolf's mention of her contemporary dictated the deletion of the reference to him, and that reassignment of the observation about Elizabethan style from Hirst to Hewet fits her undoubted plan to build up such associations for the character who was soon to become engaged to Rachel.

The result of all her work on Elizabethan literature in the novel was a clearly demarcated world in which the men became more and more associated with the Elizabethan age, while the women were regularly stripped of such associations. Rachel herself, allowed to turn some pages about that literature in Draft C, in the novel does not do even that. Yet, as I have shown, her milieu is frequently depicted as Elizabethan. Her father deals in commodities associated with Elizabethan voyages; Santa Marina, the scene of her first real contact with the world, with its reminder of Drake's expeditions, is said to be 'where it was in Elizabethan days'; there is an Elizabethan watch-tower on Monte Rosa, where Rachel first talks with Terence Hewet; his blossoming relationship with her is a journey into unknown waters; and the river up which they travel to the declaration of their love looks as it did to the Elizabethan voyagers. Within this Elizabethan milieu exists the twenty-four-year-old Rachel Vinrace, who 'had been educated as the majority of well-to-do girls in the last part of the nineteenth century were educated. . . . there was no subject in the world which she knew accurately.' Woolf continues: 'Her mind was in the state of an intelligent man's in the beginning of the reign of Queen Elizabeth; she would believe practically anything she was told . . .' (33–4). Gone is the glamour of Elizabethan literature that vitalizes Hirst and Hewet. Rachel is merely gullible. Lacking even 'the most elementary idea of a system in modern life' (34), she is trapped by an antiquated social structure she can neither understand nor transcend. She might as well be an Elizabethan woman, uneducated, without a profession, without a sense of her own importance, without the rights whose continued withholding Woolf was to decry even thirty years after writing her first novel.

It is characteristic of many writers who deprecate the present as Woolf did to resort to either a chronological or a cultural primitivism. Both can be observed in Woolf's treatment of the South American setting of her novel. In the climactic chapter in which Rachel and

Terence declare their love to each other, the English tourists, 'accustomed to the wall of trees on either side' of the river, are surprised when they come to a clearing:

On both banks of the river lay an open lawn-like space, grass covered and planted, for the gentleness and order of the place suggested human care, with graceful trees on the top of little mounds. As far as they could gaze, this lawn rose and sank with the undulating motion of an old English park.

Suddenly, they see a herd of wild deer: 'Rows of brown backs paused for a moment and then leapt, with a motion as if they were springing over waves, out of sight' (279). Thus Woolf juxtaposes civilization, with its taming of those subjected to it, and the freedom of non-institutionalized life. The basic scene has long been recognized as one Woolf found in Sir Walter Raleigh's *Discovery of the Large, Rich, and Beautiful Empire of Guiana* (1596), one of the accounts in Hakluyt's *Voyages*. Holtby commented some fifty years ago on Woolf's 'plagiarism' (78–9), and Bazin (52–3) has amplified Holtby's argument by pointing out 'the themes of conquest and virginity' common to Raleigh's account of Guiana and Woolf's treatment of her heroine.

Yet Woolf's Elizabethan source presents the scene quite differently. After describing the clearing, with its groves of trees interspersed among plains of 'grasse short and greene', the account in Hakluyt continues: 'and still as we rowed, the deere came down feeding by the waters side, as if they had beene used to a keepers call' (iv. 137). Significantly, Woolf changed Raleigh's oddly domesticated deer to the wild ones that would point a contrast to the park-like scene. She kept enough of her Elizabethan source to serve her usual purpose of establishing a milieu for Rachel; but she freely adapted to its opposite a vision of little use to her as it stood. Her own version of the wild deer remains in one's mind when, moments later, as Rachel and Terence become engaged, he tells her, 'Oh, you're free, Rachel. To you, time will make no difference, or marriage . . .' (281). The remainder of the novel tests this idea of Rachel's freedom.

When the novel opens, Rachel may be unliberated but she is quite at home in the world of her father, a ship's captain, the elements in which he lives posing no threat. She sees without alarm the 'black ribs of wrecked ships' (27) when the *Euphrosyne* sets out; and even during a storm at sea she can comment, 'Fine, isn't it?' (75). But then she changes, breaks with religion, begins to love Hewet, and immediately feels presentiments of death, significantly from her father's sphere:

Candour forced her to consider the extreme horror of feeling the water give under her, of losing her head, splashing wildly, sinking again with every vein smarting and bursting, an enormous weight sealing her mouth, and pressing salt water down her lungs when she breathed. (Draft B, E18/4)

It is as if Willoughby Vinrace's daughter were trying to be a Willoughby rather than a Rachel. But, sensing herself ill-equipped for independence and adventure, she is inevitably an ill-fated Willoughby. Woolf may have selected the father's name in allusion to the Elizabethan voyager Sir Hugh Willoughby, who died on his voyage out (MHP/Bla, 145). It is clear, certainly, that Rachel cannot survive her pathetic attempts to voyage into the world. It is as if Willoughby Vinrace's maritime empire, hitherto supportive of her life, now abandoned her to the elements it controlled. When Rachel is in fact dying, she experiences the end as if it were a drowning, her earlier premonition coming true in her imagination, with its full burden of guilt for having dared to venture into her father's realm, and with condign retribution. The scene around Rachel's death is described as 'a difficult expedition' (334); and at the centre of the expedition is the young woman who in her delirium drowns: 'She saw nothing and heard nothing but a faint booming sound, which was the sound of the sea rolling over her head' (341).

Thus Hewet's well-meaning but naïve assurances of Rachel's freedom can be seen to have exacerbated the torments she experienced for usurping her father's prerogatives. Rachel's death is Woolf's response to what she saw as the young woman's dilemma: she was unable to remain as she had been before her voyage out, naïve, sheltered, absorbed only in her music; but at the same time she was unable to join the 'brave new world' of marriage and its proffered independence. The allusions to Miranda from *The Tempest*, along with the milieu of Elizabethan voyages in *The Voyage Out* in its finished state, create a world that Rachel both is and is not a part of. When Woolf added, at a stage later than those of the extant drafts, that 'the time of Elizabeth was only distant from the present time by a moment of space' (264), she sharpened the point that the entire narrative made in its liberal use of Elizabethan elements: little progress in the condition of women had been made in the three hundred years which separated the early twentieth century from the Elizabethan age.

In the decade after the publication of *The Voyage Out* in 1915, with its brilliant use of her reading of Professor Raleigh and of the fourth volume of Hakluyt's *Voyages*, Woolf had frequent recourse to the literature of exploration. She read (or in all probability re-read) the first three volumes of Hakluyt with great care, reviewed several related books, and in addition wrote two important critical essays about sixteenth- and seventeenth-century prose, 'Reading' (1919) and 'The Elizabethan Lumber Room' (1925), both of which devote significant space to the voyagers.

The *Times Literary Supplement* sent Woolf for review in 1917 a very fine anthology of selections from Sir Walter Raleigh's letters, as well as from the *Historie of the World* (1614) and *The Last Fight of the Revenge* (1591). Although the bulk of the book is devoted to the *Historie* rather than to Raleigh's voyages, Woolf took the opportunity to discuss Elizabethan exploration, asserting that 'the world of Shakespeare is the world of Hakluyt and Raleigh . . . The navigator and the explorer made their voyage by ship instead of by the mind, but over Hakluyt's pages broods the very same lustre of the imagination.' Remembering Raleigh's *Discovery of the Large, Rich, and Beautiful Empire of Guiana*, she contended that 'those vast rivers and fertile valleys, those forests of odorous trees and mines of gold and ruby, fill up the background of the plays . . .' (*CE* iii. 27). Yet she insisted that there was more to the voyagers than the beauty of the lands they explored. The 'long days at sea, sleep and dreams under strange stars, and lonely effort in the face of death' fostered, she said, a 'meditative mood' that she found appealing (28).

Part of Woolf's reason then for returning to Hakluyt's *Voyages* again and again throughout her life is that in them she found much that was personally to the point. Thus it was that, when the *TLS* sent her another book for review which dealt with the Elizabethan voyages, she devoted much more time than was necessary to the task. The book was Froude's *English Seamen in the Sixteenth Century*, lectures the famous historian had delivered at Oxford in 1893–4, and first published in England in 1895. There were at least seven editions of this popular work before Longmans reissued it in 1918. The popularity stemmed in part from Froude's writing 'in the period of the new imperialism of the late nineteenth century', when the British would have welcomed a view that changed Hakluyt 'from the great Free Trader to the protagonist of nationalistic empire' (Quinn i. 148).

This is not to say that more serious thinkers failed to see Froude's weaknesses. In fact it is Leslie Stephen who mentions in his essay on Froude (1902) the Carlylean hero-worship that skews much of his history. Stephen repeats J. R. Green's criticism that 'in a history of

England [Froude] had omitted the English people' (*Studies* iii. 251). None the less Stephen called Froude 'the best interpreter' of the 'heroic spirit' of the Elizabethan seamen, a spirit that Stephen himself at times could only dimly discern through the 'ruffianly and the mean' qualities of the men, especially the higher ranking ones (241–2). I should think that Woolf knew her father's essay (*D.* 3 Dec. 1918); it was published while she was still living at Hyde Park Gate. But, whether stimulated by her father's essay, or by her own long-standing interest in the working man, Woolf's review of Froude rather ignored him (instead she urged her readers to buy Hakluyt—in the inexpensive Everyman edition) and investigated the world of the voyages from the point of view of the common sailors.

To accomplish this feat, Woolf returned to the primary source, Hakluyt's *Voyages*, and read three complete volumes, taking notes as she went. She appreciated the piling up of nouns characteristic of Elizabethan style, and the near-redundancy of such phrases as 'remote and farthest distant quarters'. The experience of reading was exhilarating, for she discovered that Hakluyt 'turns out on mature inspection to justify over & over again my youthful discrimination' (*D.* 7 Dec. 1918). She devotes three-quarters of her essay to those volumes, and the poor remainder to Froude. She did enjoy his occasional felicities, most particularly the swinging rhythm to be heard in his description of the small ship that took Drake around the world, no bigger, she noted, than 'a second rate yacht of a modern noble lord'. But Froude's 'heroic figures' seemed to 'lose inevitably something of the humanity which we discern in them obscurely engaged with their forgotten comrades upon those trafficks and discoveries which are recorded in the volumes of Hakluyt ('Trafficks and Discoveries' 618). She found in Hakluyt vivid accounts of titled men who lost their lives, but cited them to underline the enormous risks run by all, not just by the famous. The Earl of Cumberland's ship was hung up near the coast of Cornwall so long that the thirsty sailors drank vinegar and licked 'with their tongues (like dogges) the boards under feete' (ii. 656–7; MHP/B2d, 27).

She also found in Hakluyt a magnificent description of the departure of Sir Hugh Willoughby's ships to Russia, which first put in at Greenwich for a leave-taking that she never forgot: 'The greater shippes are towed downe with boates, and oares, and the mariners being all apparelled in Watchet or skie coloured cloth, rowed amaine, and made way with diligence.' When they got near Greenwich, the Courtiers came running out, and the comon people flockt together, standing very thicke upon the shoare: the privie Counsel, they lookt out at the windowes of the Court, and the rest ranne up to the toppes of the towers: the shippes hereupon discharge their Ordinance...and the Mariners, they shouted in such sort, that the skie rang againe with the noyse thereof. One stoode in the poope of the ship, and by his gesture bids farewell to his friendes in the best maner hee could. Another walkes upon the hatches, another climbes the shrowds, another stands upon the maine yard, and another in the top of the shippe. (i. 272; MHP/B2d, 23)

Such were the materials Woolf was working with. She quotes most of this passage in her review, and again alludes to it in 'The Elizabethan Lumber Room'. Her point was that the danger of the enterprise accounted for the solemnity of the leave-taking.

Yet she did not see the sailors as foolhardy, for their 'hopes and expectations . . . more than counterbalanced their sufferings'. She had herself sensed in Hakluyt the promise of foreign lands incredibly rich in beauty and wealth, and had used that promise in *The Voyage Out* to delineate the masculine world from which Rachel was barred. The voyagers might find gold 'in the commonest black stone', and might also see for the first time the almost legendary creatures of foreign lands. 'Marvellous was the richness of the earth', said Woolf, 'and the shapes of the creatures seen, as [the ship's captain] John Locke saw the elephant, "not only with my bodily eyes, but much more with the eyes of my mind and spirit".'

Woolf seized the precise element that fascinated the Elizabethan seamen. True, the most extraordinary sights were apt to fall to emissaries of Queen Elizabeth, but even the sailors had their share in foreign opulence. Woolf noted the 'magnificence with which the English sailors are entertained' at the Turkish court (MHP/B2d, 26), 'which was spread with carpets on the ground fourescore or fourescore and tenne foot long, with an hundred and fiftie severall dishes set thereon . . .' (ii. 290). On a voyage to Russia, the company were brought into the presence of the Emperor, 'unto whom each of us did his duetie accordingly, and kissed his right hand, his majestie sitting in his chaire of estate, with his crowne on his head, and a staffe of goldsmiths worke in his left hand well garnished with rich and costly stones . . .' (i. 352). Woolf goes out of her way to allow the reader to view the wonders of Hakluyt's world from the adventurers' point of view, the 'strange and splendid ceremonies' encountered by titled gentlemen, ships' captains, and common sailors.

She also attempts to convey some sense of the lives of ordinary men by devoting time in this review to their spiritual concerns even though piety was alien to her. She read many fine accounts in Hakluyt of desperate sea battles in which triumph was promised those who 'continually doe call on God'. 'The Divinity', she says with unconcealed wonder, 'may be addressed as if He were a temporal prince scarcely hidden by the clouds; but their piety is real enough.' She recreates in all its vividness a scene where men prepare for battle against eight enemy vessels. 'Down they fall upon their knees . . . after which drums, flutes, and trumpets sound,' and the battle begins. Woolf abandons paraphrase, for the spare language of the original could not be bettered: 'Then stood up one Grove the master, being a comely man, with his sword and target, holding them up in defiance against his enemies . . . But chiefly the boatswain showed himself valiant above the rest; for he fared among the Turks like a wood lion . . .' Years later a phrase, if not its import, recurred in her memory as she wrote that Dadie Rylands was 'as pink as a daisy and as proud as a wood-lion. Where does one read of wood lions?' (*L.* 1800, 21 Aug. 1927). Well, one reads of wood (i.e. crazy) lions in Hakluyt. And one recalls the phrase if one has incorporated it in a review meant to convey some sense of the anonymous seamen whose exploits meant more to Woolf than those of their famous compatriots. History is more than the history of Great Men.

Nor is Woolf's frequent mention of common seamen the only evidence of the heightened social consciousness she brought to this reading of Hakluyt. She balked at Froude's slant, 'those famous prejudices and opinions which colour all his writing' and make of the voyages a glorious chapter in the manifest destiny of British Protestantism. The voyagers, she maintained, 'had, as we have, a mixture of motives in their undertakings, among which the desire to justify the Protestant faith was not always to the fore'. Clearly, a major impetus to the voyages was trade, and that often for 'the good of the poor' (MHP/B2d, 26). She quotes at length from a letter written in 1582 by a cousin of Hakluyt's to urge his agent in Constantinople to promote the superior English wool, to benefit not just the merchants and shepherds but also to prevent 'the turning to bag and wallet of the infinite number of the poore people imploied in clothing in severall degrees of labour here in England'. Gilbert advocated a north-west passage in part so that they might 'settle there such needy people of our countrey, which now trouble the common wealth, and through want here at home are inforced to commit outragious offences, whereby they are dayly consumed with the gallowes' (iii. 45). Woolf used this account in praising the elder Hakluyt for promoting trade, and maintained that his efforts helped the poor ' "ready to starve for relief" more than by building them alms houses or by giving them lands and goods'. She saw in the voyages, then, a means of class mobility, rather than a perpetuation of a system that allowed the rich to salve their consciences while keeping down the underprivileged.

I do not mean to overstate the case for Woolf's social consciousness in this review of Froude's book. It is clear, for example, that she was not yet ready to decry in print the exploitation of the poor of other nations. But her social conscience was sufficiently developed for her to see the value of trade in the rise of a middle class in England. Hakluyt's letter of instruction to his agent in Constantinople was just one of the many she studied to learn about the ordinary people who engaged in the voyages, or for whose ultimate benefit many were undertaken. The volumes of Hakluyt that she read were long, but her reading notes attest to the fact that she read every page, even the humblest letters, which made 'as good reading as the more heroic passages which have become famous'. Woolf's emphasis on the common man is not unexpected at this point in her life. It was part of a growing social consciousness fostered by political events. Beatrice and Sidney Webb had visited the Woolfs in September of 1918, and in the course of conversation Virginia had asked one of her 'most fruitful questions; viz: how easy is it for a man to change his social grade?' (*D.* 18 Sept. 1918). It was the sort of question that was in the air, and that had been brought to the fore for Woolf with Leonard's founding of the 1917 club about a year earlier, following the February Revolution in Russia. The lines had become clearly drawn in her mind between imperialist exploitation and socialist betterment of the common man.

When Woolf came to review Froude's *English Seamen in the Sixteenth Century,* and decided to make of it a critical essay on Hakluyt's Elizabethan text, it is not at all surprising that she read those volumes devoted primarily to Russia and the East. In 1906, when reviewing Professor Raleigh's *English Voyages of the Sixteenth Century,* the western voyages caught her eye; these provided the setting and frame for *The Voyage Out,* thereby strengthening Woolf's feminist statement. But by 1918 another cause had come to have an equal claim on her loyalties, and the review of Froude's book evinces that cause both by its preoccupation with the improvement of the lot of the comon man, and by its selection of accounts of voyages to and trade with Russia.

Less than a year later Woolf had occasion to think again about the voyages to Russia, and several of the other accounts in the first three volumes of Hakluyt that she had read in connection with her review of Froude's book. She returned to Hakluyt in pursuance of a plan to define the impact of representative examples of sixteenth- and seventeenth-century prose on a sensitive reader of the twentieth century. The resultant essay, 'Reading', she never published as such (it was published posthumously in *The Captain's Death Bed*, repr. *CE* ii. 12–33) but incorporated into 'The Elizabethan Lumber Room'. Since the later essay neither departs substantively from the earlier, nor develops ideas quite as fully, I shall concentrate my remarks on 'Reading' with brief mention from time to time that Woolf includes a given passage in 'The Elizabethan Lumber Room'.

In its considerable coverage of Hakluyt, 'Reading' incorporates some of the review of Froude, rearranged and revised; a bit from Raleigh's account of Guiana, including the scene of the grazing deer that Woolf had used in *The Voyage Out*; and some new material drawn from the first three volumes of Hakluyt. As in the Froude essay, Woolf celebrates the exploits of 'forgotten voyagers'; but she questions, for the first time, the adequacy of the narratives: the writers in Hakluyt provide descriptions of the voyages and of the places visited, but rarely anything in the least introspective, '. . . they make no mention of oneself; seem altogether oblivious of such an organism . . .'. Yet if the sailors were incapable of analysis, they possessed an enviable 'balance, owing to the poise of brain and body arrived at by the union of adventures and physical exertion with minds still tranquil and unstirred as the summer sea' (21). Additionally, the very unprofessionalism of the writers, combined with what she had earlier called their 'veracious eye', often provided the raw materials whose significance Woolf herself was quick to grasp. She was impressed, for example, by a 'luminous' tale of the abduction of two native Americans (MHP/B2d, 29), the man one year 'shown about like a wild beast', and the next given 'a woman savage on board to keep him company'.

When they see each other they blush; they blush profoundly; the sailor notices it but knows not why it is. And later the two savages set up house together on board ship, she attending to his wants, he nursing her in sickness, but living, as the sailors note, in perfect chastity. (*CE* ii. 20; 'ELR', *CE* i. 48)

The story engaged both her sympathies and her pictorial imagination fully: 'The erratic searchlight cast by these records falling for a second upon those blushing cheeks three hundred years ago, among the snow, sets up that sense of communication which we are apt to get only from fiction' (*CE* ii. 20).

By the time that she wrote 'Reading' Woolf had read and re-read four volumes of Hakluyt. To say that accounts of voyages sometimes had the power of fiction was a high compliment, and one that suggests the evocativeness Woolf hoped to achieve by alluding to the voyages in her own fiction. The imagery that continued to stimulate her imagination was broadly speaking of two types: images of warmth and ease, and images of cold and mystery.

The former derived from accounts of voyages to South America and to the eastern Mediterranean. Raleigh's Guiana, recaptured in *The Voyage Out*, still haunted her imagination (*CE* ii. 18–19), and would find its way into 'The Elizabethan Lumber Room' as well (*CE* i. 47). The undulating lands lining the Plate, herds of deer, precious stones, and 'dusky limbs of savages' evoked the Southern warmth and plenty that, Woolf said, 'is the pleasantest atmosphere on a hot summer's day'.

They talk of their commodities and there you see them; more clearly and separately in bulk, colour, and variety than the goods brought by steamer and piled upon docks; they talk of fruit; the red and yellow globes hang unpicked on virgin trees; so with the lands they sight; the morning mist is only just now lifting and not a flower has been plucked. The grass has long whitened tracks upon it for the first time.

This vision of a rich virgin land had already served in *The Voyage Out*, where Helen Ambrose attempts to embody the red and yellow fruit in a work of art. In addition, Woolf's re-reading of the adventures of Fitch, Bodenham, and Lok, the very different richness of the eastern Mediterranean supplemented the South American scenes. Sailors experienced in towns the same sense of freshness as they saw for the first time the 'white towers . . . gilt domes and ivory minarets' of the Levant (21). These images of favoured climates, where nature poured forth riches or where man embellished the landscape with incredible wealth, had enormous suggestive power.

But as Woolf looked back with panoptic vision over Hakluyt's world, she also acknowledged that 'in the land of long winters and squat-faced savages the very darkness and strangeness draw the imagination' (19). Drawing again on the voyages to Russia she imagined 'three or four men from the west of England set down in the white landscape', trading until they were picked up again by ships 'no bigger than yachts'. 'Strange must have been their thoughts; strange the sense of the unknown; and of themselves, the isolated English, burning on the very rim of the dark, and the dark full of unseen splendours' (*CE* ii. 19; 'ELR', *CE* i. 48). Both the northern voyages and the southern ones which first drew Woolf's imagination had great immediacy for her: 'the sight upon which the English merchant, the vanguard of civilization, first set eyes has the brilliancy still of a Roman vase or other shining ornament dug up and stood for a moment in the sun before, exposed to the air, seen by millions of eyes, it dulls and crumbles away' (*CE* ii. 19). Her accolade, an ode on an English urn, suggests that in the seeming artlessness of the *Voyages* the Elizabethan seamen who recorded them achieved the permanence of art.

Woolf's reading of the southern voyages had already informed her writing of *The Voyage Out*. In two novels of the 1920s, *Jacob's Room* and *To the Lighthouse*, Woolf would reflect her thoughts about gender in relation to the phenomenon of voyaging; and finally all of her reading in Hakluyt, of both the southern and northern voyages, would enter into her last novel of that decade, *Orlando*.

In Woolf's first novel of the 1920s, *Jacob's Room* (1922), the sea is omnipresent. The action begins in Cornwall, where Betty Flanders is on holiday with her three sons; it returns there when Jacob visits the Durrants; and Woolf evokes that special locale again when Jacob sees the Greek coast. Scarborough is the scene of Jacob's upbringing and school holidays. At one point an anonymous young man imagines a Jacobean Scarborough, devoid of pier—'and how grey and turbulent the sea is in the seventeeth century!' (19)—a typically Woolfian reminder of the earlier voyagers. Furthermore, the men in Betty Flanders's life are both connected with the sea, her husband Seabrook nominally, her lover Captain Barfoot more substantially. Women, the narrator comments, might imagine the captain 'on the Bridge at night', might have 'visions of shipwreck and disaster, in which all the passengers come tumbling from their cabins, and there is the captain, buttoned in his pea-jacket matched with the storm, vanquished by it but by none other' (28). It is a version of the bravery of Queen Elizabeth's heroes, adapted to the modern world. Yet, while women are said to enjoy such bravery in men, Mrs Jarvis, the clergyman's wife, is jealous of the opportunities available to men but denied to women. Her attitude is reminiscent of Katherine Hilbery's in *Night and Day*, whose daydreams run to 'the

conduct of a vast ship in a hurricane round a black promontory of rock',
for which she has a 'surpassing ability' (45). Like Katharine, Mrs Jarvis
insists that men are not the only ones with souls to be defined by
heroism in the face of adversity; the storm is her storm as much as his
(28). Soul or not, though, she is landlocked, as are all the women in
Jacob's Room save Mrs Durrant, who recalls sailing with her fiancé
round the coast of Cornwall when she was a young woman (61).
The voyagers of *Jacob's Room* are in fact men. Archer Flanders is in
the Royal Navy; Timmy Durrant becomes a clerk at the Admiralty.
Even Betty Flanders's brother has adventured on the seas while she
remains in England: poor Morty (15, 91) is introduced into the
narrative, one assumes, solely to reinforce the gender-connection of
voyaging. When Jacob and Timmy Durrant are boating on the Cam,
they are amused over Uncle Morty's life, what with his sailing
Indian Ocean, exotically becoming a Muhammadan, and romantically
dying (38).

Jacob himself trails clouds of glory from heroic sea-adventurers, 'the
world our ship' (90). The 'battered Ulysses' at the British Museum puts
Fanny Elmer in mind of Jacob (170). At a Guy Fawkes party, dancers
wreathe Jacob's head, others 'hung glass grapes on his shoulders, until
he looked like the figure-head of a wrecked ship' (75). It is of course a
highly romantic, if premonitory, image. Earlier in the book, Jacob and
Timmy Durrant actually sail round the coast of Cornwall. While the
six-day trip is perhaps not much of a feat in itself, still 'ships have been
wrecked here' (47), and the narrator asserts that Jacob is quite capable of
'sailing round the world in a ten-ton yacht, which, very likely, he would
do one of these days . . .' (50). Three centuries earlier Sir Francis Drake
had set out from Cornwall to circumnavigate the globe in just such a
ship. Sunburnt and unshaven, Jacob is the very model of a 'modern
noble lord'.

But the association of men with voyaging in *Jacob's Room* continually
suggests disaster: shipwreck, sinking, and drowning are real possibilities.
More important, men's voyaging can imperil nations as well as
individuals. The scene at the Admiralty, where Timmy works, is thick
with preparations for England's entry into the First World War; and the
peaceful scene in Athens at the same moment, with sunset on the
Parthenon, and the Greek women 'as jolly as sand-martins', shifts
suddenly when 'the ships in the Piraeus fired their guns'. Indeed, so
firm is the association between the sea and guns that Betty Flanders, far
away in Scarborough, is not quite sure whether the sound she hears is

the battle in France, or the sea. The dull sound makes her tｈ 'Morty lost, and Seabrook dead; her sons fighting for their couｎ (175).

Woolf's treatment of the sea is part and parcel of her condemnation of the patriarchal culture she held responsible for war. The romance of the Elizabethan voyagers had for several years now been tempered by an indictment of the bellicosity of their modern counterparts. In 1910 Woolf had enjoyed her part in the Dreadnought Hoax, mocking 'the most modern and the most secret man o' war then afloat, H.M.S. *Dreadnought*' (Bell i. 157). In a story published just one year before *Jacob's Room*, 'A Society', Woolf allows one of her characters the same privilege, by way of building her case against the Royal Navy. Other characters visit other bastions of the patriarchy, all revealed to be faulty, so that they appear responsible for the outbreak of the First World War.

Although men are the culprits of 'A Society', Woolf would not be so foolish as to find fault with the entire sex. Rather, it was those in power who used only the aggressive–heroic part of their selves that were responsible for the worst features of civilization. By the end of the decade Woolf hoped for a mitigation of these problems through a development of androgyny. Demonstrated in *Orlando*, her theory was explicitly discussed in *A Room of One's Own*, where she sets up an image of two young people, one female, one male, getting into a taxi: 'and then the cab glided off as if it were swept on by the current . . .' (167). The taxi, she says, is symbolic of the androgynous mind, where the male and female elements co-operate to get somewhere.

The boat in *To the Lighthouse* (1927) can be seen in much the same light, for in this novel Brittanic men no longer rule the waves. Just as female and male are paired in other respects (for example the Ramsays, Rose and Jasper, Lily and Mr Carmichael), so are they paired on the voyage to the lighthouse. Accompanying their father are both Cam and James, his youngest daughter and youngest son. They are in league, purportedly to resist their father's tyranny, but in fact together making the trip a success. Each contributes a special quality, Cam 'womanly' imagination and sympathy, James 'manly' courage and direction.

It is a mistake to limit the significance of the attainment of the lighthouse (beyond, that is, the case of Lily Briscoe) to its meaning in the development of James alone. James and Cam experience their separate epiphanies, and both are of importance to the novel. True, Mr Ramsay makes of the voyage a triumph for James ('Well done'), but that event is immediately shifted to Cam's consciousness:

There! Cam thought, addressing herself silently to James. You've got it at last. For she knew that this was what James had been wanting, and she knew that now he had got it he was so pleased that he would not look at her or at his father or at any one . . . you've got it now, Cam thought. (306)

Cam is sufficiently perceptive to serve as the author's vehicle for interpreting the event—one of many instances of Woolf's insisting on Cam's importance in the final section of the book. In the many pages devoted to the children's thoughts in the third section, Cam's dominate the narrative about twice as frequently as James's.

Woolf prepares the way for Cam's centrality by setting up a parallel early on between Cam and Mrs Ramsay. It is worth examining two passages in some detail:

Mrs Ramsay:	*Cam:*
. . . and in pity for him [Mr Bankes], life being now strong enough to bear her on again, she began all this business, as a sailor not without weariness sees the wind fill his sail and yet hardly wants to be off again and thinks how, had the ship sunk, he would have whirled round and round and found rest on the floor of the sea. (127)	hand cut a trail in the sea, as her mind made the green swirls and streaks into patterns and, numbed and shrouded, wandered in imagination in that underworld of waters where the pearls stuck in clusters to white sprays, where in the green light a change came over one's entire mind and one's body shone half transparent enveloped in a green cloak. (272)

Clearly, Mrs Ramsay's state of mind is a metaphorical pre-echo of Cam's. Both mother and daughter would welcome an escape—an underwater escape: Mrs Ramsay from the demands of the dinner party, Cam from the demands of the voyage. The paralleling of the two raises Cam's stature for what amounts to the final lap of the novel, the progress from the midpoint between the Isle of Skye and the lighthouse.

But at the same time the paralleled passages isolate, in both manner and matter, important differences between the two females. Mrs Ramsay's mood is reported by the narrator with a distancing 'as', whereas Cam's underwater jaunt is presented with less mediation. Further, Mrs Ramsay's shipwreck is conceived of as an end to activity, whereas Cam's is the starting-point for a new mode of consciousness. And, finally, Cam's underwater world is more richly suggestive than her mother's, alive with tactile and visual imagery, and with literary allusion. So close was the connection between pearls in the sea and dead fathers (*VO*; *L*. 1348, 19 Jan. 1923), that Cam's vision of pearls must be read in that context. Having been struck by her father's 'crass blindness and tyranny' and her own sufferings (253), Cam expresses her hostility to her father in the clusters of pearls stuck to white sprays, as accurately as James expresses his although in a more attenuated fashion. Having thus voiced the death-wish, for both her father and herself, she gains a sort of freedom: 'in the green light a change came over one's entire mind and one's body shone half transparent enveloped in a green cloak.' It is 'Full Fathom Five' again, but the particular lineaments of the sea-change owe something to Marvell's 'The Garden', where the speaker achieves a oneness with nature, 'a green thought in a green shade'. Cam's imagination puts her in touch with a reality that gives perspective to the details of everyday life, and thereby helps solve some of its problems. She can cope with her ambivalence towards her father, and she can even find form below the seeming arbitrariness of life, as Rachel Vinrace, the earliest of Woolf's women voyagers, could not do (Nashashibi 199).

The trip to the lighthouse is filled with reminders of heroic Elizabethan voyagers, of what Woolf called the 'lonely effort in the face of death'. James shares his father's vision of the world, a vision tied in Woolf's imagination to Drake's rounding the Horn: 'We are driving before a gale—we must sink' (302). Cam, also haunted by thoughts of heroic disaster, attempts to give them shape, to incorporate them into stories. At that point in the journey when Mr Ramsay congratulates James on his steering, Cam achieves the perfect balance of an artist, between the world of fact and the world of vision:

. . . it seemed as if they were doing two things at once; they were eating their lunch here in the sun and they were also making for safety in a great storm after a shipwreck. Would the water last? Would the provisions last? she asked herself, telling herself a story but knowing at the same time what was the truth. (304)

If James can identify with Drake's driving before a gale, Cam can identify with the common seamen who repeatedly faced disaster. Recall Woolf's summary in the 1918 review of Froude: 'Many would come back no more; let alone the risk that a wave would swamp the little ship . . . or [that they would be] hung up by adverse winds off the coast of Cornwall for a fortnight, until, in their thirst, they licked the muddy water off the deck . . .' Cam may not know the points of the compass, but she can share imaginatively in such adventures when she herself voyages off the British coast.

In murmuring Cowper's 'we perished, each alone' (284), Cam takes on her father's heroic qualities and elevates the voyage to something more remarkable than a family outing. Although women are not generally part of that side of life, she can be said to have realized the fleeting desire of Lily Briscoe to be 'included among the sailors and adventurers' (153). When Cam trails her hand in the ice-cold sea, 'there spurted up a fountain of joy at the change, at the escape, at the adventure (that she should be alive, that she should be there)' and she begins to see the place of the 'little island' in the larger universe (280–1). Cam and Lily share the view of sailing as an 'extraordinary adventure' (303), with each other and with Woolf. And again, like Woolf, they enter the world of the voyagers via the creative imagination, through story-telling and painting. Indeed, Woolf often likened the creative effort to a dangerous voyage (*BA* 210–11). As soon as Lily solves one problem in a painting, she must face another: 'Down in the hollow of one wave she saw the next wave towering higher and higher above her' (*TL* 236). She finally solves all problems with that painting by placing on the canvas 'a line there, in the centre', the line presumably of the lighthouse (310).

The lighthouse, the central symbol of the painting and of the novel itself, generally is thought to represent Mrs Ramsay. If it is true, as Mr Ramsay believes, that 'we perish, each alone', Woolf suggests that it is also true that 'there is a coherence in things, a stability; something, she meant, is immune from change . . .' (158). That 'something', glimpsed variously as love and works of art, is demonstrated in Mrs Ramsay's dinner party, in her remaining in the memories of those who knew her, and in Lily's painting, the culmination of both her love for Mrs Ramsay and her final sympathy for Mr Ramsay.

Linking all of these is the poem which Mrs Ramsay reads earlier in the novel, William Browne of Tavistock's 'Sirens' Song' (179). Because the poem is an Elizabethan evocation of the ultimate voyager, Ulysses, it deserves full quotation:

> Steer, hither steer your winged pines,
>   All beaten mariners!
> Here lie Love's undiscover'd mines,
>   A prey to passengers—
> Perfumes far sweeter than the best
> Which make the Phoenix' urn and nest.
> Fear not your ships,
> Nor any to oppose you save our lips;

But come on shore,
Where no joy dies till Love hath gotten more.

For swelling waves our panting breasts,
  Where never storms arise,
Exchange, and be awhile our guests:
  For stars gaze on our eyes.
The compass Love shall hourly sing,
And as he goes about the ring,
  We will not miss
To tell each point he nameth with a kiss.
  —Then come on shore,
  Where no joy dies till Love hath gotten more.

Browne's song of course deliberately suppresses the sirens' motive of destruction, and would perhaps have attracted Woolf by its elimination of the misogyny implicit in Homer's tale. Instead it celebrates in two lovely verses the joys to be found on the sirens' island home. There the sailors might find 'Love's undiscover'd mines' and sweet perfumes, reminiscent of the rich lands recently discovered by British voyagers. There they offer refuge to storm-beaten mariners; and they offer not only love, but a love which denies death by always begetting more love.

The 'Sirens' Song' is quite appropriate for Mrs Ramsay. If the lighthouse to which she hoped James might sail has any meaning for her, it is as the place of restful love following whatever difficulties life may bring him.[3] Woolf once compared her father's relief at the respite provided him after the 'agony and loneliness of thought' by her mother's 'unquestionable human loveliness' to that of 'a seafarer [who] wrapt for many days in mist on the fruitless waters lands at dawn upon a sunlit shore, where all nature enfolds him and breathes in his ear rest and assurance' (*MB* 37–8). The passage might almost be considered a gloss on Woolf's quotation of the line from Browne's 'Sirens' Song'.

Mrs Ramsay's reading of the line also sets up the later identification of Cam with her mother; and the substance of the lyric speaks directly to Cam's significance in the novel. Not just a sharer in the voyage, but as much as James a beneficiary of it, she is also a contributor to its successful completion. Cam does not know the points of the compass, to her father's chagrin, but his teasing cannot unseat her love for him:

---

[3] Fleishman (106) relates the song to James's attainment of the lighthouse, but somewhat differently. Wyatt ('The Celebration' 164) interprets the mines as 'the hidden explosives that married life detonates'—though the sirens could not have in mind that meaning.

cted her more' (253). In Browne's song, Love hourly
..s, and the sirens promise that, 'as he goes about the
tell each point he nameth with a kiss'. Of that sort of
..nows a great deal. Since knowledge of the geographical
..cessary for the success of a voyage, the novel valorizes
Jam..   y to steer; and, since love is necessary for the success of
this particular voyage, the novel valorizes Cam's ability to 'tell each
point with a kiss'.

Of the six Ramsay children alive after the war, only Cam and James
actually go to the lighthouse, despite the fact that their four brothers
and sisters have returned with them to Skye. One almost hears in the
names Woolf employs for her two successful young voyagers echoes of
the voyage described in *Jacob's Room*, the English 'James' harking back
to the Latin *Jacobus*, while 'Cam' puts one in mind of the river in
Cambridge where Jacob and Timmy first planned their voyage. Sailing
was a well-nigh masculine pursuit, and the pleasures, the satisfactions,
and the perils of the patriarchy seemed to adhere to the male voyagers.
In *To The Lighthouse*, on the other hand, the possibilities of voyaging
are extended to women, and a new set of values emerges. The journey to
the lighthouse elicits sympathy for both sexes, and rewards both
appropriately. Lily Briscoe, one of Woolf's avatars in *To the Lighthouse*,
looks out to sea at the 'silent little boat [where] Mr. Ramsay was sitting
with Cam and James' (242), much as Woolf imagines herself, in *A
Room of One's Own*, watching a young man and young woman in a taxi.
Lily's vision can encompass both male and female, for 'the war had
drawn the sting of her femininity. Poor devils, one thought, poor devils,
of both sexes' (238). This conjunction of voyages and war again takes
one back to the earlier *Jacob's Room*, but with a difference, for the
androgynous voyage may be the start of something more positive.
Though a son of the Ramsays is taken by the same war that had claimed
Jacob Flanders, Woolf expresses hope, by means of the reconciliation
within the microcosm of the Ramsay family, for increased international
understanding and co-operation.

In *Orlando* (1928), the book she wrote immediately after *To the
Lighthouse*, Woolf's long acquaintance with the Elizabethan voyages is
most evident, for here she draws on both the southern and the northern
voyages, especially the latter, and that particularly in the vision of
Russia prompted by Orlando's affair with Sasha, the Muscovite
princess who arrived in London in the entourage of the ambassador.
Woolf had read two accounts in Hakluyt of the first visit from a Russian

ambassador, which occurred in the mid-sixteenth century, the narratives sufficiently vivid to have prompted some note-taking. Sasha's entertainment therefore sounds quite authentic: when she wants to see 'the Tower, the Beefeaters, the Heads on Temple Bar, and the jewellers' shops in the city', Orlando obliges, and buys her 'whatever took her fancy in the Royal Exchange' (44). The first Muscovite ambassador to the English court was 'received with fourscore merchants with chaines of gold', entertained at court, and shown the sights of London (i. 322; MHP/B2d, 24).

Orlando is justly proud of London's architectural wonders, and in his ethnocentric way assumes the worst of Sasha's compatriots:

for he had heard that the women in Muscovy wear beards and the men are covered with fur from the waist down; that both sexes are smeared with tallow to keep the cold out, tear meat with their fingers and live in huts, where an English noble would scruple to keep his cattle . . . (48)

Orlando's vision of Russia is modelled on several accounts that Woolf had read in Hakluyt. One voyager saw men 'eate rocke weedes . . . foules egges rawe, and the yong birdes also that were in the egges' (i. 326; MHP/B2d, 24). The Russians lived, even in major cities, in wooden houses. Even the detail of both sexes' smearing themselves with tallow is not too far from the truth for an English traveller reported that Russian wives 'grease their faces . . .' As for Orlando's bizarre notions that women were bearded, the men naturally furry, well, an author can allow herself some licence.

Yet it is remarkable that in this work of fancy Woolf used very little licence in her entire coverage of Russia. She knew that certain commodities were much sought after in the voyages to Russia, wax and tallow for example, so that it comes as not much of a surprise that Sasha gnaws tallow (52). The same is true of the violence Woolf attributes to Russians (drawn in all likelihood from tales of the Tartars). Sasha's Russia was a land of 'lust and slaughter', a land 'where there were frozen rivers and wild horses and men, she said, who gashed each other's throats open' (50). Even when her first 'betrayal' of Orlando is glossed over, Sasha 'barked like a wolf' (54). And eventually, she turns on Orlando, like the wolf and fox to which she was compared. Lurking beneath her wonderfully sophisticated appearance and manner is a Russian beast.

Or so it seems to Orlando, whose imagination is coloured by travellers' tales, not yet freed by experiences to come. On the night of Orlando's planned elopement, as he awaits Sasha in vain, Woolf carefully reminds the reader of those tales: the 'few seafaring men' in the parlour of the inn near Blackfriars where Orlando waits 'sit there trolling their ditties, and telling their stories of Drake, Hawkins, and Grenville . . .' (59). Lured by the enchantment of the mysterious Russia, Orlando had also been troubled throughout their time together by the Russians' reputation for treachery. When it is evident that Sasha will not arrive, in spite of their agreement, 'The old suspicions subterraneously at work in him rushed forth from concealment openly' (61). The woman who had flattered him proved to be 'faithless, mutable, fickle', a 'devil, adulteress, deceiver . . .' (64). How could Sasha be otherwise? 'The aura of intrigue' surrounding her owes something to 'the early tales brought back by travellers in Elizabethan times' (Rubenstein 169). The Russians, according to Hakluyt, were 'great talkers and lyers, without any faith or trust in their words, flatterers and dissemblers' (i. 350).

To colour Orlando's view of Sasha is the main use of Hakluyt's northern voyages in this novel. Woolf had read the tale of Anthony Jenkinson's voyage, with its account of the Russians' travel on frozen rivers: '. . . and one horse with a sled, will draw a man upon it 400 miles, in three days . . .' (Hakluyt i. 351; see also ii. p.ix). This Woolf transmuted, with the same hyperbole, into Sasha's assertion that 'In Russia they had rivers ten miles broad on which one could gallop six horses abreast all day long without meeting a soul' (44). Interestingly, there is an account of a stage erected on the ice, though for a show of military might rather than for a dramatic performance.

It is on the frozen Thames that Orlando first meets Sasha, one of the great loves of his life. From the northern voyages come many of the details concerning Sasha. The southern voyages play a small but equally significant role in *Orlando*: they provide the background for the Lady Orlando's other great love, her husband, Marmaduke Bonthrop Shelmerdine. Marmaduke's life is 'spent in the most desperate and splendid of adventures—which is to voyage round Cape Horn in the teeth of a gale' (252). Woolf knew all about that particular adventure from reading both Hakluyt's account of Drake's circumnavigation and Froude's magnificent retelling. Froude had said of the islands that make up Cape Horn, 'in the latitude of Cape Horn a westerly gale blows for ever round the globe; the waves the highest anywhere known' (118). Woolf's choice of this enterprise as Marmaduke's identifying image is inspired, calling forth visions of masts snapping off, sails torn to ribbons, shipwrecks—the panorama of adventure and courage that makes up the life of a hero.

In working out the relationship between Orlando and Marmaduke, Woolf again approaches the question of gender and voyaging broached in both *Jacob's Room* and *To the Lighthouse.* Marmaduke sets out from Falmouth, as Jacob Flanders had done, and talks the kind of talk James Ramsay, but not Cam, would be able to understand (257). His is a world of romantic masculine adventure. But Marmaduke is no more exclusively masculine than the Lady Orlando is exclusively feminine, and only 'demonstration' can establish the basic sex (252). The androgynous Orlando understands Marmaduke's talk of starboard and larboard, of booms and Bo'suns (257–8) In so far as she is androgynous, her life partakes of her husband's voyages around Cape Horn; and in so far as Marmaduke is androgynous, the essence of his life finds form in his wife's poetic images.

Orlando has been a poet since her boyhood in the sixteenth century; and now, in the nineteenth, she achieves the expression of what Hoffmann (443) calls 'the essence of the poetic vision', her comprehension of life in a toy boat on the Serpentine. As Orlando looks at her penny steamer, it seems to be an ocean liner fighting waves that 'soon become just as big as the waves on the Atlantic':

So Orlando mistook the toy boat for her husband's brig; and the wave she had made with her toe for a mountain of water off Cape Horn; and as she watched the toy boat climb the ripple, she thought she saw Bonthrop's ship climb up and up a glassy wall; up and up it went, and a white crest with a thousand deaths in it arched over it; and through the thousand deaths it went and disappeared—'It's sunk!' she cried out in an agony—and then, behold, there it was again sailing along safe and sound among the ducks on the other side of the Atlantic. (286–7)

The scene draws on Woolf's own memories of sailing boats on the pond in Kensington Gardens, where once 'my Cornish lugger sailed perfectly to the middle of the pond and then with my eyes upon it, amazed, sank suddenly' ('Sketch', *MB* 77). The Lady Orlando realizes in her imagination the extremes of danger met by the voyagers so vividly that Woolf just about enables the reader to accept as 'Ecstasy!' Orlando's relief at her husband's having once more successfully rounded the Horn. The toy boat on the Serpentine and 'Ecstasy' are, she discovers, 'interchangeable and meant exactly the same thing . . .' (287). Thus ends the exclusivity of Elizabethan voyaging. Woolf begins the process that will take centuries when, in his own person, Orlando goes as Ambassador to the Turkish court at Constantinople; in his own person he hears talk of voyages to the Azores, Spain, and Portugal undertaken by the Earl of Cumberland and Sir Richard Grenville, and of Drake's and Hawkins's exploits in the West Indies. Beyond these, and adding to them to make up what amounts to a vicarious circumnavigation of the globe, Orlando through Sasha joins Hakluyt's voyagers to the northernmost parts of Russia, and through Marmaduke goes to the southernmost parts of South America. The Lady Orlando is a part of all that she has met.

Woolf's choice of a sailor for Orlando's mate seems almost inevitable when one recalls the community she often insisted upon between the characteristic features of poetry and Hakluyt's *Voyages*. In a review written a decade before *Orlando* Woolf had justified her 'love of these old voyagers' by pointing to 'the strain of poetry—the meditative mood fostered by long days at sea, sleep and dreams under strange stars, and lonely effort in the face of death' (*CE* iii. 28). That a poet and a sailor—particularly a sailor whose 'ancestry' can be traced to Hakluyt— should marry is thus, if unconventional, surely fitting. Although the Lady Orlando entertains some momentary doubts about her marriage, the very areas of her doubts—the husband's dedication to sailing, the wife's to writing poetry—are sources of strength in the marriage. Marmaduke gives and receives the freedom to adventure into the unknown, and the androgynous husband values the poet in his wife, in whom the Coleridgean man and woman are fused. The 'meditative mood' which dominates both poet and voyager ensures the legitimacy of their union.

It is not surprising then that Hakluyt, although the object of Woolf's earliest enthusiasm, was not the only Elizabethan writer to exercise a strong appeal. Her response to poets and dramatists, as well as to other prose writers, is the subject of the next chapter.

The Variety of Elizabethan Literature

WOOLF'S first love was prose, but over the years she read works in all the major genres of early modern English literature. Her range was broad and her choices sometimes unexpected. Among prose writers, she read not only Hakluyt but also such diverse people as Bacon, Sir Thomas Browne, Sir Philip Sidney, and Fulke Greville. She read Shakespeare, but less expectedly she also read Greene and Ford and a host of lesser Elizabethan and Jacobean dramatists. And, while along with her contemporaries she rediscovered Donne's poems, she also regularly enjoyed a host of other lyric poets, and read closely four entire books of the *Faerie Queene*. Her early preference for prose gave way to poetry, which was everywhere to be found—in the lyric, in narrative poems, in prose narratives, in the verse drama. She never abandoned the prose writers; but, just as her early enthusiasms became more firmly grounded, so did her reservations.

Woolf took a professional interest in Elizabethan prose, searching out the writers' aims and investigating their techniques. If any sort of narrative was involved, one of the criteria by which she judged it was its ability to tell a story (and Hakluyt measured up in that respect—*CE* ii. 18, 20). But the enthusiasm she felt for Hakluyt's prose did not really extend to prose narratives of a clearly fictive stripe, on which she made greater demands. Although Elizabethan prose narrative was not geared to telling a story in a straightforward way, Woolf insisted that it do just that, like the novels which in time developed from it. She was ill-equipped for its leisurely pace, found its inclusions and exclusions almost inexplicable, and in consequence read very little of the enormous output in this area. Although Nashe's *The Unfortunate Traveller* was in fact one of the last things she read, it hardly seems to have made much impression ('Anon.' 435). Yet she did read one of the greatest works in the genre, Sir Philip Sidney's *Arcadia*. She took copious notes, and published an essay on it in the second *Common Reader* (*CE* i. 19–27). Reading the book was a matter of initial pleasure, for Woolf shared Sidney's joy in language, and throughout the close to three hundred large folio pages felicitous phrases kept her going. But the beautiful phrases and stately cadences were almost lost in a prolixity whose decorativeness finally cloyed. Much of the book is given over to characters telling stories, with rather little of the sort of dialogue that enlivens later fiction, and that only in the peasant characters, who rarely made an appearance.

Part of the difficulty as Woolf saw it was in Sidney's conception of fiction, an unfolding of an inordinate number of stories, one after the other, and with no end in view—or rather, not with the end in view that a novelist might have, the development of character. Although she had read Greville's *Life* of Sidney as well as modern biographies, which made it clear that his aims in narrative were appropriate to the age, she felt that a writer need not be bound by convention, and she occasionally sensed in Sidney an interest in a more modern conception of character. Gynecia's passion for Zelmane, Musidorus's anger and pain, the pathos of old Basilius—these were all proof that Sidney was capable of developing character when he gave his creations genuine emotions (22–4). Had he limited the number of stories that filled the pages of the *Arcadia*, he might have created more believable and interesting characters, clearly motivated by ideas and emotions recognizable to moderns. But Elizabethan prose accommodated and perhaps even elicited the general rather than the particular, and rarely lent itself to close observation. There were exceptions of course, a heron ' "wagling" as it rises from the marsh . . . the water-spaniel hunting the duck "with a snuffling grace" .' But such patches of realism occur almost exclusively in reference to 'nature and animals and peasants. Prose, it seems, is made for slow, noble, and generalized emotions; for the descriptions of wide landscapes; for the conveyance of long, equable discourses uninterrupted for pages together by any other speaker' (24). How frequently did Sidney actually look at his aristocratic characters, who dominated the work? To Woolf's mind, almost not at all.

It was in Sidney's verse, found throughout the *Arcadia* both in interpolated lyrics and massed at the ends of the individual books, that Woolf discovered some of the elements of the novel missing from his prose—realism, naturalistic emotion directly conveyed, urgency of expression (24–5). She claimed that verse 'performs something of the function of dialogue in the modern novel. It breaks up the monotony and strikes a high-light' (24). The 'complaint' of Plangus, from which she quotes at length (25), proves Sidney's capacity for 'vehement speaking'. Woolf's reading notes on the *Arcadia* reveal how frequently she preferred a lyric to the narrative in which Sidney embedded it. The 'interminable adventures of Pyrocles and Musidorus' were heightened and relieved by songs (MHP/B2p, 10). Woolf read the poetry with care and pleasure, even the eclogues, which modern readers frequently pass over, thinking them extraneous to the story.

But what most pleased Woolf was the occasional happy conjunction of prose and poetry, when matter and manner blended perfectly in each, and the two worked together to tell a compelling story. When, for example, Philoclea went for a moonlit walk in the woods, through the 'delightful grove & trees', said Woolf, 'poetry naturally breathed' (MHP/B2p, 11). The scene was one of the most striking examples of Sidney's narrative art at its best.

That best was too infrequent in Woolf's estimation. In general, prose and verse did not cohere, nor was Sidney likely to pursue a tale to its logical end at all expeditiously, what with interpolated stories of some length, or development of a series of paralleled structures, or elaboration and qualification of a single word. Much of what Woolf found most attractive in Sidney—his stately cadences, his poetry—vitiated the *Arcadia* as a work of fiction. His weaknesses, however, would seem to be strengths in the great writers of non-fiction prose.

Expository prose of the Renaissance was Woolf's forte. She certainly expected it to adhere to normal standards of straightforwardness and clarity, but she kept an open mind even on those matters, working assiduously to understand the most convoluted and obscure works if they promised some gain, aesthetic or otherwise. She attempted to discover how an author's purpose determined his stylistic and structural choices, sometimes she even tried to allow for an author's debt to literary convention, and she was frequently interested as a craftsman in the relationship between form and content. In a review of modern essays Woolf pointed to some nineteenth- and twentieth-century writers as well as one earlier master—Sir Francis Bacon—as exemplars of her belief that in great essayists 'some fierce attachment to an idea' makes for 'a perpetual union' between sound and sense (*CE* ii. 50).

Woolf's enthusiasm for Renaissance prose began with Hakluyt and Bacon. She asked her father for Spedding's edition of Bacon when she was young, and read him again with 'continual delight' when Thoby gave her the essays (*L.* 66, 67; 25 and 27 Jan. 1903). Thereafter she read him sporadically, and consulted him before writing her last essays on

Elizabethan literature, 'Anon.' and 'The Reader'. She saw in his ambiguity, his cleverness, and his caution what she had come in a lifetime on the fringes of political power to recognize as 'the thinking mind, the governing class mind' (MHP/B2c, 24–5). This 'aristocratic scholar' had much to say about Truth, Death, Unity of religion, Revenge, Dissimulation—in short, about 'the great world of action'.

But it was not his subject-matter alone that convinced Woolf that her earlier enthusiasm had been justified. It was his style. He got his striking effects, not from hyperbole, but rather from what Woolf called 'the poetry of prose. He was bringing the prose of the mind into being' ('Anon.' 396–7). What she meant by those phrases can be inferred from one of her favourite passages:

Nay, retire men cannot when they would; neither will they, when it were Reason; but are impatient of Privateness, even in age and sickness, which require the shadow: like old Townsmen: that will still be sitting at their street door, though thereby they offer Age to Scorn . . . (CE ii. 49–50; and 'Anon.' 397)

In contrast to much writing which is 'loose, [merely] plausible, and commonplace', this sentence is 'exact, truthful, and imaginative'. Bacon served as a touchstone of excellence in the art of writing.

Woolf certainly did not expect the polish and imagination she valued in Bacon's essays when she read other kinds of Renaissance prose. But she did expect to hear a personal voice, particularly in less 'literary' works like memoirs and in less formal contexts such as letters, notebooks, and the like. In 'Reading' she recycled reviews written earlier of *The Memoirs of Ann Lady Fanshawe* and *The House of Lyme from its Foundation to the End of the Eighteenth Century* to demonstrate the effects on prose style of a certain concept of decorum: the writers were governed by the desire to appear dignified in the eyes of posterity. They indulged in neither 'natural slips and trifles' nor any extremes of emotion; their language was stilted, all 'stiff polysyllables and branching periods' (CE ii. 14–16). Yet the problems afflicting memoirs were just as apt to burden letters written to friends and relatives. Woolf criticized Gabriel Harvey's sister Mercy for writing on the very lively topic of her attempted seduction without seeming to be personally involved. Even vulgarity would have been welcome. Or again, she noticed that Lady Sidney could barely make a simple request, so cumbersome was her language; and Sir Henry Wotton's letters (often praised as some of the best of the age) were, Woolf felt, 'pompous and ornate' (*CE* iii. 32–3). She was always hoping to find the life of the Elizabethans in their everyday prose, and that hope was generally frustrated.

In 'The Strange Elizabethans' (1932) Woolf outlines her solution to the problem: she would read the prose of someone who 'possessed to some extent the modern instinct for preserving trifles, for keeping copies of letters, and for making notes of ideas that struck him in the margins of books' (33). Her choice of Gabriel Harvey, Spenser's friend, led her to volumes rarely read these days, the *Letter-book*, the *Works*, and the *Marginalia*. She read them in their entirety, filling page after page of her notebooks with quotations, paraphrases, and brief commentary. It was a systematic, almost scholarly study. She felt rewarded from time to time with a robust and slangy passage that she found 'mellifluous' or a 'forthright' alliterative phrase. Harvey's marginalia, of necessity terse, were at least lively (42). But more representative sentences stretched to two hundred words, until Woolf felt pushed 'almost beyond the limits of human patience. The words seem to run red-hot, molten, hither and thither, until we cry out in anguish for the boon of some meaning to set its stamp on them' (37). Even the few facts she grabs in desperation are obscured by 'the fumes of Harvey's eloquence' until all is 'windy, wordy, voluminous, and obsolete' (38). The seriousness of her effort to come to terms with Elizabethan prose is evident in her attempts to formulate a theory accounting for Harvey's style: she contended that 'we are reading what we should be hearing', and that the many 'amplifications and the repetitions . . . are for the benefit of the slow and sensual ear which loves to dally over sense and luxuriate in sound . . .' (38).

Woolf arrived at this theory of the origin of Elizabethan prose style after reading Donne's funeral sermon on Magdalen Herbert, in which she discerned an architecture, a 'climbing up by use of the same word: repetition of Arches'. She noted Donne's description of Mrs Herbert's attire, '. . . always agreeable to her *quality*, and agreeable to her *company*; Such as shee might, and such, as others, such as shee was, did weare . . . It may be *worse*, nay, it may be a *worse pride*, to weare worse things, than others doe.'

Woolf realized that 'when you are speaking, you make things much too plain' (XI. 20). In the same funeral sermon she came across frequent amplifications, as in this description of Mrs Herbert's wit: '. . . her inclination, and conversation, naturally, cheerfull, and merry, and loving facetiousnesse, and sharpnesse of wit . . .' She could account, then, for Harvey's tendency to both amplification and repetition by recourse to sermon style. It was unusual for Woolf to theorize in this way, but her ear was telling her something. Without a background in classical rhetoric, the source of both written and spoken style in the Renaissance, she could only assume that Harvey had learned his art in church. She did not care for the result when he was at his most prolix, but she tried to be understanding.

In the essay Woolf is as interested in Harvey the man as in Harvey the prose stylist. In the process of coming to know him, however, she actually abandons literary criticism and slips back into the role of novelist. Basically, two fictive procedures are involved: first, she takes sentences that Harvey copied from others and attributes them to Harvey himself, positing a two-sided man to account for discrepancies, 'the sedentary Harvey' always giving sage advice to his other self, 'the ambitious but uneasy youth'. She plays off various quotations against each other, concluding, 'So runs the dialogue that we invent between the two Harveys—Harvey the active and Harvey the passive, Harvey the foolish and Harvey the wise' (CE iii. 41–2). Woolf's second fictive procedure is to stock the mind of Harvey in his old age with material properly belonging to an earlier period. As Woolf paints a picture of the man in his retirement at Saffron Walden, she supplements the known facts with fictitious 'consolations' and 'dreams' culled from marginalia Harvey had written anywhere from twenty to fifty years earlier. She can thus declare that 'a singularly humane view of learning survived in the breast of the old and disappointed scholar' (43). Perhaps.[1] If Elizabethan prose refused to yield up the everyday life of the times, if it could not 'make people talk, simply and naturally, about ordinary things' (32), a skilful modern novelist might nevertheless get it to whisper a few secrets.

The faults Woolf found with Harvey's prose she regarded as widespread during the Renaissance, not only in minor figures, but even in the great. In the Defence of Poesie Sir Philip Sidney was guilty of much amplification (long accumulations and catalogues) and little that was natural-sounding, quick, or colloquial. When the prolixity of Sidney's prose exasperated her, and she bemoaned its inflexibility, her most vehement charge was merely that it was 'poetry without the wings' (CE i. 49–50). Even in writers she criticized rather seriously Woolf generally managed to find some merit (as the Danes were said to do with

[1] Professor J. O'Brien Schaefer has suggested to me that Lytton Strachey had used the same technique in the conclusion of his Queen Victoria.

Hamlet, dipping his faults in their affection). Hugh Latimer stumbled and repeated himself, true, frequently losing the thread of his argument; but his rural plainness and humour were quite winning. Lady Anne Clifford wrote endless inventories; but 'the sense of the body permeates her pages' ('Anon.' 387, 427). Frequently she found more matter for amusement than for censure in the excesses of her favourites. Although she worshipped Sir Thomas Browne almost to the point of idolatry, she had to admit when reviewing a new edition that he did actually state that 'afflictions induce callosities' ('Sir T.B.'). She enjoyed mimicking Browne's Latinity: there were fine things, she said, in his *Christian Morals* 'among many hints and exquisite adumbrations' (*L.* 378, 18 Aug. 1907).

By the same reckoning, Thomas Dekker was 'not to be taken too seriously', either when he heaped up clauses or when he created all sorts of hyperboles and metaphors in his compulsion to 'enlarge, generalize, beautify'. His was 'the same habit of aggrandisement' that Woolf found in most Elizabethan prose writers. Yet Dekker could 'swoop with the true Elizabethan gusto upon some dunghill, could brawl & bawl & be as bawdy & plain spoken & hearty & frank as Shakespeare or Chaucer'. Therefore, even though he could not adopt the tones of ordinary discourse, in *The Wonderful Year* Woolf found a 'bounding & curvetting speech' (MHP/B2p, 3) that at times was precisely what she wanted, 'all that I love most at the moment. I bathed myself in Dekker last night as in my natural element. Surely this is a nobler instrument than Scott or the 18th Century' (*D.* 3 Sept. 1931). She saw in Dekker both the glories and the faults of his age: 'When Dekker sets out to tell us how Queen Elizabeth died in the spring, he cannot describe her death in particular or that spring in particular; he must dilate upon all deaths and all springs . . .' (*CE* i. 35–6). Certainly Woolf is somewhat amused, but in quoting a representative passage from the work she also reveals her admiration for the prolixity, the figurative language, and the diction of Elizabethan prose.

Just as Woolf herself frequently used metaphor to pin down meaning and to make it vivid, so she discovered the same capacity, a great inventiveness and freshness in writers of Renaissance prose. Gabriel Harvey's sister, for example, protested to the married nobleman wooing her: 'Good Lord, that you should seek after so bare and country stuff abroad, that have so costly and courtly wares at home.' Rhetoric must have been in the air which Mercy Harvey breathed, 'the sway of the Elizabethan convention' and 'the accent of their speech' so powerful that it was possible for a milkmaid to sound as good as a trained writer (*CE* iii. 35–6).

In fact it was possible for a writer to be too sophisticated. Fulke Greville, whose *Life of Sir Philip Sidney* was one of Woolf's earliest review books for the *Times Literary Supplement*, was long-winded, convuluted, and rhetorically dense. But Woolf admired his 'passages of the ripest melody . . .' (*L*. 355, 22 Mar. 1907). Greville had 'fashioned a monument to [Sidney], carved and decorated it, twisted and plaited it, in the best style of the early seventeenth century prose' ('Philip Sidney' 173). Her favourite passages were one where Greville said that Sidney's 'end was not writing, even while he wrote', and another where he called Sidney 'a sea-mark' on the English coast. Nor did her judgement change appreciably twenty-five years later when she again read the book and singled out the same passages. Her second reading again stressed metaphor: Sidney, she noted, was 'our unbelieved Cassandra', while the word 'gold' was 'an attractive adamant' to draw men into risky investments (xx. 38–9). Greville's pride in a brilliant display, however, sometimes got the better of his judgement. Then he might overindulge his penchant for figurative language and, as Woolf said in the review, be 'closely throttled in the embraces of a sinuous metaphor' (174).

More consistently fine in the use of metaphor was Sir Walter Raleigh:

From the sea he takes his most frequent and splendid imagery. It comes naturally to him to speak of the 'Navigation of this life', of 'the Port of death, to which all winds drive us'. Our false friends, he says, 'forsake us in the first tempest of misfortune and steere away before the Sea and Winde.' So in old age we find that our joy and our woe have 'sayled out of sight'. (*CE* iii. 29)

Woolf drew all of these examples of metaphor from the Preface to Raleigh's *Historie of the World*, impressed with the aptness of the figures of speech and the ease with which he employs them. She suggested that the Preface be read after many other pieces of Raleigh's prose, thus ending 'as one leaves a church with the sound of the organ in one's ears' (28). Greville might occasionally be uneven in conception and execution of metaphor, but Raleigh was thoroughly dependable.

Other rhetorical devices, while of less interest to Woolf, certainly had their appeal—for example, the sort of alliterative passages she singled out in Gabriel Harvey, or one or another author's use of personification. The master of rhetoric in Woolf's eyes was Raleigh, who not only created a large array of consistently fine metaphors but also raised the relatively feeble device of personification to beautiful heights, as can be seen in the following example. The Elizabethans, Woolf knew, thought of death as 'not an idea but a person . . . And to Raleigh in particular, death was a very definite enemy—death, "which doth pursue us and hold us in chace from our infancy".' The repetition, with slight amplification, in this statement has none of the tediousness Woolf found objectionable in Harvey. Raleigh simply knew what he was about. And nowhere more so than in a passage that deftly employs personification, apostrophe, alliteration, and parallel structure. It was the passage from *Historie of the World* with which Woolf ended her review of the Raleigh anthology: 'O eloquent, just and mightie Death! whom none could advise, thou hast perswaded; what none hath dared, thou hast done' (31). Raleigh's structuring of this sentence is itself eloquent, the simplicity of its rhythmic elements (whom none . . . thou hast . . . what none . . . thou hast) enriched by the repeated 'D' sounds that echo the key word 'Death'. Raleigh was a master of the time-honoured device of a series of balanced words or phrases, a device that Woolf herself often used. To cite just two examples: Woolf points to a reader's interest in Raleigh's life, 'His adventures by sea and land, his quest of Eldorado and the great gold-mine of his dreams, his sentence of death and long imprisonment . . .' (28); she maintains that Harvey had 'a face like ours—a changing, a variable, a human face' (43).

Woolf's frequent use of balanced structure made her especially sensitive to its appearance in her reading, but also rather severe in her judgement. She expected the achievement of perfect balance—the effect of conscious craft—to seem a natural consequence of the ideas being expressed. She was very impressed by the balanced structure of the following sentence written by Mercy Harvey to her would-be wooer: 'The thing you wot of, Milord, were a great trespass towards God, a great offence to the world, a great grief to my friends, a great shame to myself, and, as I think, a great dishonour to your lordship' (36). It is a remarkably fine sentence. In contrast, Woolf believed that Sidney himself (who elsewhere advocated *sprezzatura*) failed to find the right pitch when he created balanced prose, the most representative example of that failure occurring in a love scene in the *Arcadia* when the young lady Philoclea speaks:

If I had continued as I ought, *Philoclea*, you had either never been, or ever been *Zelmane*: you had either never attempted this change, set on with hope, or never discovered it, stopt with despair. But I fear mee, my behaviour ill governed, gave you the first comfort: I fear mee, my affection ill hid, hath given you this last assurance . . .

'The extraordinary pattern of words,' Woolf commented, was 'built up like the flourishes of a design. almost meaningless, passionless . . .' (MHP/B2p, 16).

In contrast there is an equally rhetorical passage in Raleigh's preface to the *Historie of the World*, quoted in Woolf's review as an example of 'natural symmetry of form':

. . . let him but take the accompt of his memory (for wee have no other keeper of our pleasures past) and trulie examine what it hath reserved, either of beauty and youth, or foregone delights; what it hath saved, that it might last, of his dearest affections, or of whatever else the amorous Springtime gave his thoughts of contentment, then unvaluable; and hee shall finde that all the art which his elder yeares have, can draw no other vapour out of these dissolutions, than heavie, secret and sad sighs . . . (*CE* iii. 30)

The difference between these passages goes beyond the disparate requirements of fiction and non-fiction. Sidney's parallel structures are too exact to ring true, whereas Raleigh's are actually fit, as Woolf maintained, 'for the tenderness of noble human intercourse'. The parallel clauses and phrases seem to open out from one another because of the demands of sense; and the final cadence is onomatopoetic and almost musical in its rhythms. Woolf said that 'in its melody and strength, its natural symmetry of form, it is a perfect speech . . . It reaches us almost with the very accent of Raleigh's voice.' The occasional problems that Woolf found in, say, Sidney, or in his biographer, Fulke Greville, which probably came from their overindulgence in certain rhetorical techniques—what Woolf loosely terms 'characteristic Elizabethan conceits'—did not beset Raleigh's prose. She granted that his style in the travel literature was less pleasing to her than that in his more meditative works (28, 30), but it was in his account of Guiana that she had found the passage she lifted to describe the South American scene in *The Voyage Out*. Even at his less impressive, then, Raleigh was very fine. At his best he was one of a fairly select company of Elizabethans who, to Woolf, exemplified the beauty of the age.

The Renaissance prose Woolf most favoured had a sonorous quality. She found it not only in Raleigh, but also in such places as the opening of Greville's *Life* of Sidney and in Dekker's description of the plague (xx. 38; xi. 11). Woolf believed that the phenomenon was widespread because 'a noble biblical cadence' beat in their brains, a rhythm that the prose of the time was pliant and plastic enough to profit from. A certain 'freedom of stroke' made for 'a beautiful water-like liquidity & melody'.

Although her terminology is rather impressionistic, the 'rhythm' and the 'melody' can be heard in such a passage as the following: 'but all was more calme than a still water, all husht' (MHP/B2p, 3). This passage from Dekker's *The Wonderful Year* illustrates, among other traits, the Renaissance tendency to 'beautify' (*CE* i. 35–6).

But no one was more musical than one of her earliest favourites, Sir Thomas Browne, whom she read 'fairly often' over the years (*D.* 12 Sept. 1919). She has Orlando compare the achievements of his ancestors with those of Sir Thomas Browne, and Sir Thomas wins: 'Like an incantation rising from all parts of the room, from the night wind and the moonlight, rolled the divine melody of those words' (81). Although the narrator jealously refuses to quote Browne, Woolf did so when reviewing a new edition:

But the iniquity of oblivion blindly scattereth her poppy, and deals with the memory of men without distinction to merit of perpetuity . . . Darkness and light divide the course of time, and oblivion shares with memory a great part even of our living beings; we slightly remember our felicities and the smartest strokes of affliction leave but short smart upon us . . . The Egyptian mummies, which Cambyses or time hath spared, avarice now consumeth. Mummy is become merchandise, Mizraim cures wounds, and Pharaoh is sold for balsams.

Most readers would agree with Woolf, that the words do 'revive the old amazement' in their 'splendour of sound'. Browne's prose is a cathedral organ which 'goes plunging and soaring and indulging in vast and elephantine gambols of awful yet grotesque sublimity' ('Sir T.B.'). Qualifications notwithstanding, this is the praise of a worshipper, not blind in her faith but no less a worshipper for that.

Sir Thomas Browne was the first writer on whom Woolf ever spoke in a professional capacity as literary critic, a lecture to working women at Morley College on the relationship between music and poetry, for which she read a book on the subject (EN, 18 Jan. 1905, 13, 14). When, just a few years later, Woolf began drafting her first novel, the heroine owned and read a copy of Browne's *Religio Medici*, 'for the title together perhaps with some stray word or portrait had charmed her when she was first beginning to read'. The appeal of the book was to the imagination:

. . . the words lured her on, with a promise distinct though not definable, of wondrous caverns, and vast luminous vistas concealed below them, and in time they came to undermine her visible world with a labyrinth of dark channels, and to expand her heaven. Even now that she was a grown woman she could start herself on some whimsical flight infinitely pleasant to her, by reading certain words.[2]

When preparing the 1923 review of Browne Woolf commented that 'if certain words are said, the mind supplies the rest', suggesting that Browne's prose is poetry. In 'Reading' she distinguishes between Renaissance memoirs and travel literature on the one hand, what she calls the deposit of daily life, and, on the other, 'what is timeless and contemporary' in the period, its poetry, the sole example the well-crafted prose of Sir Thomas Browne. In such a work as the *Religio Medici* the cumulative pleasure of prose and the immediate pleasure of poetry are both found (MHP/B2q, 70). Thus it is that that book, and Browne's *Vulgar Errors* as well, are the poetry that Woolf discusses in 'Reading' (*CE* ii. 26–32).

Her interest in the *Religio Medici* is twofold, part Browne's style, part his content. As 'the first [writer] to talk of himself', he gave a 'splendid picture of his soul'. In addition, his interests were almost boundless, and writing was an opportunity for him 'to speculate and fantastically accumulate considerations' (28). He seemed the most imaginative and stimulating of the Renaissance prose writers because of the great variety of subjects that he treated in his books, and the immense differences between those books, one from another. *The Garden of Cyrus* combined scientific rigour and religious orthodoxy, bizarre experiments and ingenious theories ('Sir T.B.'). His *Vulgar Errors*, replete with the unnatural natural history of his time, appealed to 'the English mind', Woolf theorized, because it is 'naturally prone to take its ease and pleasure in the loosest whimsies and humours' (*CE* ii. 27). Browne's mind was capacious, fascinated with 'life in general [and] . . . his own life in particular' (29). Ordinary things became extraordinary in Browne's treatment of them: Even 'flowers and insects and grasses at his feet' seemed, in the *Garden of Cyrus*, to be surrounded by 'a halo of wonder' ('Sir T.B.'). The result, says Woolf, is that we 'stand still in amazement' as Browne's prose 'raises the vault of [our] mind' (*CE* ii. 29).

It is the ability of well-written prose to stimulate the imagination that Woolf celebrates in her favourite Renaissance authors. Nor did they forget life's austerities and terrors for their prose repeatedly calls such topics to mind; but in the hands of a Browne or a Raleigh they are

---

[2] Quoted in *Melymbrosia* Appendix B, 267. De Salvo (Melymbrosia, p. xviii) dates the draft Winter and Spring 1908. Moore (in Marcus, *New* 84–6) finds in this version an image derived from the *Religio Medici*, Cynthia as an 'amphibious creature'.

transmuted, and the reader can perceive man's stature as he faces what is after all inevitable. Sir Walter Raleigh's final letter to his wife is a model of the 'magnificence with which such a being relinquishes his hopes in life and dismisses the cares of "this ridiculous world". . .'. Woolf quotes with keen appreciation what she calls his 'deeply burdened sigh' (*CE* iii. 30). Raleigh and other Renaissance men generally triumphed over their fears, but it was their openness and artistry in expressing them that was at least as ingratiating to Woolf.

Sir Thomas Browne constantly enters the 'dark world' of his inner self, confesses to doubts, to 'a hell within' much as Robert Burton does in *The Anatomy of Melancholy*. But the unhappiness thus revealed serves 'to chequer the immediate spectacle' and thereby to enhance the pleasure of contemplation, these masters of the imagination calling forth one's own imaginative powers ('Anon.' 429). Woolf shows the effect on a 'contemporary' of Browne's, Orlando. After his first trance, Orlando visited the crypt beneath his house, for he 'took a strange delight in thoughts of death and decay', a point upon which Woolf elaborates in a parody of *Urne Burial*:

It was a ghastly sepulchre; dug deep beneath the foundations of the house as if the first Lord of the family . . . had wished to testify how all pomp is built upon corruption; how the skeleton lies beneath the flesh; how we that dance and sing above must lie below; how the crimson velvet turns to dust . . . 'Nothing remains of all these Princes . . . except one digit, and he would take a skeleton hand in his and bend the joints this way and that. 'Whose hand was it?' he went on to ask. 'The right or the left? The hand of man or woman, of age or youth? Had it urged the war horse, or plied the needle? Had it plucked the rose, or grasped cold steel?'

Orlando cuts short the catalogue because his imagination is too fecund, and 'he shrank, as his wont was, from the cardinal labour of composition, which is excision' (71)—a problem also for 'Thomas Browne, a Doctor of Norwich, whose writing upon such subjects took his fancy amazingly'. But why is the lazy Orlando willing to expend the labour necessary to read 'the delicate articulation of one of the doctor's longest and most marvellously contorted cogitations' (72–3)?

Woolf answers that question in 'Reading'. To exercise one's mind on the difficult first chapter of *Urne Burial* is a point of pride: 'We must stop, go back, try out this way and that, and proceed at a foot's pace.' Browne simply does not 'conciliate his reader'; his books 'are dull if he chooses, difficult if he likes, beautiful beyond measure if he has a mind that way'. Woolf's proof of that beauty is drawn also from *Urne Burial*, from the opening words of the 'Epistle Dedicatory' (*CE* ii. 32): 'When the Funeral pyre was out, and the last valediction over, men took a lasting adieu to their interred Friends.' She probably had in mind such a passage for Ralph Denham's reading in an edition of Browne when he visits William Rodney in *Night and Day*, 'a passage which he knew very nearly by heart' (*N&D* 75). Beyond question this puts the seal of approval on that young man. Woolf later contended that 'few people love the writing of Sir Thomas Browne, but those who do are of the salt of the earth' ('Sir T.B.').

Given Woolf's fondness for poetic prose, the appeal of poetry itself was only to be expected. From her youngest days she had read and re-read lyrical poetry, including some anthology pieces of Donne, and Spenser's two great odes, 'Epithalamion' and 'Prothalamion'. But only in the early 1930s did she sit down to read Spenser or Donne in a concentrated way over a period of months, after which she wrote an essay on each.

Published by Leonard Woolf in *The Moment* six years after his wife's death, the essay on the *Faerie Queene* has gained wide currency and is frequently quoted by specialists and non-specialists alike (Patrides; Pomeroy 499–500). Parts are eminently quotable, but probably the chief reason for its popularity with specialists is the articulateness of Woolf's appreciation for a Renaissance poet who is not particularly favoured by the reading public. The diaries record her early delight (23 Jan. 1935), flagging interest (27 Feb.), a 'standstill' in the reading (11 Mar.) at the end of Book IV after some 24,000 lines of Spenser's poetry, and then a decision to return to the poem and finish it (13 June).

Narrative in Spenser's verse was very much more to Woolf's liking than narrative in Sidney's prose. The plot seemed to move more smoothly (*CE* i. 14), and the verse was of such a high calibre that Woolf not only took delight in it but actually seems to have been fascinated by Spenser's technique. The poem's stanza, eight lines of iambic pentameter followed by an Alexandrine, is ideally suited to the requirements of the narrative. The reader can enjoy for long stretches what Woolf called 'the beautiful free-stepping measure' (MHP/B2m, 6), the stanza breaks regularly providing brief rests. Eventually Woolf tired of the regularity and contended in the essay that the verse is 'a celestial rocking-horse, whose pace is always rhythmical and seemly, but lulling, soporific' (17). In an essay on Gibbon she was to use the image again, developing it as Keats had done in another context: in

Gibbon's prose the rocking-horse sometimes becomes a Pegasus (*CE* i. 115). In Spenser's case the rhythm is more down-to-earth, but is none the less functional, for it sustains the reader through an extremely long poem: 'On no other terms,' Woolf said, 'could we be kept in being' (17–18). Some years later she devoted several pages to Spenser in her final essays, and devised a more exact image for the Spenserian stanza: '. . . the metre flings its curve of sound, to break, like a wave on the same place, and like a wave to withdraw, to fill again. Folded in this incantation we drowse and sleep; yet always see through the waters, something irradiated' ('Anon.' 391).

The freshness of Spenser's language makes for some of the glow. Woolf singles out in the earlier essay words like 'fry and rascal and losel, the common speech that was current on the lips of the women at the door' (17), and this interest in Spenser's 'word-conscious' artistry did not wane. She enjoyed the epithets in 'lamping sky' and 'the builder Oake', and like Keats she noticed the 'sea-shouldring Whales'. But often a line of great simplicity would catch her eye, as for example the statement that, at a certain betrothal, 'music did apply her skill the warbling notes to play'. She paid special attention to Spenser's figures of speech, some to her taste, some not. After she had met all too many similes to various animals she became quite discriminating: she criticized commonplaceness on the one hand (men like tigers fighting over food), a forced quality on the other (a knight's vulnerability being likened to a vulture's when missing the heron at which he hurled himself). But some of Spenser's epic similes were welcome because they combined aptness with exact observation: a battle with clear victory going to neither knight is compared to the varying tides of the River Shannon; the mingled cries of a heroine, other women, and boys is 'Such as the troubled theaters oftimes annoyes'. These were similes on which one writer could commend another.

Woolf's pleasure in reading the *Faerie Queene* came as a surprise. True, she had long savoured the odes: she had alluded to the 'Epithalamion' in an early draft of *The Voyage Out*; and as a teenager she had copied into her diary (EN 4 Aug.–23 Sept. 1899) lines from the 'Prothalamion' (a poem that would figure briefly in the last novel, *Between the Acts*). But Woolf had probably sampled just enough of the long narrative poem to confirm her prejudice against allegory ('Lady Fanshawe's Memoirs'; *CW* 47). In *Freshwater* she had ridiculed the Victorian preoccupation with allegorical rendering of almost everything. So she advises readers in the Spenser essay:

At the mere mention of chivalry shiver and snigger; detest allegory; revel in direct speech; adore all the virtues of the robust, the plain-spoken; and then, when the whole being is red and brittle as sandstone in the sun, make a dash for The Faery Queen and give yourself up to it. (14)

It proved very easy to give herself up to Spenser's poem. Instead of stick figures, she met the Redcrosse Knight and Una, whose immediacy prompted in her 'the simple wish . . . to feel their heat and cold, and their thirst and hunger'. To read the first two books of the *Faerie Queene* was to have 'the natural quiet feelings of liking and disliking tolerantly and gently excited' (14–15), for it is not difficult to keep the characters straight. In books three and four, however, easily confused characters are engaged in quite a large number of interwoven events. She began to feel some exasperation and then boredom, 'Because these figures dont have the weight of the book behind them. They taper off. Also the repetition of battles, loves becomes monotonous' (MHP/B2m, 17). Even then, however, specific scenes created a characterization that was every bit as compelling as in the earlier books: Scudamour, for example, became identifiable and interesting when the allegory externalized the internal—in this case a visit to the blacksmith Care, whose dreadful noise keeps awake throughout the night the anxious husband of an abducted wife.

The essay on the *Faerie Queene* reflects Woolf's ambivalence towards Spenser's characterizations. On the one hand, she complained that Spenser, unlike dramatists, never had to bring his characters 'to the surface', but could let them 'sink back into [his] mind' without gaining definition. On the other hand, she recognized that Spenser was not a failed dramatist but a successful allegorist, who could create symbols. A character 'draws natural breath, living breath' from Spenser's world, 'which offers him the use of dragons, knights, magic; and all the company that exist about them; and flowers and dawn and sunset' (17). The poet can accomplish a great deal, depicting a character's despair, for example, not from his thinking in print—as Woolf does with Septimus Smith—but rather from his meeting someone typifying the quality of despair. Spenser 'has the fullest sense of what sorrow is', and conveys that sense as an allegorical poet would naturally do, 'on a larger, freer, more depersonalized scale' than the novelist's. 'By making the passions into people, he gives them an amplitude. And who shall say that this is the less natural, the less realistic?' (16). It was enough that (as she said of an immortal's lament for her unconscious son) 'the voice of human pain [came] out of the clouds' (MHP/B2m, 15). Spenser insisted on 'the qualities that agitate living people at the moment; spite, greed, jealousy, ugliness, poverty, pain . . .' (18).

These are the qualities that make up what Woolf called 'the adventures of a soul', and all great books (the *Faerie Queene*, the *Odyssey*, the *Divine Comedy*) tell that story and no other. The second book of the *Faerie Queene*, the tale of Sir Guyon, knight of Temperance, seemed especially rich in that respect. In Guyon's adventures in Hell Woolf found illustrations of the temptations of greed and pride. Another episode that appealed was one involving the 'merry mariner' Phaedria, who sings 'Behold . . . the flowrs', a parody of the Sermon on the Mount's lilies of the field. She concludes that man should not waste his hours in pain, but should rather choose present pleasures. Here Woolf found 'some adumbration of the difficulty of life: temptation—passion' (MHP/B2m, 11). Spenser realized in the *Faerie Queene* what was only latent in much of Sidney, the development in a narrative of the psychology of its characters and 'the adventures of the soul' (*CE* i. 27).

Many of these adventures seemed to have a contemporary relevance for Woolf that is not at all far-fetched. Her feminist reading of the poem, already discussed, is a case in point. Another is her seeing in Mammon's offer of riches the corrupt attractions of monarchy and empire, and in Guyon's refusal the integrity of modern democracy. She had noted with approbation an earlier observation of the narrator, who decried royal excess and pomp (*FQ* I. xii. 14). Now in Guyon's words, 'All that I need I have; what needeth mee |To covet more then I have cause to use?' she heard a sort of democratic socialism. Such interpretations were possible because in Spenser's poetry 'more is imagined than is stated . . . so that after four hundred years it still corresponds to something which we . . . feel at the moment' (*CE* i. 15).

Access to the minds of his readers is possible because Spenser is more than 'merely a thinking brain; he is a feeling body, a sensitive heart', and in reading him 'we feel that the whole being is drawn upon . . .' (16). Woolf contended that 'the faculty we employ upon poetry at the first reading is sensual'. In such lines as

> oft from the forrest wildings he did bring
> Whose sides empurpled were with smyling red

she found the reason for Spenser's success: he 'rouses the eye'; and, even if parts of the poem are dull, before long the verse rouses the ear as well. In almost every respect, then, the *Faerie Queene* was ideally suited

>enser's technique was superb, his ideas important, his
ct enough to sustain interest but flexible enough to allow
.ty.

cal of Woolf that she should expect a goodly amount of
lyricism in a narrative poem, for in general she did not care for the
genre. She raced through Shakespeare's major narrative poems,
recording some scattered examples of pictorial beauty and exactness,
but was held by neither the story nor the characterizations (xxv. 35–6).
She had some feeling for ballads: in *A Room of One's Own* she alludes to
'Marie Hamilton', in *Between the Acts* to 'The Wraggle-Taggle Gypsies,
O!' And she read at least parts of Spenser's *Shepheardes Calender* (xxv.
54). She even once professed the desire to read long poems by Spenser,
Daniel, and Drayton (*L.* 1976, 29 Dec. 1928), though there is no
evidence that she in fact read either Daniel or Drayton. Woolf's
admiration for the *Faerie Queene* was, then, an exception to the rule, for
in Renaissance poetry she preferred lyric to narrative, the smaller
compass apparently precluding what she took to be the characteristic
excesses of the time. The compression of popular forms also encouraged
the poet to select the most telling words and images, and to load every
rift with ore. It mattered not whether a lyric poem were musical or
harsh, frequently anthologized or barely known, idiosyncratic or
conventional. Woolf's taste was catholic, as long as a poem had
intensity, a quality that she found omnipresent in the Renaissance lyric.

One of the most idiosyncratic of the poets, John Donne, was a late
taste. Woolf seems to have begun to take him seriously when she was
working on *Jacob's Room* (in 1921), attracted to the 'savagery' of the
elegies and satires. Bonamy reads Donne for the vigour of the language
(*JR* hol. i. 233, May 1921); and Jacob gives Sandra a copy (273, Nov.
1921)—as he does in the published novel (160–1). Woolf found in
Donne the same 'queer individuality' that she considered her own 'only
interest as a writer' (*D.* 18 Feb. 1922), and developed a sort of affection
for him compounded of the poems, the biography, and perhaps even an
early portrait in which he looks out on 'a world that half allures, half
disgusts him . . .' (*CE* ii. 4; *CE* iii. 59–60; 'Indiscretions', *W&W* 72,
76). Yet this particular taste took some cultivating. After thinking for
ten years about writing an essay on Donne, she finally did so only for
the tercentenary of his death. To a much greater degree than in
her approach to others, Woolf consulted the experts, particularly
Saintsbury's *History of Elizabethan Literature* and Grierson's editions of
the poems. Thus equipped she read through the complete elegies and

admired their beauty, intensity, wit, even crabbedness (XIX. 56). Although she devotes several pages of the essay to her first favourites, the elegies and satires (*CE* i. 33–8), she eventually read most of the poems and came to appreciate more than 'savagery'. She admired the brusqueness of the songs (32), and used a line from 'The Relic' to good effect in *Orlando*: 'He became the adored of many women and some men' (125). Even in the first and second 'Anniversaries', whose length and intellectualism probably daunted Woolf (reading was a 'duty', *D*. 13 Feb. 1932), she found a congenial mind whose 'rare and remote speculations' were worth the untangling (43).

The essay praises each of Donne's masterpieces and quotes liberally from most of them. It is in fact little more than a mass of well-selected quotations, in Woolf's view 'a great but I think well intentioned grind' (*D*. 16 Feb. 1932). But in it she puts her finger on what was for her the salient feature of Donne's variously motivated poems: their intensity. Divine poems as well as love poems dealt in the complexities of emotion of a man who 'must always speak from his own centre' (35). His was 'a bold and active mind that loves to deal with actual things, which struggles to express each shock exactly as it impinges upon his tight-stretched senses' (34).

It is easy to see why Woolf would feel some attraction for Donne. His was an earned differentness:

It is this desire for nakedness in an age that was florid, this determination to record not the likenesses which go to compose a rounded and seemly whole, but the inconsistencies that break up semblances, the power to make us feel the different emotions of love and hate and laughter at the same time, that separate Donne from his contemporaries. (36)

This is an honest assessment of a poet whom Woolf respected and admired, but it is not the overwhelming enthusiasm that she reserved for Donne's contemporaries and immediate successors who recorded 'the likenesses which go to compose a rounded and seemly whole'. Poems for which she cared deeply left frequent traces in her other essays and novels.

A large number of lyrics were a permanent part of Woolf's mind. Sidney, Shakespeare, and Jonson; Herrick, Campion, and Marvell—all illustrious names, all known from her earliest years, and all makers of 'seemly wholes'—entered into her essays and novels in significant ways. Included in their number must be the anonymous author of a poem that in fact left several traces, the lyric that Louis repeats in *The Waves* (200–3):

> Western wind, when wilt thou blow
> The small rain down can rain?
> Christ, if my love were in my arms
> And I in my bed again!

So familiar was the quatrain to Woolf that she could employ it in a variety of contexts, in the novel, in her diary for the sheer fun of it (*D.* 14 Mar. 1934), and in two essays 'How Should One Read a Book?' and 'Byron and Mr. Briggs', for quite another purpose. In both essays she treats the poem as quintessential, one which, despite all the kinds of poetry that exist, is representative. Similarly, despite all the kinds of readers that exist, her reactions to the poem are meant to demonstrate precisely what is involved in any reader's response to poetry.

Unlike in her reaction to fiction, she is immediately immersed and does not seek any biographical details about the author, or even his name: '. . . there is no other sensation except that of the poem itself.' She is not inclined while reading to think about historical or literary milieu, for 'the poet is always our contemporary. Our being for the moment is centred and constricted, as in any violent shock of personal emotion' (*CE* ii. 6–7).

In an earlier analysis, 'Byron and Mr. Briggs', she tallies reaction with line, thus:

That is passionate; direct; a cry to apply to everything. Western wind, when will thou blow—how wistfully it begins, with a sort of weary delaying compared with the direct attack of the concluding lines—the alliteration of course helping. The 'small rain' is exquisite—the fine rain that comes on the western wind, blowing white sheets over the orchards. Some sailor wrote it, far away looking towards England. 'Christ if my love were in my arms and I in my bed again!' (337–8)

Woolf recognizes that her statement is an attempt to focus her mind, but no sooner does she write this than she discovers that the very act of analysis diminishes the emotion she has felt. Later she thinks 'involuntarily' of the most striking detail of the poem, the 'small rain'. That phrase is impressive because, although she has seen such rain, she 'never thought of calling [it] small'.

Yet even this insight, accurate though it may be, is not really satisfying, for it is a far cry from the emotion she felt. Woolf values the capacity of the poem to evoke emotion in the reader, but that emotion is what she calls 'general', what human beings share rather than what is particular to a given poet or a given reader. 'Western Wind' makes the reader 'feel for all lovers and for all partings' rather than for his own or those of people he knows. 'The great writers require that we shall cease to be so-and-so, [but] shall retain only the truth of our emotions, which we have in common with others' (340). The difference between 'Western Wind' and a lyric by Donne is obvious: the intensity derives, not from the poet's being 'consciously and conspicuously himself', as Woolf contended Donne always was, but rather from his voicing emotions that everyone shares.

That the author of 'Western Wind' did just that is in a sense demonstrated by a scene in *The Waves*, in which the emotions embodied in the lyric are shared by Louis. He reads the poem and thinks of the losses he has endured, Rhoda's desertion and Percival's death, and withal his strong sense of the necessity to carry on. His situation is not in the least that of the implied speaker of the lyric, whom Woolf envisions as a sailor longing for home and his love; but such is the power of these four lines that, read by a man who has experienced the emotions that are part of having loved and having known the pain of separation, they elicit a strong response. Louis can enjoy 'Western Wind' precisely because it evokes what is true, what we have in common, and precisely because it is 'at enmity with my mahogany table and spats, and also, alas, with the vulgarity of my mistress'—that is, with those parts of his life which are false to his inner reality. The experience is broken down into its component parts, and concludes with the four lines together, Louis now empowered to resume his 'curious attempt' to bring into harmony the petty details of today and the important realities of the past.

The quotation in one of Woolf's novels of an entire poem is unique to this scene in *The Waves*. But she frequently alluded to poems whose ideas related to her major themes or whose imagery perfectly expressed her own meaning. For example, in another episode found in *The Waves*, Bernard mentions in his summing-up a very familiar image from one of Ben Jonson's odes (Schlack, *Continuing* 126, 152 n) in order to illustrate what people generally say about a person's dying young: it's the quality of a life and not longevity that counts; although an oak may stand three hundred years (as in another novel Orlando's in fact does), 'A lily of a day | Is fairer far in May'. Jonson's 'To the immortal memory and friendship of that noble pair, Sir Lucius Cary and Sir H. Morison', is an elegant tribute to Morison, who died at twenty-one, and who like Percival was 'a perfect patriot and a noble friend'. Like Cary, Bernard is left behind, but, unlike Cary, he is both the bereaved and the writer. In that double role he is self-conscious, and he can hear in the austere classicism of Jonson's beautiful ode something artificial, a consolation a bit too slick, which he uses by way of contrast to his own earlier, and genuine, response to the real Percival, 'whom I wanted to lose his hair, to shock the authorities, to grow old with me . . .' (265).

More to Woolf's personal taste than Ben Jonson, and the poets to whom she most frequently turned, were Herrick and Marvell—and of course Shakespeare. Their poetry is especially rich in images and metaphors that stimulate 'the eye of the mind and of the body'. This couplet from Herrick's 'To Electra' is illustrative:

> More white than are the whitest creams,
> Or moonlight tinselling the streams

Herrick evokes a strong visual response by pairing the simple white with 'the glittering, sequined, fluid look of moonlit water' (*CE* ii. 241). As she makes clear in 'Byron and Mr. Briggs' (342–3), the essay in which can be found much of the theoretical underpinning of her practice, Herrick's power can be attributed to an accuracy of both observation and feeling in the poet. The little epitaph on his maid Prudence satisfies the mind's longing for 'some finality, something stated':

> In this little urn is laid
> Prudence Baldwin, once my maid;
> From whose happy spark here let
> Spring the purple violet.

She revelled in the accuracy and exactitude of the wonderful lines in 'His Grange, or private wealth' about the hen who 'goes her long white egg to lay'.

These few lines illustrate Woolf's appreciation of the Renaissance habit of reaching for the actual. The poets thereby avoided vagueness, and at times managed to express metaphorically what might otherwise remain unexpressed. Their lyrics, filled with closely observed detail, remained in Woolf's mind and fed her creative imagination.

Woolf knew Herrick's 'Gather ye rosebuds while ye may', from her youth (*L.* 5, 24 Feb. 1897), and had Orlando do just that in his, for 'Girls were roses, and their seasons were short as the flowers'. Plucked they must be before nightfall. . . .' Lest the reader miss the joke, the narrator comments that 'what the poets said in rhyme, the young translated into practice'. Woolf also alludes to Campion's translation of

Catullus' poem to Lesbia, another *carpe diem* lyric: 'The moment is brief . . . the moment is over; one long night is then to be slept by all' *Orl.* 27).[3]

Another of these lyrics often in Woolf's mind (alluded to casually in her diary and letters) was Marvell's 'To His Coy Mistress', especially the four lines that open the middle movement of the poem:

> But at my back I always hear
> Time's winged chariot hurrying near;
> And yonder all before us lie
> Deserts of vast eternity.

In a meditation on time in *Orlando*, the hero cannot define the meaning of his life 'even when it stretched longest and the moments swelled biggest and he seemed to wander alone in deserts of vast eternity . . .' (99–100). Woolf thus puts readers in mind of the poem's contrasts between limited time and the larger stretches available through the imagination—thereby reinforcing a central conceit of *Orlando*.

Woolf always used Marvell in a functional way. In *The Years* North recites 'The Garden', the only poem he knows by heart, while visiting his cousin Sara. Old, unresolved tensions between them are underscored by the particular lines North reads, 'Society is all but rude— | To this delicious solitude' (339). He just might be telling Sara that he prefers to be alone.

But Woolf's favourite lines from the poem were the description of the viewer's immersion in a garden until the mind annihilates 'all that's made | To a green thought in a green shade'—an image of perfection. She always thought of 'The Garden' when she saw the sun making leaves 'transparent green' (*D*. 14 Sept. 1925). Again in *The Years*, when Woolf wants to suggest that only in the country does Kitty Lasswade come fully alive, she echoes Marvell's image. Kitty walks into the morning-room, where 'The green light dazzled her . . . It was as if she stood in the hollow of an emerald. All was green outside.' Total immersion in the green shade undoubtedly represents the oneness of physical state with mental state. An interesting version of Marvell's lines also occurs in a late essay on Sir Francis Bacon. Woolf describes Bacon walking in 'delicate groves', where his thought is 'coloured, embodied . . . given concrete form' ('Anon.' 397). Green-coloured

---

[3] A line from the original Latin appears in *The Years* (394). Leaska ('Virginia' 196–7) notes that in the holograph of that novel Woolf mentions both Herrick and Campion.

thought is Woolf's metaphor, then, for Bacon's concreteness and exactness in the essays.

Woolf's uses of the images of vast deserts and green shades are a tribute as well to Marvell's concreteness and exactness, qualities Woolf frequently found in the best Renaissance verse. They accounted for much of her attraction to the poetry of the period, just as the high-flown and inexact exasperated her. When Orlando is sixteen and still a fledgling poet, his failings are the failings of the time:

> He was describing, as all young poets are for ever describing, nature, and in order to match the shade of green precisely he looked (and here he showed more audacity than most) at the thing itself, which happened to be a laurel bush growing beneath the window. After that, of course, he could write no more. Green in nature is one thing, green in literature another. (16–17)

Orlando will not achieve the competence of a Herrick or a Marvell; he will remain a lesser poet, blessed with a natural facility but without the genius to be original.

Although Woolf stresses the hero's slavish reliance on poetic convention, from time to time she reminds the reader that many poets of the era spoke more individually. In both the manuscript and the finished novel she illustrates individuality through allusions to Ben Jonson's 'A Celebration of Charis'. In the holograph Orlando and Sasha hear some lines from section four of this set of ten lyric pieces, beginning 'See the Chariot at hand here of Love'. Orlando thinks the description 'the very image of his lady'. When Woolf decided to emphasize instead the theme of jealousy at this juncture, she substituted the more appropriate scene from *Othello* with which we are familiar in the novel (57). But placed at a later point in the novel Jonson's poem still could serve a purpose, for it provides a model of poetic excellence in the evocation of female beauty: snow's whiteness 'before the soil hath smutch'd it', the softness of 'the wool of the beaver', the sweetness of 'nard in the fire' or 'the bag of the bee'—these images are clear and exact, and culminate in the tribute to Charis that concludes the poem: 'O so white, O so soft, O so sweet is she!' All of this is behind the description of the beautifully gowned, bejewelled Lady Orlando: 'so dark, so bright, so hard, so soft, was she' (185–6). In a sense Orlando has become after a couple of centuries what he once had admired in Sasha, a vivid Elizabethan beloved.

As a young man all those years ago—and here is the point of the contrast—he had been incapable of Jonson's freshness. He wrote as everyman wrote. The most standard ways of describing female beauty suited him in his sonneteering, 'as stale as the women who inspired them . . .' (47). He writes sonnets to Clorinda, Favilla, and Euphrosyne, 'to give them the names he called them in his sonnets' (32), and is linked romantically with Doris, Chloris, Delia, or Diana, 'for he made rhymes to them all in turn' (28).

Woolf's handling of Orlando is gentle, the slight mockery simply her way of registering a modern reaction to the outdated conventions of the Elizabethan love sonnet. But she felt that the attitudes towards women suggested by those conventions should not be encouraged in the twentieth century, and she later attacked academics for wasting time in studying such things as 'the evolution of the Elizabethan sonnet' when in effect Rome was burning (*CE* ii. 282–3). In the relationship between the sexes today, persistence of attitudes neatly symbolized by sonnet conventions can be devastating, as Woolf demonstrates in *Night and Day*. Her vehicle is Sidney's *Astrophil and Stella* (in spite of its great poetic merit and of Woolf's long familiarity with it). Enlivening William Rodney's dialogue is one of the best-known sonnets from the sequence, 'With how sad steps, O moon, thou climb'st the skies!' (67). By means of the allusion he is satirized for espousing the outmoded view of women held by the speakers of sonnet sequences in the Renaissance. Astrophil complains of Stella's pride: women love to be loved, but disdain those who love them. Katharine, Rodney asserts, is nothing without marriage; but she scorns him ('we write sonnets to your eyebrows, you cruel practical creature'). The lines from Sidney, beautiful enough to make Katharine's brief engagement to Rodney seem a bit less ludicrous than it might otherwise be, none the less place him squarely in an old-fashioned context from which Katharine must struggle to free herself. He is inappropriate for someone who can think, and will be replaced by Ralph Denham.

Not all of the sonnet sequences expressed stereotyped views of women, just as not all were addressed primarily to women. Shakespeare's were ideologically more comfortable for Woolf, and had all the intensity that she demanded, with their resonant vocabulary, exactness of description, and compelling story. Although she once admitted that she found the sonnets difficult, a strain to her 'reasoning power', she felt the lure of Shakespeare's 'tremendous phrases' and the embedding of his thought in 'music' (AEFR v. 9). If someone in one of her novels were to disapprove of the sonnets, it would be a mark against him, as it is for example in the case of Richard Dalloway. Richard believes that decent people should not read the sonnets 'because it was like listening at keyholes (besides the relationship was not one that he approved)' (*Mrs. D.* 113). In the same way, Bernard's mere mention of Sonnet 116, 'Let me not to the marriage of true minds admit impediments', is a point in his favour (*Waves* 259).

Beyond this use for characterization, by means of a specific sonnet Woolf contributes to large themes in two of her novels. In *Between the Acts*, when all the actors of the pageant appear onstage during the scene of the mirrors that expose the audience, each repeats a bit of his part. One line is a version of 'and maiden virtue rudely strumpeted', from Shakespeare's Sonnet 66, 'Tir'd with all these, for restful death I cry'. Woolf's version, 'and the maiden faith is rudely strumpeted' (185), a conflation of Shakespeare's lines, retains the force of the original; and, although inadvertent error just might be involved, Woolf's version accords with the strained marriage vows of Giles and Isa, as well as with the repeated account of a gang rape. It is just one of the many continuities that the novel establishes with the past, in this case a fearsome continuity. Perhaps Woolf is showing that art gives structure to experience, however grim, and in the case of this particular sonnet to the death wish itself.

She uses another Shakespeare sonnet, 98, 'From you have I been absent in the spring', in *To the Lighthouse*. This sonnet takes on a far greater reality than the one in *Between the Acts* since Woolf lavishes much care on its presentation, keeps it more insistently before the reader, and assigns it to one of the major characters, Mrs Ramsay. She reads it while her husband reads Scott, he weeping and slapping his thigh, she becoming more and more peaceful. The first line that she singles out, 'Nor praise the deep vermilion in the rose', is part of all the richness of the spring which the discontent speaker of the sonnet cannot enjoy in the absence of his beloved. The experience of reading the sonnet has the glamour of an ascent to a mountain top, from which one can see the world in all its beauty:

> . . . she was ascending, she felt, on to the top, on to the summit. How satisfying! How restful! All the odds and ends of the day stuck to this magnet; her mind felt swept, felt clean. And then there it was, suddenly entire; she held it in her hands, beautiful and reasonable, clear and complete, the essence sucked out of life and held rounded here—the sonnet. (181)

Mrs Ramsay can appreciate the complete work of art, first the specificity of the quoted line, and then the more general image of the couplet, simple yet powerful, which gives perspective to the lines preceding it:

Yet seem'd it winter still, and, you away,
As with your shadow I with these did play.

Like the 'Sirens' song', which Mrs Ramsay also reads, the poem is an affirmation of love, and of love arrived at and maintained by imagination and intelligence. The passage leads directly to a satisfying scene between the Ramsays. But it also leads, by means of repetition of the final line, to some sense of foreboding, which is finally articulated in Mrs Ramsay's thoughts: '. . . the shadow, the thing folding them in was beginning, she felt, to close round her again' (183–4). It is in fact the last scene in which Mrs Ramsay is alive.

Later in the novel, when Lily Briscoe is thinking of Mrs Ramsay and attempting again to paint a picture she started years ago, the two major meanings of 'shadow' in Shakespeare's sonnet inform Lily's thinking, shadow in the sense of something lacking substance, and shadow in the sense of portrait, the latter of course predominating. These meanings attract a third, and that is shadow in the sense of area darkened by an opaque object, a meaning that is completely appropriate to the form Mrs Ramsay and James take in the painting. Perhaps to remind the reader of Mrs Ramsay's satisfaction in Shakespeare's sonnet, Lily's thoughts echo its final line: 'Ghost, air, nothingness, a thing you could play with easily and safely at any time of day or night, [Mrs Ramsay] had been that.' But such play is dangerous, the lack of substance finally revealing 'a centre of complete emptiness' (266). The shadow of the sonnet next becomes, by a transition almost linguistic, a 'shade' moving across flower-filled fields (270), then a triangular shadow cast by some body (299), and, finally, when Lily completes the painting, the 'shadow' regains its Elizabethan sense of portrait, for the painting is an abstract portrait of Mrs Ramsay (310).

Among the many differences between Woolf's reactions to the drama, the prose, and the poetry of the Renaissance, one of the most basic is manifested in the decisions she made about writing criticism. Her responses to the various kinds of poetry were scattered in essays and novels, with separate essays on Donne and Spenser; but she made no attempt to survey the genre. She approached the prose of the era more frequently (essays on Hakluyt, Harvey, Sidney) and more systematically (in 'Reading' and in 'The Elizabethan Lumber Room'). But she never embarked on a full-blown study. Only the drama seemed to demand such treatment. With a view to writing a definitive account of the drama, over a year and a half she read a large number of plays, on thirty of which her reading notes are extant. This extraordinary amount of preparation culminated in a major essay on the drama, 'Notes on an Elizabethan Play' (1925), published first as a leading article in the *Times Literary Supplement*, and then, with very slight revision, in the first *Common Reader*.

The essay focuses on a small group of playwrights, most of them born during Elizabeth's reign although flourishing during James's and even as late as Charles's. Since only one of the plays was published during the reign, the word 'Elizabethan' in the title should be taken broadly, to include everything from late in the sixteenth century up to the closing of the theatres. In addition to deciding on the span to be covered, Woolf made two other important decisions: although she had read a goodly number of playwrights, she would devote her analysis to lesser dramatists; and, although she had read works in the three major genres, she would limit her discussion to tragedy, briefly bringing in a couple of comedies for the purpose of contrast. Her focus is on the following: Kyd, *The Spanish Tragedy* (1592); Chapman, *Bussy d'Ambois* (1607); Webster, *The White Devil* (1608); Beaumont and Fletcher, *The Maid's Tragedy* (1619); Dekker, Ford, and Rowley, *The Witch of Edmonton* (1623); Ford, *The Broken Heart* (1633) and *'Tis Pity She's a Whore* (1633). Woolf probably selected these particular plays because, given the assortment of dramas with which she was for one reason or another familiar, they presented in exaggerated form all that she thought was both the best that could be said about the lesser drama of the time, and the worst. Together they made up the construct that she dubbed 'an Elizabethan play'. She knew perfectly well that hosts of plays existed from the time that called into question many of her assertions, and she could not have believed that her coverage was exhaustive. But she suspected that 'a typical' play, 'a bad one, or the skeleton of the good' would bring out essential qualities (*D*. 3 Feb. 1924) unobscured by the characteristically magnificent language. The views expressed in 'Notes on an Elizabethan Play' are Woolf's primary ones, but opposing observations, suppressed for a variety of reasons, none the less constitute an important part of Woolf's evaluation of these plays.

The 'greatest infliction that Elizabethan drama puts upon us', said Woolf, is the plot, 'the incessant, improbable, almost unintelligible convolutions' that 'confuse and fatigue a reader'. She demanded that a plot 'agitate great emotions; bring into existence memorable scenes; stir the actors to say what could not be said without this stimulus' (*CE* i. 56)—reasonable demands all, and a perceptive analysis of the functions of plot in a drama. As she was reading through some of the plays that contributed to the essay, she found them lacking in these various areas: Chapman's *Bussy d'Ambois* was often incoherent (MHP/B2o, 15, 16); Webster's plot in *The White Devil* seemed too busy, 'the usual chop & change so intolerable to read' (XIX. 29), the more frustrating because the play otherwise fascinated her with its vigorous speeches and sympathetic main characters. Webster was a fine writer, yet he seemed unable to resist such convolutions of plot (XXV. 2).

As Woolf read Beaumont and Fletcher's *The Maid's Tragedy*, on the other hand, she found a highly functional plot, interesting in itself, and capable of 'springing people's passions', thus meeting one of her central demands. Another, that the plot bring into existence memorable scenes, was surely met in such a scene as 'Evadne's revelation that she is the king's mistress [and] has only married Amintor to get her child a father'—one Woolf singled out in her notes as illustrative of the 'great deal of life' in the play (XIX. 52). And the plot of *The Maid's Tragedy* certainly stirred characters to remarkable dialogue: one speech in particular, an old busybody's lament for his daughter's death, always impressed Woolf, she said, as 'a stroke of genius' (53). Yet in the essay she faults both *The White Devil* and *The Maid's Tragedy* for plots unrelated to the emotions aroused (56). She lumps Robert Greene's plots with Kyd's when in fact she privately called the only of Greene's plays that she read, *Friar Bacon and Friar Bungay*, 'very interesting' and 'easy to follow' (XIX. 41). One can only assume that the enthusiasm Woolf felt while she was reading waned later when she discovered that very little stuck in her memory. Or perhaps she silently suppressed certain of her enthusiasms for the sake of a unified and hard-hitting essay.

The matter of the relationship between plot and characterization is probably another instance of Woolf's eliminating certain discrepancies as she moved from reading to writing. In the essay Woolf asserts that, because of the complexities of 'Elizabethan' plots, 'there are no characters in Elizabethan drama, only violences whom we know so little that we can scarcely care what becomes of them' (*CE* i. 57). She excepts only Shakespeare 'and perhaps Ben Jonson' from this accusation. And she cites two examples of the 'violences' that replace characters in the drama as a whole, Bel-imperia in Kyd's *Spanish Tragedy* and Annabella in *'Tis Pity She's a Whore*. Woolf read Kyd's play twice (XXV. 25–6; XIX. 34–5), but was not convinced that she could care any more for Bel-imperia than for 'an animated broomstick', in spite of her 'running the whole gamut of human misery to kill herself in the end' (57). Annabella in *'Tis Pity* goes 'from pole to pole in a series of tremendous vicis-situdes', but 'we do not know how she reaches her conclusions, only that she has reached them. Nobody describes her. She is always at the height of her passion, never at its approach' (57). Thus Woolf supports her contention with solid evidence, and the essay would very likely con-vince a reader unfamiliar with a broader range of Elizabethan and Jaco-bean plays that characterization is minimal.

But interestingly enough Woolf was herself acquainted with plays in which the characterizations were deftly handled. Webster's *The White Devil*, despite an involved plot, held her interest throughout because of the extremely attractive Vittoria; held it even to the end: 'sympathy goes straight to Vittoria & Flamineo, dying game' (xxv. 3). And Webster's *The Duchess of Malfi* was 'far better, & more tightly strung than The White Devil'. The play was an exception to Woolf's rule in two respects, its plot 'as good as can be & the characters more subtle than usual' (xix. 23). Webster builds the character of the Duchess in a series of scenes, beginning early (as Woolf noted) with 'the strength and directness' of her proposal to her steward, Antonio. When the Duchess learns that she has been banished, she envies 'the birds, that live i' the field | On the wild benefit of nature', for they can freely choose their mates. She decides that Antonio and one son must go elsewhere for their safety, and accepts his platitudinous assurances with her magnificent 'naught made me e'er | Go right but heaven's scourge-stick'. She tells her brother's henchman, Bosola, that she will teach her children how to curse: 'since they were born accurs'd, | Curses shall be their first language.' She is not cowed by the misfortunes that befall her, but faces them with enormous bravery and a certain style. Woolf recorded all the lines I have quoted commenting on their appropriate-ness for the impetuous aristocrat (xix. 23–4). In *Night and Day* (57) she singles out the death scene of the Duchess for special mention; and several years after writing 'Notes on an Elizabethan Play' she would include the Duchess among the dramatic heroines who 'have burnt like beacons in all the works of all the poets from the beginning of time' (*Room* 74). Even the characterization of Bosola, who is unrelievedly nefarious for four acts, won Woolf's approval, for his sudden reformation added the complexity she expected in good drama. She appreciated a play in which the characters 'are not always absolute . . .' (xix. 24). Clearly, then, Webster should have joined Shakespeare and Ben Jonson as an example in the essay of a playwright whose characterizations met Woolf's specifications.

Those specifications included not only the complexity that real flesh and blood contains, but also certain trappings of reality that anchor readers to a play and thereby free their imaginations. In 'Notes on an Elizabethan Play' Woolf sets up a contrast between everyday reality—a Liverpool inhabited by 'some knight called Smith, who succeeded his father in the family business of pitwood importers'—and the world of the 'Elizabethan' play, an Armenia inhabited by angry unicorns and horn-seeking jewellers (the example is from *Bussy d'Ambois*). In these plays 'their Smiths are all changed to dukes, their Liverpools to fabulous islands and palaces in Genoa' (*CE* i. 54–5). They are the sort of plays Orlando habitually wrote around the end of the sixteenth century:

He was fluent, evidently, but he was abstract. Vice, Crime, Misery were the personages of his drama; there were Kings and Queens of impossible territories; horrid plots confounded them; noble sentiments suffused them; there was never a word said as he himself would have said it . . . (16)

But then Orlando would probably rank as the least of the lesser dramatists, on a par with, say, Thomas Sackville (Schlack, *Continuing* 83), and such a cast of characters, not necessarily fatal in other writers, was lifeless in his hands. He might have done better had his Smiths remained Smiths.

When Woolf asserted in 'Notes on an Elizabethan Play' that *all* 'Elizabethan' Smiths were changed to dukes, she was of course exaggerating, as she was in *Orlando*, and probably had in mind the efforts of amateurs and others whose place in literary history is undistinguished. From her own experience there was another side to the story: beside the royal personages and aristocrats of *The Maid's Tragedy* or *The Duchess of Malfi*, commoners abounded in much comedy (admittedly not her province in the essay) and in a play from which she actually quotes lines, *The Witch of Edmonton*. She commented in her notes on the oddness of its being about 'real people, of the lower classes, & at the present time—all unlikely in Elizabethan drama . . .'. Therefore it is fair to say that, while she was certainly more accustomed to aristrocratic characters, she knew that Smiths could be found among the dramatis personae.

In addition, she rethought the matter of class and setting just a couple of years later and reached a more tenable conclusion than she had in 1925. In 'The Narrow Bridge of Art', an impressive essay on aesthetics, she asserted that the more usual high-born characters—and even the exotic settings—of the 'Elizabethan' drama were highly functional: 'It was a natural device which gave depth and distance to their figures. But the country remained English; and the Bohemian prince was the same person as the English noble' (*CE* ii. 221). Freed from the self-imposed restrictions of the earlier essay, and rising above its literary provincialism, Woolf could see very clearly indeed the rationale for this important element of the drama, especially when the light of Shakespeare (whose Bohemian prince probably furnished the example) reveals in the lesser dramatists a lustre she had before failed to notice.

Even those plays most deficient in plot and characterization shared with plays that were unexceptionable in those respects a quality that was pre-eminent among Woolf's critical requirements. Because it was a verse drama, all that she found most praiseworthy in Renaissance poetry, the 'moments of intensity' and the 'phrases of astonishing beauty', quite naturally redounded to the credit of the drama as well (*CE* i. 58). 'Notes on an Elizabethan Play' is full of such quotations. There was an embarrassment of riches, so that successive drafts of the essay show Woolf including now this set of lines, now that, wondering how to incorporate her favourites, and to do so without depriving them of the force they have in context. She hated to let go of a prize, and in 'How Should One Read a Book?' lines of verse from Renaissance plays are treated as poetry; in fact, Woolf does not even bother to mention that the lines are taken from plays. She cites them, just as she does lines from *The Prelude* and the 'Rime of the Ancient Mariner', to support her contention that 'the intensity of poetry covers an immense range of emotion'. To illustrate its 'force and directness' she cites a couplet from Beaumont and Fletcher's *The Maid's Tragedy*; and in contrast she quotes eight lines of 'wavering modulation' from Ford's *The Lover's Melancholy* (*CE* ii. 7).

That same emphasis on the drama as poetry informs the entire 'Notes on an Elizabethan Play'. Woolf quotes from Ford's *The Broken Heart*, Chapman's *Bussy d'Ambois*, Beaumont and Fletcher's *The Maid's Tragedy*, Dekker and others' *The Witch of Edmonton*, and Webster's *The White Devil*. From some of these she selects two quotations, from *The White Devil*, four. All of these passages affected Woolf because in them the emotion was 'concentrated, generalized, heightened' (*CE* i. 58). The individual character's experience is of wider significance because the medium of verse reveals essence. The playwright 'goes beyond the single and the separate, shows us not Annabella in love, but love itself', and 'ruin and death and the soul . . .' (59). The lines that especially attracted Woolf dealt less frequently with love and rather more frequently with death, with death 'in general'. This was the special province of Renaissance tragedy, and those authors who were most melancholic were most pleasing, even when indulging in the very practices Woolf decried in 'Notes on an Elizabethan Play'. If she really did dislike the plot of *The Maid's Tragedy* as she said she did (*CE* i. 56), the quality of Beaumont and Fletcher's verse more than compensated. Few lyrics tap the beauty in disappointment and death as well as this song from that play:

> Lay a garland on my hearse
>   Of the dismal yew;
> Maidens, willow branches bear;
>   Say I died true.
> My love was false, but I was firm
>   From my hour of birth.
> Upon my buried body lie
>   Lightly, gentle earth.

Woolf's reactions to the first quatrain of this attractively melancholic song reveal precisely how she believed verse drama gets its power: in its 'perfect marriages of sense and sound' it can depict 'extremes of passion', and can reveal character not by description but by 'illumination' (58). The secret was in such a song as 'Lay a garland on my hearse', 'the sort of thing only the Elizabethans can do' (xix. 52).

But the best example of Woolf's inclination to forgive supposed faults can be found in her response to the plays of John Ford, whose verse demonstrated the characteristic virtues of beauty and generalized emotion. For the purposes of discussion, at the outset in the essay she attacks the characterization of Annabella in *'Tis Pity She's a Whore*; but within pages she recognizes the inappropriateness of judging with novelistic criteria, and praises Ford's depiction of 'love itself' by means of 'crises and calamities'. His *The Broken Heart* seemed even better: the plot could be grasped easily, he made 'some attempt at psychology', and in his language she found 'a kind of beautiful fitness' as well as 'an exactitude and spareness' (xix. 39–40). In 'Notes on an Elizabethan Play' Woolf quotes some lines from the play to illustrate the vanity of human wishes and the desirability of death (*CE* i. 60). She recorded the long speech in her reading notes, impressed by Ford's tenderness and the beauty of his writing, especially in the remedy proposed, 'a winding-sheet, a fold of lead, | And some untrod-in corner in the earth'. His preoccupation with death, his depiction of characters at the extreme edge of despair, suited her perfectly. It did not matter that people were named Ithocles and Calantha, or that they were royal. What mattered was that someone could say,

> O, my lords,
> I but deceived your eyes with antic gesture,
> When one news straight came huddling on another
> Of death! and death! and death! still I danced forward.

—and these lines she quotes in the essay (58). From the very opening of *The Lover's Melancholy*, Woolf heard 'a very musical melancholy', and everything was bathed in attractiveness. A young lady's going to Cyprus dressed as a man was 'charming', and indeed 'the charming unreality' was actually 'one source of pleasure' (XIX. 50–1). The world seen from a melancholic perspective, and given expression in lovely poetry, was precisely what Woolf wanted. John Ford was therefore a great favourite.

So too was Webster. Woolf disapproved of the highly convoluted plot of *The White Devil* and approved the characterization of the leads. But what captivated her was the poetry. As is evident from the frequent quotations in 'Notes on an Elizabethan Play', to Woolf's mind it was quintessentially 'Elizabethan'. Isabella's lines beginning 'You have oft for these two lips | Neglected cassia' illustrate the moments of intensity; the lines 'My soul, like to a ship in a black storm | Is driven, I know not whither' reveal emphasis on the general; and to illustrate the preoccupation with death, Woolf selects both 'Lord, Lord, that I were dead!' and 'O then soft natural death that art joint-twin | To sweetest slumber!' (*CE* i. 58–60). Woolf felt a fascination in Webster's combination of horror, violence, and remarkably strong blank verse, and filled up six pages of notes with quotations from *The White Devil*, for there was 'greatness all scattered about' (XXV. 2–4; XIX. 27–9).

A Webster play filled with the kind of horrors Woolf so often decried, but filled as well with magnificent verse, was *The Duchess of Malfi*. Woolf called the dead hand 'very typical of the Elizabethan's physical horror'. But when the Duchess decides that she will not pray, 'No, I'll go curse,' Woolf saw that Webster piles up the horrors to such an extent that a single word such as 'curse' is effective (XIX. 24). She valued the way certain playwrights handled death, with bitter-sweetness (Beaumont and Fletcher in 'Lay a garland on my hearse' and 'I shall fall like a tree, & find my grave' from *The Maid's Tragedy*; Ford in 'Minutes are numbered by the fall of sands' from *The Lover's Melancholy*). But she valued even more Webster's handling of that theme, for in his plays all was starkness and splendour. Even reasonless deaths could 'be made the occasion for poetry', as in Ferdinand's response to his sister's death: 'Cover her face; mine eyes dazzle; she died young' or Bosola's numbed answer to the question of how Antonio died, 'In a mist, I know not how' (xix. 25). *The Duchess of Malfi* was a 'magnificent play' with 'its sudden direct sap: pounce: stroke. Its culminations & whirlwinds' (xix. 23). It was 'Elizabethan' tragedy precisely as she preferred it.

When Woolf decided to limit her coverage in 'Notes on an Elizabethan Play' to tragedy, she was eliminating what was never really a strong interest. But, while she was engaged in the concentrated reading, she did read quite a few comedies, and discovered merit in several of them, verse of a high order, and 'an intermittent bawling vigour' that she could not resist. She recorded some lines from Robert Greene's *Friar Bacon and Friar Bungay* that are a perfect illustration of 'the coloured and the high-sounding':

> In frigates bottom'd with rich Sethin planks,
> Topt with the lofty firs of Lebanon,
> Stemm'd & incas'd with burnished ivory
> And overlac'd with plates of Persian wealth,
> Like Thetis shalt thou wanton on the waves,
> And draw the dolphins to thy lovely cup,
> To dance lavoltas in the purple streams.

True, she said, this is a 'purple patch' (xix. 41); but she herself was as charmed by this 'characteristic Elizabethan extravagance' (*CE* i. 49) as a putative contemporary audience, even if she could confess to the taste only in a draft since it was 'slightly to our discredit we feel & should not be acknowledged openly . . .' (*Mrs. D.* Corr. 67). She found such extravagance, to her surprise, even in Ben Jonson, in a passage where Volpone offers Celia gifts of 'the juice of July flowers, of the milk of unicorns and panthers' breath, of ropes of pearl, brains of peacocks and Cretan wine' (*CE* i. 61).

The brief allusions in 'Notes on an Elizabethan Play' to Greene and Jonson serve merely to point up differences between the poetry to be found in Renaissance comedy and, her primary interest, tragedy. Woolf certainly enjoyed both, the passionate intensity and beauty of tragic verse, and the occasional rhetorical extravagance of comic. But for Woolf comedy was, with very few exceptions, a world of non-hyperbolic prose. As such she read it only intermittently; and, although she alluded to it from time to time in essays on a variety of subjects, she never devoted an entire essay to the genre. She did, however, write reviews of individual plays, one of particular interest, of a new edition in 1920 of *Gammer Gurton's Needle* for the *TLS*. She loved the 'Englishness' of the play, the direct language, 'wholesome and natural' indecency, the village setting, and such simple characters as 'Diccon, the rascally tramp . . .'. So English is the play that it struck Woolf as just right for one of the productions at the Oliver family's Pointz Hall (*BA* 59). It was 'a very coarse play', but 'none the worse for that' (*L*. 3498, 14 Mar. 1939).

Woolf also admired the 'swing and directness' of the plot: 'The story rattles itself off without a hitch', the writer making a single detour, and that for one of her long-time favourites, 'the splendid drinking song' of 'I can not eat but little meat'. The down-to-earth quality and rough humour of this song have earned it a place in many anthologies, where she probably first met it. But for the rest, something was lacking, and that was poetry. Verse there was aplenty; but the playwright 'was no poet. He sang his song in praise of ale with splendid vigour, but for the majority of human pleasures, for the look of things, for love and for death he had no sense at all.' The absence of what seemed to her the characteristic Elizabethan topics and extravagance may account for the curious fact that Woolf consistently got her chronology wrong, placing the play far earlier than her sources placed it (she has John Paston see the play close to sixty years before it was written, and she lumps it with Chaucer and *Piers Plowman* in a draft of *BA*). It did not seem Elizabethan.

Less than a year after reviewing *Gammer Gurton's Needle*, and before she finally decided to focus on tragedy in 'Notes on an Elizabethan Play', Woolf read several more comedies, presumably with the end in view of having a solid basis for the essay. As a young woman she had read Ben Jonson (*L*. 39, 5 Nov. 1901), and he was an enduring favourite of Lytton Strachey and his family (Sanders 23; *D*. 18 Jan. 1918). When Woolf decided to 'read like an expert' for the book of criticism that would become *The Common Reader* (*D*. 23 May 1921), she quite naturally began with a Jonson play, *Bartholemew Fair*. She thought it a 'difficult scattered work' but very much enjoyed the first three acts; and, although she was not quite sure how she felt about Jonson's 'hard clever dialogue', she liked the language of Ursula (MHP/B2d, 32).

At this point, June of 1921, she had completed her first draft of *Jacob's Room* and was adding scattered pages to her manuscript before revising the whole. She used the opportunity to have a character express one or another of her views on *Bartholemew Fair*, as she often did with books that she was reading (and just as characteristically she would go on to delete the literary criticism from her final draft of the novel). When Richard Bonamy is upset, for example, he always reads one of 'the ancients'—'for though a number of people write well enough nowadays, what we have lost entirely is vigour of language'. Now he selects Ben Jonson, and not surprisingly *Bartholomew Fair*. Sure enough, Bonamy points to the fat 'pig-woman', Ursula, as Woolf herself had done:

There is a scene for example in Bartholomew Fair of a fat woman scolding which could not be pieced together by twenty of our young men writing in concert; . . . when this torrent of language gets its way, the chances are that it sweeps down with it something . . . astonishing. (*JR* hol. ii. 233)

This evaluation of the language of the play probably represents Woolf's most positive approach to Jonson's 'hard clever dialogue'. But she was not happy with it, and put in a word for beauty over cleverness by creating a scene in which Clara Durrant sighs romantically when she hears Jonson's lyric 'Drink to me only with thine eyes' (cf. *JR* 88). Neatly enough, the two friends who most love Jacob, Richard Bonamy and Clara, represent two distinct critical preferences. When deleting from the novel Bonamy's bit of literary criticism, Woolf also deleted the Jonson lyric, and substituted for it a more appropriate one from a Shakespeare play. But she retained Bonamy's general preference for classically precise dialogue: 'I like books whose virtue is all drawn together in a page or two, I like sentences that don't bulge though armies cross them. I like words to be hard.' In contrast there were Jacob and Clara, and probably Woolf herself, 'those whose taste is all for the fresh growths of the morning, who throw up the window, and find the poppies spread in the sun, and can't forbear a shout of jubilation at the astonishing fertility of English literature' (140). After the novel was published, Lytton Strachey wrote to Woolf, 'Of course you're very romantic—which alarms me slightly—I am such a Bonamy' (*Woolf–Strachey Letters* 144). Strachey saw correctly enough that his friend's enjoyment of such classical writers as Jonson did not run very deep.

Yet some time before publishing *The Common Reader*, probably early in 1924, Woolf tried again. She frequently found Gregory Smith's study of Jonson helpful while re-reading *Bartholomew Fair* and reading four other plays, but her notes on all the plays are a record of almost constant frustration. Jonson was no Shakespeare, but, like many 'lesser dramatists', she said, he 'worried one with too many scenes'. Neither

The Alchemist nor *The Silent Woman* could keep her attention, so ingenious were the plots (XIX. 42). She finally realized that for such works as *Volpone* or *The Alchemist* she had 'a natural disinclination' (46). It became increasingly clear that she preferred humour to wit.

She resented Jonson's intellectualism, the more so the more she came to understand his satiric purpose with the help of Smith's book. She wondered why he should want to satirize the Puritans in *Bartholomew Fair*, or whom he really was attacking in *The Alchemist*. She later came to the conclusion that a greater complexity of vision (such as Shakespeare's) would lead an author to genres other than satire (D. 6 May 1935). Jonson's vision was less rounded, and satire its natural expression, for 'an intellectual must have something to pick to pieces' (XIX. 42). His criticism of foibles she could tolerate better than his more subtle and recondite attacks on sinfulness. So it was that she could appreciate the obvious satire in Sir Epicure Mammon's *Playboy* fantasy in *The Alchemist* (42) or, in *Volpone*, 'the character of Sir Politic, who is a know-all, busybody fool, & finally shut up in his own tortoise. Also Lady Pol. in her first scene with Volpone is first rate, asking the maids to prepare her, then rattling off all her book learning.' She did not read *Volpone* as 'a study of human depravity' (45), and preferred the first act of *The Silent Woman* as 'a kindlier comedy than Volpone. It is more a comedy of curious traits. Morose's love of silence does not cut so deep as the avarice & cupidity in Volpone' (46).

Years later in the pageant of *Between the Acts*, her Restoration comedy, whose most obvious source is *The Way of the World*, harks back as well to the Renaissance. She recalls *Volpone*, but not the greedy birds of prey. Rather, her Sir Spaniel Lilyliver and Lady Harpy Harraden resemble the characters that she had preferred, Sir Politic Would-be and his Lady Pol. The name of a clergyman, Sir Smirking Peace-be-with-you-all, has a decidedly Jonsonian ring, recalling Zeal-of-the-land Busy from *Bartholomew Fair*. Again the tone derives from the relatively brighter part of Jonson's palette. Woolf wanted a kindlier view of the human race, the people reprehensible, not depraved.

She also wanted to discover character in the process of being revealed, with gradualness and complexities one might meet in real life, or in the novel. Only Shakespeare, 'and perhaps Ben Jonson', she said in 'Notes on an Elizabethan Play', managed to create flesh and blood characters (*CE* i. 57). She was almost willing to admit Jonson's characterizations on the basis not only of Ursula the pig-woman and Sir Politic Would-be, but also of the more comples Mosca, whose co-operation with

Volpone not only showed his remarkable cleverness, but slowly and gradually revealed other traits as well, notably the subtlety of his hatred, and his greed (XIX. 44–5). He was, in short, not one-dimensional. But nether was he a rounded character. And that was generally how Woolf viewed Jonson's characters that she favoured: Subtle, Mammon, and Doll in *The Alchemist*, for example, behaved just surprisingly enough to be considered lively, but finally were dismissed as 'not real people' (42).

Given her disappointment in the best of the comic dramatists, Woolf's emphasis on tragedy in 'Notes on an Elizabethan Play' is understandable and may have contributed to the success of the essay even with academics (*D.* 4 May 1925). She confined her commentary on the drama thereafter, however, to incidental observations or at most to isolated paragraphs, until the very end of her life, when she again studied the drama with some thoroughness. Until then, if extant notes and the usual external evidence are to be relied on, she read Shakespeare steadily but the lesser dramatists only during one period, the fall of 1935.

Over the years there were remarkably few changes in Woolf's reactions to the drama. When she had read Ford's *The Lover's Melancholy* in the 1920s she admired the 'musical melancholy' and pleasurable unreality; in the mid-1930s she preferred Ford's tragedy to the memoirs of a contemporary, enjoying the play's beauty and remoteness (*D.* 29 Sept. 1935). Yet there were some changes in Woolf's views, some based on wider acquaintance with Renaissance drama and some probably coming from a developing capacity to appreciate the drama on its own terms. When towards the end of her life Woolf once again studied the drama, in preparation for her history of English literature, she included two plays in drafts, one by Marlowe and the other by Heywood. Heywood was a new acquaintance, his *A Woman Killed with Kindness* the sort of domestic tragedy of which Woolf had been largely unaware earlier. Not only was the play set in Yorkshire, but its characters had ordinary names (Anne, Frankford) and spoke like ordinary people. When Frankford said 'O God! O God; that it were possible | To undo things done; to call back yesterday!', Woolf realized that his words 'are our own' ('Anon.' 423–4). She found this the more remarkable because, in the prose of the time, the words of real people were 'shadowy and suppressed', full of 'contortions [and] evasions' (423). She was more surprised by the playwright's interest in theme and character. He eschews extremely convoluted plots, 'separates himself from his audience', and allows himself to consider 'the motive behind the action'. He asks 'what is the effect of mercy?—if the adulterers are confronted not with death but with a guilty conscience?' (423). The very psychology which Woolf found lacking in, say *'Tis Pity She's a Whore* she encountered in *A Woman Killed with Kindness*. Could she have simply looked in the wrong place? A change in critical judgement was in order.

If changes in Woolf's attitudes about Renaissance drama came in part from a wider acquaintance with the genre, some were a function of her maturity as a reader. She knew Marlowe's plays, for example, from rather early on (*L*. 39, 5 Nov. 1901), and her own Jacob Flanders wrote essays on Marlowe, ranking him with Shakespeare (107, 122). Eliot had recently celebrated Marlowe in an influential essay when Woolf read four of the plays in preparation for 'Notes on an Elizabethan Play'.[4] But she read inattentively and without profit. Lines that showed startling directness, 'material splendour', and intensity convinced her that Marlowe was 'undoubtedly a poet' (xxv. 31). Yet, when a phrase from the play stuck in her mind ('religious caterpillars'), it somehow attached itself in her imagination not to Marlowe but to Webster, the playwright she preferred (*L*. 2916, 8 Aug. 1934).

Nor did the hasty reading of the four plays in 1923, lead Woolf to include Marlowe in 'Notes on an Elizabethan Play' or in the more general essays immediately following it in which she quoted from some of her favourites. In 1923 her primary interest was clearly in language, and some fifteen years later in a draft of *Between the Acts* Mrs Swithin echoes that interest. She thinks of books as roads, Marlowe's more circuitous and more exotic than his predecessors: 'The road curled; the sentence once more became serpentine; and bore the mind on its proud back.' Marlowe 'stuck his verse with sonorous words, many syllabled', the travels of the time enriching the language (*BA* TS 29–30). When Woolf read Marlowe again a year or two later, she became aware of something that had eluded her earlier. She related language to the humanist push for knowledge: high-sounding rhetoric was functional, she discovered, commensurate with the vastness of the universe of the play, as was the boastful language of those whose achievements were in fact great. She came to see in short that there is nothing discreditable in a reader's love of such extravagance.

Woolf had always appreciated the richness of Renaissance drama, but

---

[4] 'Notes on the Blank Verse of Christopher Marlowe' (repr. in *The Sacred Wood* (1920)), read in this collection by Woolf in 1924 (*L*. 1495, 3 Sept.). Some earlier undated notes on the book, from around the time of its publication, are in MHP/B2d, 20.

she had been only dimly aware of the extent of its diversity, its ability to capture the everyday as well as the grand, to use the resources of language in the widest spectrum of expression. Now, with her reading of *A Woman Killed with Kindness* and re-reading of *Tamburlaine* while the Second World War raged around her, she arrived at a fuller and deeper appreciation. Of course no playwright could measure up to Shakespeare, but other playwrights have an honourable place in her esteem. Together they make up the age of Elizabeth she celebrates in her final novel, *Between the Acts*.

In the 'Elizabethan' pageant she does not develop character at all, but instead deftly stresses the unique ability of the poetic drama to generalize: when a young prince sees his beloved approach the scene, Isa Oliver concludes that 'Love embodied' has entered (91). This derives from Woolf's earlier contention that such a play as *'Tis Pity She's a Whore* gives the reader, not the sort of character found in the novel, but rather 'love itself'. In the originals the intensity of the verse was largely responsible. Woolf's own verse in the pageant lacking that power, she gets something of the effect by means of frequent allusion. Twice she quotes lines from *The White Devil* that illustrate the kind of poetry characteristic of those plays. She had noted back in the 1920s (xxv. 3) Flamineo's eerie contention that wives will remarry

> Ere the worm pierce your winding sheet, ere the spider
> Make a thin curtain for your epitaphs.

Now in the mirrors scene of the pageant in *Between the Acts* Woolf included a curiously conflated version of the lines: '*Where the worm weaves its winding sheet*' (185). Perhaps Woolf thought Webster's words would be heard as a comment on the tenuousness of the marital bond in contemporary life, adumbrated in Mrs Manresa and developed more fully in the desires of Giles and Isa. Another line from *The White Devil* is actually quoted in the 'Elizabethan' part of the pageant, '*Call for the robin redbreast and the wren*', the dirge from Webster's tragedy fitting nicely into the priest's benediction at the end of the play (92).

One perceives the play from the point of view of Isa Oliver, whose thoughts interrupt the action. She summarizes the plot:

About a false Duke; and a Princess disguised as a boy; then the long lost heir turns out to be the beggar, because of a mole on his cheek; and Ferdinando and Carinthia—that's the Duke's daughter, only she's been lost in a cave—falls in love with Ferdinando who had been put into a basket as a baby by an aged crone. And they marry. (88)

Yet we see almost nothing of the action here summarized, for, as Isa realizes, 'the plot was only there to beget emotion'. Not the 'greatest infliction that Elizabethan drama puts upon us', as Woolf once asserted, the plot calls up, in its recounting of the difficulties and joys of young love, the emotions of love and hate, and, in its acceptance of death, the emotion of peace (90, 92). 'Love. Hate. Peace. Three emotions made the ply of human life' (92).[5] Isa realizes furthermore that the writer of the pageant shares her view of Elizabethan drama: 'Don't bother about the plot: the plot's nothing.' There is a recognition scene (an old crone identifies a prince) and the prince and princess greet each other. That suffices, and 'all else was verbiage, repetition' (91).

Such treatment was enough to capture the special fitness of Renaissance drama for depicting 'love itself' and for doing so with a dramatis personae largely composed of royalty. Woolf had long since abandoned her strictures against 'Kings and Queens of impossible territories', and here illustrates the point she had made in 'The Narrow Bridge of Art' that playwrights 'gave depth and distance' to their figures by making them princes and princesses (*CE* ii. 221). But she had also become aware, in such plays as *The Witch of Edmonton* and *A Woman Killed with Kindness*, of the presence of commoners in early plays, and these she features in the pageant by giving the only lengthy speeches to an aged crone and a priest. Old, deaf, and given to remembering the past, the crone is at that point in life which fascinated Woolf, and her primary purpose in the pageant would seem to be to die. Behind her emphasis in *Between the Acts* on Elsbeth, the aged crone, rather than on the young lovers whose story it is supposed to be, is Woolf's belief, articulated early and still maintained, that 'to die and be quit of it all' is the desire of Renaissance characters: 'the bell that tolls throughout the drama is death and disenchantment' (*CE* i. 60).

Elsbeth's death in fact prompts the other lengthy speech, '*From the distaff of life's tangled skein, unloose her hands*' (92). In this speech, delivered by the priest, Woolf epitomizes the worlds of early modern English tragedy and comedy. It begins as a dirge, a form Woolf frequently remarked in Elizabethan and Jacobean tragedies, and achieves authenticity by incorporating the opening line of the dirge from *The White Devil*, 'Call for the robin redbreast and the wren'. For Woolf as for her predecessors, death was often made 'the occasion for poetry'. But life, 'the other presence of Elizabethan drama' (*CE* i. 61),

---

[5] In drafts of this section of the novel (*BA* TS 119–21), Woolf works gradually towards the third 'emotion', experimenting with fear, then sorrow, then death.

also has its place in *Between the Acts*, the de-emphasized plot being after all a comic one. The priest moves from tragedy to comedy as he ends his speech (and the 'Elizabethan' pageant) with benediction on a happy couple and the words 'Lead on the dance!' (92–3).

Both the plot and the ending are typical of much Renaissance comedy, including Shakespeare's comedies and dramatic romances. Indeed, all that most attracted Woolf in general to the drama of the time can be found in Shakespeare, intensified, brought to perfection, writ large. Her developing appreciation of Shakespeare, and the incorporation of elements from his plays into her fiction, form the subject of the following chapter.

4

Shakespeare

SHAKESPEARE was a part of Woolf's atmosphere. Her family and their friends, and later her own friends, read and quoted him as a matter of course. Leslie Stephen additionally wrote essays about Shakespeare and the other Elizabethans, and his lengthy essay 'Shakespeare as a Man' (*Studies* iv. 1–44) started many hares she was also to chase. His biographical and critical sources remained on the shelves to be taken down occasionally when Virginia needed facts or a sense of the standard interpretation of one or another play. Familiarity with Shakespeare at Hyde Park Gate was easy and unostentatious. Woolf remembered that once when reading *Hamlet* aloud to Julia she mistook a word in Gertrude's account of the drowning of Ophelia: '. . . her instinct, for books at least, seems to me to have been strong, and I liked it, for she gave a jump, I remember, when . . . I misread "sliver" "silver" . . .' ('Sketch', *MB* 86).

None the less Woolf resisted Shakespeare for some time and claimed to find his plays 'antipathetic. How did they begin? With some dull speech; about a hundred miles from anything that interested me.' Once, to prove her point, she selected a play at random—*Twelfth Night*—but instead of dullness there was the duke's beautiful opening speech, 'If music be the food of love, play on'. It 'downed' her ('Sketch', *MB* 119). But still the plays of Shakespeare seemed to be the property of others, not her own, although she knew that she should take pleasure from them.

Her brother Thoby venerated Shakespeare. She wrote to him at Cambridge, 'I find to my immense pride that I really enjoy not only admire Sophocles. So after all there is hope for Shakespeare' (*L*. 36, July 1901). Finally she capitulated (*L*. 39, 5 Nov. 1901). She was ready 'to take back a whole cartload of goatisms which I used . . . in speaking of a certain great English writer—the greatest . . .'. She had read *Cymbeline* 'just to see if there mightnt be more in the great William than I supposed. And I was quite upset! Really and truly I am now let in to [the] company of worshippers—though I still feel a little oppressed by his—greatness I suppose.' But she needed Thoby's help, for, although the 'smaller characters are human', the major ones seemed superhuman: 'Why aren't they more human? Imogen and Posthumous [*sic*] and Cymbeline—I find them beyond me—Is this my feminine weakness in the upper region? But really they might have been cut out with a pair of scissors—as far as mere humanity goes . . .' None the less, Shakespeare's language was clear sailing ('Of course they talk divinely'). She singled out for Thoby's delectation the 'best lines in the play—almost in any play I should think—' in which Imogen asks her husband why he threw her from him.

IMOGEN. Think that you are upon a rock, and now
  Throw me again.
POSTHUMUS.   Hang there like fruit, my soul,
  Till the tree die!

While the few sentences in this letter to Thoby are not remarkable, they have in their favour honesty and enough sensitivity to Shakespearian metaphor to augur well for future criticism. The objection to the characters of dramatic romance is shared by some reputable critics even today, just as some share Woolf's interest in the interchange quoted above (Lenz *et al.* 14). It is important that she read the play at all, since it is not one of the most popular in the Shakespearian canon, and that she ventured some criticism. The step had been taken that was to be followed by many more in a lifetime of reading Shakespeare.

Late in 1908 Woolf began a serious reading of five Shakespearian tragedies, *Romeo and Juliet, Hamlet, King Lear, Othello,* and *Macbeth.* Her reading notes begin with two questions, 'Who shall say anything of Romeo & Juliet? Do I dare?—in private . . .' (HRN/*N&D* 2). From one point of view such timidity is hard to understand. She had heard allusions to the play frequently enough while a youngster to employ one herself in a short story written for the family newspaper when she was only ten: 'I philosophically say with Shakespear "What's in a name."?' (*A Cockney's Farming Experiences* 5). Yet being from a literary family seems to have bred in Woolf a certain diffidence when it came to critical pronouncements about Shakespeare, and there was some lingering belief in 'my feminine weakness in the upper region'. Even when she was convinced that as a writer she understood the 'desire of the mind for change', she could not contemplate making the point in print: 'Now if I

ever had the wits to go into the Shakespeare business I believe one
would find the same law there—tragedy comedy, & so on' (*D*. 26 Jan.
1933). Nor would Leslie Stephen's views on Shakespearian criticism by
either sex have encouraged Woolf to write. Stephen declared that 'no
one should write about Shakespeare without a special licence. Heaven-
born critics or thorough antiquaries alone should add to the pile under
which his "honoured bones" are but too effectually hidden' (*Studies* iv.
1). Woolf herself felt 'that unless one is possessed of the truth, or is a
garrulous old busybody, from America, one ought to hold one's tongue'
(*L*. 2831, 10 Dec. 1933). Being neither heaven-born critic nor antiquary
of any sort, neither possessed of the truth nor a garrulous American, she
never wrote a critical essay devoted exclusively to Shakespeare. But she
alluded casually to him in letters and diaries, used him to suggest in her
essays a standard for evaluating other writers, and brought him into the
conversations, thoughts, and explicitly-mentioned reading, of characters in her fiction.

Academics tended to write books and articles about Shakespeare.
These 'middlebrows' sauntered 'now on this side of the hedge, now on
that, in pursuit of no single object, neither art itself nor life itself, but
both mixed indistinguishably, and rather nastily, with money, fame,
power, or prestige' (*CE* ii. 199). Lowbrows should not turn to the
professors.

All you have to do is to read [Shakespeare]. The Cambridge edition is both
good and cheap. If you find Hamlet difficult, ask him to tea. He is a highbrow.
Ask Ophelia to meet him. She is a lowbrow. Talk to them, as you talk to me,
and you will know more about Shakespeare than all the middlebrows in the
world can teach you . . . (201)

Woolf shows much faith in the power of the ordinary reader to
understand an unmediated Shakespeare. Her attitude here is completely
consistent with her long-lasting belief in the capacity of Shakespeare to
yield some meaning to any reader who makes an effort, with his
faculties unimpeded by something extraneous such as the desire for
gain. Yet even the most disinterested readers will not see Shakespeare
'whole', for their own personalities and the times in which they live
must in the very nature of things dictate what they see. In a draft of *The
Years* a character's thoughts so interfere with his reading of a
Shakespearian play that he begins to wonder what Shakespeare would
have thought about trade unions. He realizes that 'all sorts of irrelevant
odds & ends' vitiate his criticism ('Pargiters' vii. 13).

In even the best of the Shakespearian critics Woolf noticed the tendency to indulge in what she termed 'autobiographical criticism':

It is a commonplace to say that every critic finds his own features in Shakespeare. His variety is such that every one can find scattered here or there the development of some one of his own attributes. The critic then accents what he is responsive to, and so composes his own meaning, in Shakespeares words. ('Anon.' 431)

Woolf would have seen the process up close, in herself and in her father. When Leslie Stephen tried to understand the ageing Shakespeare, he saw a poet who, although he no longer wrote sonnets, none the less could 'appreciate gentle, pure, and obedient womanhood . . .' (*Studies* iv. 41). Whatever this may say about Shakespeare, it says a great deal about Sir Leslie, and suggests why Woolf looked to others, the few times she looked at all, for help in understanding Shakespeare.

Those critics who had anything of real interest to say were almost invariably writers themselves. Presumably their considerable natural sensibilities were further heightened by their own creative acts: such a critic 'feels his way along a line spun by his own failures and successes . . . it is the Keats, the Coleridge, the Lamb, the Flaubert who get to the heart of the matter' (*CE* i. 316). Woolf once called Coleridge the only critic worth reading 'with the sound of the play still in one's ears'; his notes on Shakespeare have 'the power of seeming to bring to light what was already there beforehand, instead of imposing anything from the outside' (*B&P* 33). Yet even Coleridge, she later said, was confined to some extent by who he was, as all Shakespearian critics must be: 'The Johnson S[hakespeare] the Coleridge S. the Bradley S. are all contributions to our knowledge of what Shakespeare looked like, if you see him through a certain vision. But there always remains something further. It is this that lures the reader' ('Anon.' 431–2). Whatever the value of a particular piece of criticism, and whether or not one agrees with it, it perforce steps between the reader and the text; it 'takes the zest from our reading of Shakespeare, because we know someone has said it before, or said it better' (*CE* iv. 200). Woolf believed that the interference is especially damaging because the response to Shakespeare is potentially far fuller than the response to any other writer. The 'exactitude' of his images makes them seem 'the cap & culmination of the thought: its final expression'. By means of metaphor Shakespeare 'enlarges, intensifies, makes new & strange', while the rhythms and sounds of his verse 'stir the mind as wine & dance stir the

body' ('How Should One Read a Book?' hol. 5–6). Mind and imagination are engaged by means of the intimate relationship between
reader and text:

> The vitality, the intensity, the compression and pressure of every page keep one
> on the stretch almost to the exclusion of comment, and as for saying [as critics
> do] that this is 'ornament' or that 'structure' such phrases if we remember them
> float like feathers on the blast of a storm at sea. ('Byron and Mr. Briggs' 346).

Woolf wanted to retain the violence of direct impression, but
criticism softens the impact.

> . . . it is rashness that we need in reading Shakespeare. It is not that we should
> doze in reading him, but that, fully conscious and aware, his fame intimidates
> and bores, and all the views of the critics dull in us that thunderclap of
> conviction which, if an illusion, is still so helpful an illusion, so prodigious a
> pleasure, so keen a stimulus in reading the great.

Taking one step further Leslie Stephen's suggestion that a special
licence be required for writing about Shakespeare, Woolf thinks that 'a
paternal government might well forbid writing about him . . .'. Short of
such a solution, though, illness will do to diminish the timidity
generally fostered in the reader by Shakespeare's greatness and the
critics' authority, and take one to the 'undiscovered countries' to which
we are ordinarily denied access (*CE* iv. 193). Then 'the barriers go
down, the knots run smooth, the brain rings and resounds with Lear or
Macbeth, and even Coleridge himself squeaks like a distant mouse'
(200–1).

If Coleridge's Shakespearian criticism deserves such a fate, it is not
surprising that Woolf chose to eschew making full-fledged critical
pronouncements. But she did read critically, and her reading notes on
over half of Shakespeare's plays are extant, beginning with the five she
read in late 1908 and 1909. All were tragedies, and *Romeo and Juliet*
was the first of the plays on which she actually tried to write a piece of
criticism, though she managed only the following paragraph:

> Who shall say anything of Romeo & Juliet? Do I dare?—in private: it seems to
> me very immature work: very weak joinings, & no care of individualism in
> hero & heroine. They are the two parts of Love. But the Nurse! old
> Capulet—shaking his head—bustling—decided in the wrong places, like old
> age; beyond words. There is also a marvellous passage about a druggists
> shop—It is not true, of course, that Romeo & Juliet are without character; I
> mean that . . . in their relation with each other they have very little that is

individual; she is 14: they fall in love at sight: Love is their bond. But in their relations with other people, they have a great deal of character. Take the scene in which Juliet tests the nurse: the nurse pretends that Paris is as good a man as Romeo: Juliet pretends to agree—turns away, has her first insight into old people's baseness. (but this is fragmentary) (HRN/*N&D* 2)

    Subtleties of characterization in the young lovers, evidence of growth, thematic concerns—none of these struck Woolf. Although Romeo and Juliet could not really have been cut out with the same pair of scissors Woolf complained of in her reading of *Cymbeline*, the young lovers never captured her imagination as the older characters had done. She rarely gave them much thought, and years after that first reading, prompted by a forthcoming performance, she opined that 'Shakespeare spoil[s] his psychology' in having Romeo fall in love with Juliet 'so soon after Rosalind' (*L.* 3084, 26 Nov. 1935). The nurse, on the other hand, was alive and at hand whenever Woolf needed an illustration, as for example for comparison with Wagner's musical statements. Shakespeare 'makes an old nurse the type of all the old nurses in the world, while she keeps her identity as a particular old woman' (*B&P* 21).

    The broadly done characters obviously had greater appeal than the romantic leads, for Woolf knew little of romantic love, while first-hand experience obviously informs her comments about Capulet 'decided in the wrong places, like old age', and the nurse's affording Juliet 'her first insight into old people's baseness'. As Woolf pursued her own career, she developed a sensitivity to the language of the play which is obviously absent in the 1908–9 reading and notes (*CE* iii. 17). Yet when she read the play again while preparing the first *Common Reader* (*D.* 21 June 1924), the only notes she took involved old Capulet, and she commented on the 'perfect character drawing in Capulet & the old nurse' (MHP/B2o, 47). In 'The Pastons and Chaucer', one of the *Common Reader* essays, Woolf's appreciation for the nurse stands her in good stead. She denigrates the 'decency' of English literature beginning in the eighteenth century, and praises the earthiness of characters in earlier works, pointing to Shakespeare's nurse along with Chaucer's Wife of Bath (*CE* iii. 11).

    The only real change in Woolf's assessment of *Romeo and Juliet* came, not from a developing ability to see Shakespeare's handling of the young lovers, but from a new orientation towards characterization itself. When Isa Oliver speculates about the arrival of the heroine in the 'Elizabethan' pageant: 'Who came? Isa looked. The nightingale's song?

The pearl in night's black ear? Love embodied' (*BA* 91), she scrambles Romeo's first glimpse of Juliet (Wyatt, 'Art' 99):

> She hangs upon the cheek of night
> Like a rich jewel in an Ethiope's ear.

By thus alluding to the great moment of ecstatic recognition in the classic story of love, Woolf in a sense sanctions Isa's belief in the primacy of the basic emotions. Woolf never wavered in her belief that Shakespeare failed to individualize the lovers in their relation to each other. But by the time of *Between the Acts* what had once seemed a defect became a virtue. She came around to seeing the power of Shakespeare's approach.

Perhaps the relative stability of Woolf's reading of *Romeo and Juliet* owes something to the fact that she was least personally involved in its issues. Of her responses to the remaining plays read in 1908-9, *Hamlet*, *King Lear*, *Othello*, and *Macbeth*, two things can be said: they exemplify what she herself termed 'autobiographical criticism', the tendency of every critic to find in Shakespeare her or his own features; and, as those features changed over the years, so did her responses to the plays.

Woolf read the other tragedies in this group while at home, with notebook in hand, but *Macbeth* she read while on a train in Europe, after having spent an especially traumatic time with her sister and brother-in-law in Florence in the spring of 1909. From the time of Vanessa's marriage to Clive Bell in 1907, Woolf had been jealous of him, resentful of him, and, more recently, attracted to him and jealous of her sister. Unmarried herself at this point, she envied the obvious happiness of the two people who seemed terribly well suited to each other, loving to her, often ruthless to others. She set off from England on 23 April planning to spend a month with the Bells, but the visit was emotionally distressing and she left after just two weeks (twenty years later she still remembered how unhappy she had been at the time and 'bitter in all my judgments'—*D*. 21 Aug. 1929). She had both flirted and quarrelled with Clive; and 'he took his revenge for her coldness in a way that hurt her abominably, that is to say by the simple expedient of making love to his wife'. Of her sister's departure from Florence Vanessa said, 'It was rather melancholy to see her start off on that long journey alone leaving us together here! Of course I am sometimes impressed by the pathos of her position & I have been so more here than usual' (Bell i. 143–4).

It was at this point that Woolf read *Macbeth*. She recorded her reactions after returning to London: reading 'by the light of sunset in Switzerland' and 'the steady glare of midday in France', she missed 'innumerable subtleties of character & beauties . . .' (HRN/*N&D* 12). Reading *Macbeth* 'simply for the story', Woolf might be expected to go on to mention some of the highlights of the plot, say the vivid scenes showing the killing of Duncan, of Macduff's wife and family, of Banquo; or Macbeth's encounters with the witches; or Malcolm's victorious return; or Birnam Wood's coming to Dunsinane. But she never explicitly mentions a single one of the events of the narrative. Rather, she comments on characterization: 'Macbeth is the most human of the villains—Does one call him villain? no—nor even Lady Macbeth. Extraordinary relationship between Macbeth & his wife. They bring out each other's best & worst—reveal different sides of the same tragedy.' The analysis is certainly justified, for the closeness of Macbeth and Lady M. is apparent in his writing to her before his return from the opening battle of the play and in her immediate understanding of the import of that letter. At the same time they feed each other's ambition, and they are both—to oversimplify a bit—ruthless. Yet Woolf's analysis none the less shows a curiously idiosyncratic emphasis, given the proportions of the play. And again, although marriage was not her sole interest in *Macbeth*, it is surely significant that of the three scenes which she singled out as impressive, one is the scene in which Macduff learns of his wife's death (IV. iii). It seems likely that Woolf's experiences immediately before reading *Macbeth* aroused her sensitivity to the play's depiction of marriage, and that her criticism was—as she maintained criticism generally is—'autobiographical'.

As her circumstances changed, the focus of her later interest in the play changed. There is, it is true, a faint glimmer of interest in the Macbeth marriage later in Woolf's life, but it is really quite faint (*3Gs* 224 n). Indeed, although 'Lady Macbeth's terror or Hamlet's cry' was proof of Shakespeare's 'pity or sympathy or intuition' (*D.* 10 Sept. 1918), Woolf paid almost no attention to Lady Macbeth, whose characterization she came to question: she no more believed in Lady Macbeth as woman, than in most of the other tragic heroines (an exception would be Cleopatra). She addressed the question of the depiction of women in literature in 1920: '. . . it is becoming daily more evident that Lady Macbeth, Cordelia, Ophelia' and the heroines of eighteenth- and nineteenth-century fiction 'are by no means what they pretend to be. Some are plainly men in disguise; others represent what men would like to be, or are conscious of not being; or again they embody that dissatisfaction and despair which afflict most people when they reflect upon the sorry condition of the human race' (*B&P* 28–9). The specifically feminist question had come to seem more important to Woolf than the 'extraordinary relationship between Macbeth & his wife'.

With changes in her own marital status and the attenuation of marital involvement between Vanessa and Clive, her interest in other things intensified. She had singled out in her first reading of *Macbeth* the 'passage about the martin', that is, Banquo's mention to Duncan, as they approach Inverness, of 'the temple-haunting marlet [martin]' (I. vi. 3–6). Very soon after this scene of great tranquillity, Duncan is done to death and a reign of terror begins in Scotland. The poignant passage remained in Woolf's imagination over the years, to be evoked tellingly in *Between the Acts* during a lull before the storm of war (182–3).

Always in her mind also was Macbeth himself, not as husband but as one of those 'twisted characters' who Woolf believed 'have the great illuminations—seem to get some queer vision of the whole'. What she called after the 1909 reading 'his speech about tomorrow' exemplifies that vision, and of course it was a part of her vocabulary. 'Queer' or not, Macbeth was always eloquent. In Woolf's attention to that eloquence one can discern her taking a professional interest in Shakespeare as a fellow craftsman. Out of nowhere will come a quotation that pays tribute to Shakespeare's use of language. The brief scene with the doctor in the fifth act when Macbeth is beset with gloomy reports furnishes two examples, the first Macbeth's saying that his 'way of life | Is fall'n into the sere, the yellow leaf'—a perfect metaphor for Woolf's own use (*D.* 22 Oct. 1930; *L.* 3155, 22 July 1936). And the same scene opens with a line that is a favourite of Jacob Flanders, who quotes (with slight inaccuracy) Macbeth's words to a servant, 'The devil damn thee black, thou cream-fac'd loon!' (126). When Woolf was writing *Jacob's Room* she praised the very aspect of Shakespeare's language herein exemplified: it 'shoots out ready primed with the qualities of the speaker' ('Byron and Mr. Briggs' 346).

Shakespeare knew better than anyone how to exploit the resources of language. The intrusive narrator of *Jacob's Room* goes so far, during Jacob's time in Greece, as to point out the absurdity in saying 'that any Greek comes near Shakespeare' (138). One of Woolf's favourite instances of the originality and total aptness of his language occurs after the murder of Duncan. Macbeth carries away the daggers, and then, after his wife takes them from him, stares at his bloody hands:

> Will all great Neptune's ocean wash this blood
> Clean from my hand? No; this my hand will rather
> The multitudinous seas incarnadine,
> Making the green one red.

The appeal of these magnificent lines for writers is well known. They represent the pinnacle of the art. Woolf recalled them when judging Lawrence years later, criticizing his vocabulary ('After all English has one million words: why confine yourself to 6?') and his 'preaching'. 'Art is being rid of all preaching: things in themselves: the sentence in itself beautiful: multitudinous seas . . .' (*D*. 2 Oct. 1932). The phrase was a touchstone, and the entire line a testimony to Shakespeare's art, for 'only a great writer knows that the word "incarnadine" belongs to "multitudinous seas" ' (*CE* ii. 249).

The context of the line also had its interest, for Macbeth's horror over his deed is intensified by the knocking he hears. It continues when Lady Macbeth returns, her hands the same colour as her husband's, but her cool efficiency unimpeded. Macbeth's final words, 'To know my deed, 'twere best not know myself. | Wake Duncan with thy knocking! I would thou couldst!' are succeeded by the comic scene of the Porter. As Woolf was well aware, beginning with 'On the Knocking at the Gate in *Macbeth*' by De Quincey, 'Critic after critic points out the effect of change from tragedy to comedy in the scene of the porter . . .'. When talking about the scene with Sara in *The Years* (345–6), North, 'remembering something he had read', says that Shakespeare followed the killing of Duncan with comedy by way of contrast, 'the only form of continuity'. In Shakespeare could be found a model for the professional writer, in everything from word choice to imagery, from characterization to structure.

Once freed from the angle of vision that her preoccupation in 1909 with her sister's marriage forced on her, Woolf was able to read *Macbeth* as a fine example of Shakespeare's art, and it lived in her imagination to a far greater extent than *Romeo and Juliet* ever did. But the three remaining tragedies which she read at the time, *Othello*, *King Lear*, and *Hamlet*, had an even greater impact on her. Woolf's early familiarity with *Hamlet*, both in performance and in print, can be assumed. At any rate, the play was often in her private communications in the early years (*L*. 28, 19 Apr. 1900; *L*. 88, 30 June 1903); and there is even a playful allusion to Polonius's scheme of dramatic classification in 'Friendship's Gallery' (278).

When she finally mentioned *Hamlet* in print (in 1916), it functioned as a representative great work of art, which changes with us. 'To write down one's impressions of *Hamlet* as one reads it year after year, would be virtually to record one's own autobiography, for as we know more of life, so Shakespeare comments upon what we know.' A real work of art 'will serve a generation yet unborn with a glass in which to measure its varying stature' ('Charlotte Bronte' 169). Here Woolf first enunciates the 'autobiographical' notion of Shakespearian criticism that she often voiced. She later added that, although all great writers' characters have 'the seed of life in them [and] change as we change', Hamlet, unlike a Scott character, lived both 'profoundly' and 'fully' (*CE* i. 141). She believed that, of all Shakespeare's plays, *Hamlet* is the one which invariably elicits autobiographical criticism: it is the play read 'between the ages of twenty and twenty-five. Then one is Hamlet, one is youth . . . Thus forced always to look back or sidelong at his own past the critic sees something moving and vanishing in *Hamlet*, as in a glass one sees the reflection of oneself . . .' ('On Being Ill' 42).

When she herself read *Hamlet* in 1909, she was writing *Melymbrosia* (to be published in 1915 as *The Voyage Out*); she had practised journalism for five years; and she had by then gone through the deaths of four members of her immediate family. When Thoby died, Woolf found it 'very fitting' that a friend said of him what Fortinbras said of the dead Hamlet, 'he was likely, had he been put on, | To have prov'd most royal' ('Sketch', *MB* 119–20). The premature loss of her mother, and then Stella, and then Thoby, and the agonized time of her father's slow death from cancer in 1904, made almost inevitable a certain amount of identification with the melancholic hero, particularly in his relationships with members of his family.

As she finished reading the play, she saw Hamlet, like Juliet, as a young person 'amazed at the baseness of the world' (HRN/*N&D* 5). The particular lines and scenes on which Woolf focused correlate remarkably with her perception of the members of her immediate family and her own place in it. Polonius and Laertes in their advice to Ophelia, 'careful of the honour of their name', exemplified the 'masculine character' as found in her family. Her father, who 'hated impropriety', believed 'that women must be pure and men strong'; George Duckworth was a 'perfect fossil of Victorian society'; and between them they built 'the machine into which [Vanessa and

Virginia] were inserted in 1900'. The men of the Hyde Park Gate world 'knew the rules and attached immense importance to them' ('Sketch', *MB* 130-2).

In reaction, Woolf either talked incessantly or not at all, perhaps involuntarily, perhaps from a combination of social ineptitude and a certain perverseness, very much under her control. When Woolf read *Hamlet* in 1909 she identified not with Ophelia, whose madness was genuine, but rather with Hamlet, who 'put an antic disposition on'. Katharine Hilbery's relatives actually debate the question of whether or not Hamlet was insane (*N&D* 348), but Woolf herself seems to have been sure of his sanity. (When years later she raved self-consciously in a letter, she continued to identify with Hamlet (*L*. 2909, 5 July 1934); Vivienne Eliot, on the other hand, acted like Ophelia (*D*. 2 Sept. 1932).)

In 1909, when she read the great scenes of Ophelia's madness, her only comment was that 'Ophelia makes one pity old Polonius'. The comment is at the very least peculiar, for Polonius is no longer among the living in the fourth act, having been dispatched by Hamlet in the third. But the statement makes a kind of sense given the self-referential nature of all Woolf's comments in this reading of *Hamlet*. The key is her tendency to see her father in Polonius, and thus to feel towards the old counsellor many of the same emotions she had felt towards Leslie Stephen. Prominent among these was pity, for Laura, the child of her father's first marriage, was incorrigible, either seriously retarded or mentally ill, and finally had to be institutionalized. 'The history of Laura is really the most tragic thing in his life' (*L*. 199, 6 Dec. 1904), and a source of pity from all around 'the Old Man' (as Woolf referred to him). Thus her comment on Ophelia's madness, 'Ophelia makes one pity old Polonius', must be viewed as a most telling part of her autobiographical reading of *Hamlet*.

Gertrude, on the other hand, benefited from sharing traits with Woolf's mother. When she interrupted the euphuistic Polonius ('getting to the root of the matter. Came this fr. Hamlet?'), she resembled Julia Stephen in 'clearness of insight, sound judgement, humour, and a power of grasping very quickly the real nature of someone's circumstances' ('Reminiscences', *MB* 34-5). Yet when her admired mother died, the thirteen-year-old Virginia was overpowered by 'a desire to laugh' and not to cry ('Sketch', *MB* 92). The only other thing Woolf singled out from the second act besides Gertrude's practical nature is Hamlet's soliloquy 'O, what a rogue and peasant slave am I', which opens with his envy of the player who could weep for Hecuba when he himself, as Woolf commented, 'cant do anything . . . can only use words'. Twenty years later his self-criticism still rang in Woolf's ears (*L.* 2031, 18 May 1929). The only incident in the third act on which she commented was the Closet Scene (she noted 'the strength—almost brutality' of Hamlet's treatment of Gertrude). If she condemned him, it was to no greater extent than she condemned herself, for she knew what it was to be beset with a sea of troubles and to stay afloat only by the use of words. She admired Hamlet for 'work[ing] through different states in his imagination, perceiv[ing] all possibilities'. As she said when she set the book down, 'Hamlet sees round everything. The unknown seems to press at all points. overwhelmingly. Immense size & grandeur of the thing: Such depths in his voice.' It is those depths that she would most value in later years.

Her final comment in 1909 had to do with the perennial issue of Hamlet's procrastination. She was ready to believe that Hamlet was 'a man of vigour & action', but if that were so, why did he not act sooner? Unaccustomedly, Woolf turned to a critic, A. C. Bradley, who attributed the procrastination to the shock of Hamlet senior's death, on the heels of which 'the sudden call to action, by the ghost, found him unprepared'. Bradley was useful in providing information, for example about the religious element in the play, and she felt that his theories brought out much of the humanity and complexity of the hero. But she objected to his criticism none the less because in 'isolating things' it destroyed 'all the atmosphere, which explains, as you read; but cannot itself be explained'. She simply believed that there was in Hamlet 'something deeper' than could be reached by analysis (HRN/*N&D* 7).

Woolf's interest in the play never diminished. She frequently went to performances (in 1923, 1930, 1932, and 1935; and many performances would have gone unrecorded). One of her favourite fantasies was of 'strolling down the Strand' in Elizabethan times, bumping into Shakespeare, and asking him 'what he meant by *Hamlet*' (*CE* iii. 33). But after the 1909 reading she developed some strong feelings about lines of enquiry that should not be pursued. For example, she would not worry Shakespeare with questions about family relationships, nor specific models ('Small Talk about Meredith'); nor would she ask Shakespeare whether and to what extent Hamlet was his mouthpiece (she once complained that 'There is never an essay about Hamlet which does not make out with some confidence the author's view of what he calls "Shakespeare the man" ' (*CE* ii. 275)). She knew from a number of essays on the subject (her father's among them) that authors construct a purely imaginary Shakespeare from words which 'may, after all, have been Hamlet', that is, words appropriate to the character and not necessarily to Shakespeare. What did repay speculation was the remarkable process that must have been involved in Shakespeare's writing. He had a consummate command of the language, and also an ability to enter a skin other than his own, to 'run his hand into character as if it were a glove' (*CE* ii. 8); having entered the skins of the widest variety of characters (she mentions Hamlet, Falstaff, and Cleopatra), their individuality 'rushed him' into the knowledge of 'every sound and syllable in the language', every nuance of 'grammar and syntax' (193); his supreme command of the language enabled him to express fully Hamlet's thinking in some of the best soliloquies ever written (*CE* iv. 194).

She once humorously remarked that, had Shakespeare lived early enough to have been canonized, the soliloquies would have become part of the Anglican liturgies, 'sliced up and interspersed with hymns . . .' (*3Gs* 273 n). Luckily that never happened and they are known in context, the perfectly conceived expression of character, never more impressive than in the case of Hamlet, to Woolf's mind 'the complete figure' ('Anon.' 422 n).

Some twenty years after her first reading, Woolf thought about what Shakespeare accomplished by means of the Hamlet–Ophelia relationship. She had never been especially curious about their romance, and she had given only passing thought to Bradley's insistence on Hamlet's chagrin over Ophelia's abrupt dismissal of him. But she had come to believe that the playwright used the specific case, compelling as it was, in order to explore more fundamental issues, 'to transcend the particularity of Hamlet's relation to Ophelia and to give us his questioning not of his own personal lot alone but of the state and being of all human life' (*CE* ii. 225).

Hamlet is a highbrow, a man 'of thoroughbred intelligence who rides his mind at a gallop across country in pursuit of an idea', whereas Ophelia is a lowbrow' 'a woman of thoroughbred vitality who rides [her] body in pursuit of a living at a gallop across life' (*CE* ii. 196–7). Jocular tone and modernity of instance to the contrary, Woolf is perfectly serious in her classification. Hamlet is proof that the intellectualism of highbrows can be dangerous since, 'for some reason or another [they] are wholly incapable of dealing successfully with what is called real life. That is why . . . they honour so wholeheartedly and depend so completely upon those who are called lowbrows' (197).

Hamlet's disappointment in Ophelia may or may not be that of the spurned lover, but it is most certainly that of an intellectual whose chief means of access to the world has been inexplicably cut off.

At the same time his ability to function in the world of ideas makes his every thought attractive. If the reader sees himself or herself in Hamlet, part of the reason lies in the richness of his characterization. His celebrated inaction is just one of the many fundamental traits of human beings that is mirrored in *Hamlet*. To the extent that Hamlet lives the life of the mind, he accurately holds up a mirror wherein we see our own features. Thus it is that 'the life which is increasingly real to us is the fictitious life . . . Each of us is more Hamlet, Prince of Denmark, than he is John Smith of the Corn Exchange' (*CE* iv. 234). As Woolf took stock towards the end of her life, identifying those characteristics of intellect and temperament that made her a writer, she acknowledged the kinship she felt with Hamlet, his intellectualism like the artist's capacity to discover order and to 'make it real by putting it into words'. For that reason, she said, *Hamlet* 'is the truth about this vast mass that we call the world' ('Sketch', *MB* 72).

If Woolf's first reading of *Hamlet* lacked the maturity of these subsequent readings, it was merely eccentric rather than completely inept, very possibly because from the start she could identify with a young man struggling against 'the baseness of the world'. In a play such as *Hamlet* support for the hero saves the reader from outlandish responses. No such identification with Lear saved Woolf from decidedly queer judgements at the outset, and she lurched this way and that during her first reading of *King Lear* before she responded in the later acts to Shakespeare's overall scheme. The difficulty seems to have arisen from the similarity she perceived in the relationships between father and daughters in *King Lear* and in the Stephen family.

Woolf's first reaction to King Lear reads like a thumbnail sketch of Leslie Stephen: 'One realises that Lear has always been stormy. His daughters have suffered from it. This is done partly, I suppose to excuse or account for his extraordinary actions in dividing his kingdom—an arbitrary imperious old man' (HRN/*N&D* 8). Like Lear, Leslie was 'stormy', even before the death of Julia; following it 'the eccentric storms' were more frequent and more tempestuous ('Reminiscences', *MB* 46); his rages were 'sinister, blind, animal, savage' ('Sketch', *MB* 126). Like Cordelia (and, in Woolf's view of things, Goneril and Regan), Stella Duckworth, Virginia, and Vanessa suffered acutely when he acted irrationally, 'without strict regard for justice or magnanimity' ('Reminiscences', *MB* 34, 48); and during Stella's engagement he became 'increasingly tyrannical', all the while expecting sympathy as 'the lonely; the deserted; the old unhappy man' ('Sketch', *MB* 106). He was, in short, what Woolf found Lear to be, 'an arbitrary imperious old man'.

Despite these difficulties, however, Leslie Stephen's daughters recognized his genius and there were times when they loved 'this unworldly, very distinguished, lonely man . . .' ('Sketch', *MB* 136). Each of the daughters met his rages at one time or another with silence, especially Stella, with her 'perfectly simple unostentatious unselfishness'. She made Woolf think of 'those large white roses that have many petals and are semi-transparent' ('Sketch', *MB* 96–7). In the opening scene of *King Lear*, the silence and mild response of Cordelia to Lear's baffled accusation of untenderness, made her seem another Stella: 'a simple honest mind, somewhat stubborn; without imagination, perfectly transparent.'

The 'autobiographical' element did not lead Woolf astray in this particular analysis; but if Stella took the role of Cordelia, who might Goneril and Regan be (if indeed they *were* members of the Stephen family)? Clearly, Virginia and Vanessa—at least, such an identification could account for Virginia's otherwise-inexplicable sympathy with the 'bad' daughters (Hawkes in Marcus, *New* 43). She was willing to take their word for it that Lear's 'poor judgment' was a long-standing problem. Like the Stephen household with its three actively-participating daughters suffering from Leslie's 'tyranny', all three daughters of Lear had much to endure. So receptive was Woolf to the 'bad' daughters that she contended that 'even Regan & Goneril though they scold like fishwives are passionate women'. She could sympathize with passionate commitment as an antidote to a father's severity ('Sketch', *MB* 127–8).

But if identification with Goneril and Regan interfered with Woolf's sympathies for Lear at the beginning of the play, before long the magnificence of his characterization set her straight. He endures the storms without and within, awakes to find Cordelia by him, and knows it is he and not she who needs forgiveness.

> Pray do not mock me.
> I am a very foolish fond old man,
> Fourscore and upward, not an hour more nor less;
> And to deal plainly,
> I fear I am not in my perfect mind.

The last two lines were the 'most pathetic', but the whole speech, Woolf said approvingly, was in both idea and language as 'simple as a childs'. The entire scene between Cordelia and Lear seemed to Woolf 'as great as any'. It is easy to agree. Woolf also loved the 'wonderful speech after the battle, when Lear & Cordelia go to prison together', and she quoted

> so we'll live, & pray & sing &c.
> And take upon's the mystery of things,
> As if we were Gods spies.

The father and daughter are envisaged in mutual forgiveness, and the father speaks with the full authority of his greatness words of transcendent beauty.

When she wrote down her reactions after finishing the play, there is no mention of the 'arbitrary imperious old man'. She came to believe that Shakespeare did not want such 'definiteness', that he was not aiming at a clarity of characterization by means of which the reader could attribute Lear's downfall to personal flaws. Whatever Lear's deficiencies of character, they seemed irrelevant in the face of the malevolence of outside forces, symbolized by the storm one feels raging 'all through' the play, with 'all human kind exposed on the heath'.

For Lear is not the only one to endure pain; indeed the breadth of suffering in the play is almost unbearable. In the 1909 reading Woolf remarked on the situation of Edgar on the heath, naked and impersonating a Bedlam beggar, and she noted Lear's conclusion, that 'unaccommodated man is no more but such a poor, bare, forked animal as thou art'. Edgar's father, Gloucester, like Lear himself, sustains far more punishment than his deeds could possibly warrant. Woolf sensed the 'presence of the Gods' throughout the play, but especially in the harrowing fourth act. She recorded Gloucester's words to the Old Man after his blinding and his long-delayed recognition that he had judged his sons entirely incorrectly: 'As flies to wanton boys are we to th' gods, | They kill us for their sport.' Such suffering made Woolf ask herself many years later: 'Shall I read King Lear? Do I want such a strain on the emotions? I think I do' (D. 16 Nov. 1921). The strain was bearable in that the 'presence of the gods' need not always spell doom. Albany maintained that the just gods venged 'our nether crimes'. Gloucester is kept from suicide by his son Edgar, who lectures his father on having been saved by 'the gods'. Gloucester vows to bear future affliction 'till it do cry out itself | "Enough, enough," and die' (a cry that Woolf was wont to quote—L. 2003, 17 Feb. 1929; L. 2254, 16

Oct. 1930). Divine justice, Woolf agreed with Albany, is done, 'as the events prove'.

After the shaky start in reading the first half of *King Lear* when parallels with family members skewed her interpretation, Woolf gained entry into the play and formed judgements which did not budge thereafter. She compared this experience to the always-changing world of *Hamlet*: in *King Lear* 'the centre is solid and holds firm whatever our successive readings lay upon it' ('On Being Ill' 42). Having come round to Lear's greatness as a human being, she was able to give him the accolade bestowed on Hamlet: Lear was 'probably a "highbrow" '; and Woolf knew how 'profound, elemental, and worthy of [Shakespeare's] study' he was ('Dickens by a Disciple'). His great speeches, noted in 1909, remained in her imagination for the rest of her life, from the immediate use of the 'poor, bare, fork'd animal' to describe George III (*B&P* 51) to—some thirty years later—her use of Lear's taking on the mystery of things with Cordelia, 'as if we were God's spies', noting who at court is in, who out, in order to inform her vision of Sir Francis Bacon and court spies ('Anon.' 422 n).

Two problems arose in the 1909 reading of *King Lear*, one having to do with language. Woolf complained that the writing was 'tumultuous, sometimes absolutely turgid with meaning' (HRN/*N&D* 8). But she worked on it then; and, the more she read the play, the closer she got to its remarkable language. She recognized that by means of metaphor Shakespeare creates 'moments of astonishing excitement and stress' which enable the reader to take a 'dangerous leap through the air without the support of words . . .' (*CE* i. 7). The metaphors are such that, in reading *King Lear*, we '[strip] the branch of its flowers instantly' (11). *King Lear* was poetry of the very highest order. When she advised readers to 'compare each book with the greatest of its kind', for poetry the touchstones she recommended were *Phèdre*, *The Prelude*—and *King Lear* (*CE* ii. 8–9). The language of the play, then, commensurate with its oversize characters and theme, had come to be quite accessible, and together these made for the 'violent direct impression' one gets from the play (MHP/B2q, 73), what Woolf called Lear's 'loudness', probably echoing Coleridge, who praised its 'ear-cleaving thunder-claps' (*Shakespearean Criticism* i. 109).

The second problem encountered in the 1909 reading had to do with the function of the Fool and his 'gibberish', possibly 'a contrast to the raving of Lear' (HRN/*N&D* 8). She suggested by the time of 'On Not Knowing Greek' (1925), that Shakespeare's 'fools and madmen' functioned like a Greek chorus, to help one grasp 'the meaning of the play': the chorus 'can comment, or sum up, or allow the poet to speak himself or supply, by contrast, another side to his conception' (*CE* i. 5–6). She had herself used a 'madman', Septimus Warren Smith, to give the 'insane' side of the conception whose 'sane' side was embodied in Mrs Dalloway (*D*. 14 Oct. 1922; the novel like the essay was published in 1925). In the last two novels she used 'fool' figures and allusions to 'wild' speeches. She alluded also (as early as 1897 in her diary, and as late as 'Anon.' and 'The Reader' 376) to the Fool's song 'He that has and a little tine wit', an acceptance of the inevitability of adversity, a secular balance to Lear's great speech about God's spies, which envisages Lear and Cordelia triumphing over adversity by affirming their filial relation to God. Perhaps in juxtaposing these allusions Woolf realized more fully than she had in her earliest reading of the play precisely how Shakespeare used a fool.

In her stint of reading the tragedies in 1909, the fifth and last, *Othello*, differed enormously from the others. The villainy of Edmund in *King Lear* could be grasped, but she could find no believable complexity in Iago, and thus could not 'get him clear—too much of the consistent devil?' (HRN/*N&D* 11). The aspect of Iago's personality which many readers believe adds to the complexity of his characterization, his own sexual problems, never occurred to Woolf. Nor was she able to deal adequately with the sexual nature of the jealousy Iago stirred in Othello. She said, unconscious of pun, that 'the handkerchief is such a thin device to have such effects' (11; see also MHP/B2q, 73). If Iago's words popped into her mind in later years, she defused them (and so did her friends) by making a joke of sex. For example, she used Iago's brilliant phrase, in a letter calculated to arouse Vita's jealousy over Ethel Smyth and Lady Oxford, the latter having demanded 'that my next book shall be dedicated to her. What Poppy or Mandragora—no, its keep away [used with bitches in heat] I'm thinking of—the room still ringing with Ethel on the phone. So to bed. And whats bed without—?' (*L*. 2403, 8 July 1931). Lytton Strachey complained that Woolf omitted 'tupping' from *Night and Day*. Remembering Iago's incendiary statement to Desdemona's father that 'an old black ram | Is tupping your white ewe' she told him she 'had meant to introduce a little in that line, but somehow it seemed out of the picture—still, I regret it. Never mind; I've an idea for a story where all the characters do nothing else—but they're all quadrupeds!' (*L*. 1087, 28 Oct. 1919). The image evoked by

Iago to provoke disgust and fury in Desdemona's
trivialized back to 'real' quadrupeds.

Yet, in spite of Woolf's manifest inability to cope with sexu
she did respond to Othello's love for Desdemona. Although si.
as a love virtually devoid of a sexual component, it is sufficiently i.
with fig leaf to have fascinated her. She especially admired the 'lov
scene on Cyprus when he is reunited with Desdemona. She accepted, as
Othello himself did, Iago's assessment of his situation, and was attentive
to any hints Othello gave of deficiencies in his own person and character
that might explain his fall: 'He is no longer young—did not wish to
marry . . . Something noble, simple, of course, & southern in him; we
feel that he is a moor. There is a kind of shrinking from him, which
makes his jealousy all the more painful—he is reminded of his physical
defect' (HRN/*N&D* 10). It is terribly unpleasant to encounter so racist
a statement. But Shakespeare's art enabled Woolf to transcend her
bigotry. She was bound to admire intensity of feeling, and Othello 'is
completely possessed' by 'the passion of love'. Woolf could see 'the
wonder' in the Moor, 'the rage of his jealousy, & then the thunderclap
of his despair'. Woolf considered *Othello* a 'simpler' tragedy than the
others she had read for two reasons: first, because Othello and
Desdemona dominated it more than the other central characters did
their plays; and, second, because it was 'a tragedy of individuals' rather
than of fate or whatever one might call the outside forces she felt
pressing in on such heroes as Hamlet or Lear. 'I think that the horror of
the thing may come from the fact that Othello is in the wrong; a great
nature may go to ruin—be tortured to damnation—for one fault, & all
the rest be high & noble' (11).

But Desdemona was flawless, as 'heavenly true' as Emilia said she
was. In fact Desdemona seemed to be of the Stella Duckworth/Cordelia
type, 'childlike', but with great potential and already 'gracious &
conscious of power' (10; cf. 'Reminiscences', *MB* 50-3). Woolf worked
out her own ideas about women by means of Desdemona's relationship
with Emilia, similar to the sort she called for years later in *A Room of
One's Own* (142). When Desdemona is accused of infidelity, the
discussion reveals the great differences between them. Emilia, 'the
coarse honest bold-tongued woman, who will stand no nonsense', tries
to make some sense of what is happening. Desdemona can only wonder
ineffectually at 'these men—these men!' Woolf concluded that
Desdemona could not conceive of any woman's committing adultery
because 'one's belief in ones own sex corresponds to ones belief in

oneself'. Hawkes (in Marcus, New 35) contends that for Woolf Desdemona's perplexity is exacerbated because 'she has no confirmation for her perceptions from other women . . .'. Woolf saw the poignance in Desdemona's 'most painful words' to Emilia: 'Faith half asleep . . . Who is thy Lord?' It seemed 'as though everything were a dream round her' HRN/N&D 10–11). For Woolf and her friends the contrast between the passive and the active woman was to become a topic for discussion, and this particular example especially so (D. 4 June 1923).

Only occasionally are there cavils with the play. Woolf recalled that Thoby 'thought possibly Shakespeare was "sentimental" ' when, after Othello has smothered Desdemona, she comes to life again ('Sketch', MB 119). And Woolf herself, not only in the 1909 notes, but also later in her life, could be critical even as she praised. She read the play once on Shakespeare's birthday, and next day remarked that, although she 'was impressed by the volley & volume & tumble of his words', she would criticize that very luxuriance 'were I reviewing for the Times. He put them in when tension was slack. In the great scenes, everything fits like a glove. [But] the mind tumbles & splashes among words when it is not being urged on . . . the mind of a very great master of words who is writing with one hand' (D. 24 Apr. 1928). That Woolf went on to allude to the play frequently, however, suggests her sensitivity to the so-called 'Othello music'.

Woolf continually found in the play the perfect expression for ideas applicable to her own life, to society, and quite naturally to the lives she portrayed in her fiction. The outcome of some trial and error when she was writing Orlando is illustrative. She thought of having the hero and Sasha attend some typically Elizabethan performance, 'a masque by one of the popular Elizabethan poets—Jonson, Shakespeare, or another . . .' (Orl. hol.). But she eventually chose to use Othello instead (56–7), and the choice was excellent. One night when Orlando and Sasha are out skating, they come upon a performance of Othello, and 'the astonishing, sinuous melody of the words stirred Orlando like music'. Neither the 'rough' staging nor the unruliness of the audience can distract him from the intensity of the final scene, in which Othello tells Desdemona that he is about to kill her for committing adultery: 'The frenzy of the Moor seemed to him his own frenzy, and when the Moor suffocated the woman in her bed it was Sasha he killed with his own hands.' After the play ends, Orlando recalls a bit of the dialogue,

> Methinks it should be now a huge eclipse
> Of sun and moon, and that the affrighted globe
> Should yawn—

—Othello's amazement that there has been no disruption in nature to match the horror of his murder of Desdemona. Here in a novel, and in her own life as well, *Othello* and other of the greatest Shakespearian plays added resonance to her own voice. At the beginning of the last scene Othello, standing over the sleeping Desdemona, imagines her murder. In his beautiful speech 'It is the cause', he likens killing Desdemona to snuffing a candle: 'Put out the light, and then put out the light.' Woolf once tried to imagine the sensation of being killed by a bomb, 'the crushing of my bone shade in on my very active eye & brain: the process of putting out the light' (*D.* 2 Oct. 1940).

During the war it had become increasingly evident to Woolf that mankind would always be destroyed unless something could deflect what she took to be innate aggressiveness. In August of 1940, during the Battle of Britain, she wrote 'Thoughts on Peace in an Air Raid', an extension of the argument of *Three Guineas*. She asserted that schemes intended to establish and maintain peace following the war must prove futile because a 'subconscious Hitlerism' is instinctive. Drawing on the play in which the hero, no longer a military man, commits murder, she said, 'Othello's occupation will be gone; but he will remain Othello'. She here alludes to Othello's farewell to 'the plumed troops and the big wars | That makes ambition virtue'; now, 'Othello's occupation's gone'. Woolf heard in his words of regret at losing the 'pomp, and circumstance of glorious war' a clear statement of the need to 'compensate the man for the loss of his gun' (*CE* iv. 175).

Just as she herself thought of *Othello* during an air raid, so she has Sara allude to the play during the dinner at Maggie and Renny's in the war chapter of *The Years*, '1917'. Sara, Nicholas, and Eleanor visit, only to have the evening disrupted by an air raid. The conversation that night centres on dictators, man's ignorance of his own psychology, and pacifism. At dinner, when Maggie tells Eleanor she got her dress 'in Constantinople, from a Turk', Sara murmurs: 'A turbaned and fantastic Turk' (284). Her thoughts are on Othello's final speech, enumerating, among other services, killing a 'malignant and a turban'd Turk [who] beat a Venetian and traduc'd the state'. He now kills himself, for Othello, as Woolf observed 'will remain Othello'. Sara's seemingly fanciful literary allusion lines up neatly with her criticism of the military mind, 'unconscious Hitlerism', for she goes on to call her cousin North 'that damned fool' for serving in the military (284–5).

Woolf's despair is voiced in an allusion to the same play that provided *Mrs. Dalloway* with an expression of exultant sisterhood. The lines were taken from Othello's words to Desdemona when he sees her again, at Cyprus, after their separation:

> If it were now to die,
> 'Twere now to be most happy; for I fear
> My soul hath her content so absolute
> That not another comfort like to this
> Succeeds in unknown fate.

These she was to use to express her happiness with Leonard (*D*. 8 Apr. 1925). In the 1909 reading Woolf called these 'lovely words', but knew that they 'presage sorrow', that there must be 'this kind of solemnity in the utmost joy' (HRN/*N&D* 10). The lines have an almost generic value in a draft of *The Waves* (hol. 669), when Bernard remembers a pang Susan once gave him, and thinks of 'what one owes the people who have made one say if it were now to die twere now to be most happy; yet it ended in satiety . . .'. In *Mrs. Dalloway* the same beauty, the same solemnity, and indeed the same evanescence surround Woolf's evocation of Othello's lines. Yet in this novel they enhance a scene not of heterosexual love, but rather of sisterhood. Clarissa remembers 'the purity, the integrity, of her feeling' for Sally Seton, a feeling that 'was protective, on her side; sprang from a sense of being in league together, a presentiment of something that was bound to part them (they spoke of marriage always as a catastrophe) . . .' (50). Clarissa recalls that, as she was about to meet Sally, she felt, ' "if it were now to die 'twere now to be most happy." That was her feeling—Othello's feeling, and she felt it, she was convinced, as strongly as Shakespeare meant Othello to feel it . . .' (51). The ensuing scene is modelled on the one in *Othello*, for, just as Iago plans to 'set down the pegs that make this music' when he sees Othello and Desdemona kiss, so Peter Walsh interrupts Clarissa's exultation over Sally's kiss with 'his determination to break into their companionship'. Clarissa has 'known all along that something would interrupt, would embitter her moment of happiness' (53). Although it is possible to read more sexual content into this scene than I have done (Schlack, *Continuing* 63), Woolf's asexual reading of the Othello–Desdemona relationship at the least suggests caution.

This allusion to *Othello* would be serviceable again in *Mrs. Dalloway*, ultimately providing a link between Clarissa and Septimus Smith. As Woolf was working out a rationale for the enlistment of Septimus and others like him, and it occurred to her that for many 'there were better things than growing old' (MS 51,046, 88), she would have seen the kinship with Clarissa. For Clarissa herself clearsightedly recognized that 'closeness drew apart', but that 'there was an embrace in death'. Using this link, Woolf has Clarissa, alone in a little room during her party, ask herself: 'But this young man who had killed himself—had he plunged holding his treasure? "If it were now to die, 'twere now to be most happy," she said to herself once, coming down in white' (281). The allusion establishes an unmistakable parallel between Septimus's suicide and Clarissa's desire for death at the most exultant point in her life. It also transmutes what could have been a morbid fascination with death in both characters into a positive holding on to the most intense moment in life.

In the same scene of Clarissa's retreat to the little room, Woolf employs another allusion to *Othello*, which can be understood in the literary context in which she embeds it, *Cymbeline*. She quotes a favourite line from the play in *Jacob's Room* (126), published just three years before *Mrs. Dalloway*. The allusion to *Cymbeline* in *Mrs. Dalloway* is the frequently anthologized dirge:

> Fear no more the heat o' th' sun,
> Nor the furious winter's rages,
> Thou thy wordly task hast done,
> Home art gone, and ta'en thy wages.
> Golden lads and girls all must,
> As chimney-sweepers, come to dust.

The as-yet unrecognized heirs to the British throne, brothers of the disguised princess Imogen, recite the dirge over the unconscious, male-attired young woman (called Fidele), thinking her dead. The machinations of an Italian have led to her marital difficulties, flight, and apparent death; the help of another Italian will lead to her rebirth.

The crucial importance of the lyric itself cannot be doubted. As Wyatt contends (*Mrs. D.* 440), the allusion, 'appearing at five key points, supplies the novel's central structure'. It also supplies the novel's central image, the androgynous Fidele, a dead male, who rises up as someone who will prove to be Imogen, a live female. Although in Shakespeare's play the words of the dirge stress the quiet peace of death following the heat and rage of life, to Clarissa Dalloway they are, more simply, a reminder of death. When she first sees the lines in a bookshop window, she thinks of the dead of the First World War (*Mrs. D.* 13). Richard's having been invited to dine without her makes Clarissa think of what his life will be when he is a widower; and the shock makes her 'fear time itself' (44). The first two soundings of 'fear no more' thus establish the need for consolation at this particular time (five years after the close of the war) and for this particular woman (heart trouble caused by the flu).

Of some consolations available (for example the religious one suggested by the third and fourth lines of the dirge) Woolf says nothing, preferring to focus on only two, the first adopted by Clarissa Dalloway, the second by Septimus Smith. As the final couplet of the stanza assures us, golden girls (such as Clarissa) and lads (such as Septimus) must come to dust. Both know it; and both sense something personal in the natural world that mourns the fact. But there the similarity ends. Woolf had early intended *Mrs. Dalloway* as 'a study of . . . the world seen by the sane & the insane side by side' (*D.* 14 Oct. 1922). The paralleled passages in which 'the heart in the body' of both Clarissa and Septimus says 'fear no more' (*Mrs. D.* 58–9 and 211–12) diverge sharply: the sane Clarissa reacts to the monotonous sameness of motions in her stitching, suggesting to her the recurrence of waves, and thus of lives. To the insane Septimus, recurring patterns of light and shadow are actual pronouncements by a fully personified Nature (a seductive dancing-girl); 'fear no more' becomes the 'meaning' of Nature, who is letting the privileged Septimus hear a secret denied to others. In a draft of the novel Septimus believes that he is to meet Shakespeare at the top of a mountain, and hear him talk (MS 51,044, 63–4). 'Fear no more', presumably, is what the poet would say. The consolations the two find in Shakespeare's line thus differ considerably: Clarissa believes in continuation through others; Septimus believes that the 'message' is intended for him alone, a person whose specialness makes him the confidante of Nature and the companion of Shakespeare.

The dirge from *Cymbeline* has to do with endings, with the inevitability of death for all (as in fact the successive verses make clear). One hears it once again at the ending of *Mrs. Dalloway*, coupled with the words Othello says before killing Desdemona, 'put out the light'. The allusions can both be found in the scene of Clarissa in the little room, apart from her party. She hopes that Septimus died at a moment of great happiness, much as she had wished to do when she was overwhelmed by love for Sally Seton: 'If it were now to die, 'twere now to be most happy' (281), Othello's words on being reunited with Desdemona. Woolf has now prepared the scene for the introduction of a whole series of symbolic challenges for Clarissa. The sky is not beautiful, but instead 'ashen pale'; yet Clarissa can perceive it as 'new'. Most important, she sees the old woman next door quietly going to bed, an activity that she early in the book equated with her own death; and the woman is surrounded with conventionally disquieting images, blinds pulled down, striking clocks. Finally, the reader is reminded of Othello's line, 'There! the old lady had put out her light!' Clarissa's final understanding of the dirge from *Cymbeline* is valid, and she has been right in believing in personal continuity through the lives of others, for she now experiences reinforcement in her own reactions to the death of Septimus and the symbolic death of the old woman. Life goes on. Septimus has killed himself, but 'she did not pity him, *with all this going on*. There! the old lady put out her light! the whole house was dark now *with this going on*, she repeated, and the words came to her, Fear no more the heat of the sun' (283). The verbal repetition (my italics), and the repetition of allusion to *Othello*, and the repetition, now for the fifth time, of allusion to the dirge from *Cymbeline*—all emphasize the principle of recurrence which is Mrs Dalloway's answer to extinction.

YEARS OF MATURITY

In Woolf's reading of five Shakespearian tragedies in 1909 her response was often shaped by a rather limited experience of the outside world and her consequent tendency to dwell on the extremely vivid people who made up the Stephen family. Yet, if these restrictions skewed her readings, they rarely led to misreading, and she developed the capacity in later years to weigh character using more of Shakespeare's evidence and to respond to ideas with greater subtlety. The experiences of just a single decade following the 1909 reading reveal just how drastically her life changed. She married, published her first novel, won a certain amount of critical acclaim from it, published several short stories and her second novel, thereby establishing her reputation even more firmly, and of course extended the range of her friendships immeasurably. The prolonged adolescence was at an end at last, and along with it exaggeratedly autobiographical criticism of Shakespeare as well. It is a measure of Woolf's development as a reader that she was no longer given to speculations about Shakespeare's revealing, say, 'the baseness of the adult world'. She began to feel at home with Shakespeare, who gave her a way of seeing her life in some perspective. Vanessa became 'a Shakespeare character' (*L.* 825, 6 Mar. 1917); and when friends laughed, gossiped, and were in general sensitive, Woolf decided that Shakespeare would have approved of them (*D.* 7 Jan. 1923; *L.* 1805, 2 Sept. 1927)—a sentiment also given to Neville in *The Waves* (hol. 263). Shakespeare's sympathies, for the commoner and the king, for both men and women, for the mad and the sane, showed the comprehensiveness of his vision and the bedrock 'rightness' of his values.

Beyond the impact of the sheer passing of the years, and her own development as a writer, two other circumstances helped Woolf to grow as a reader. The first was that she continued to read Shakespeare's plays, some of them old favourites, others new acquaintances. In addition to this reading, occasional but fairly steady, there were two periods of concentrated reading, one in the early 1920s and the other in the early 1930s. She also enjoyed increased opportunities for discussing the plays. Like Bernard in *The Waves*, she visited friends to 'talk endlessly about books', until she came to 'know that particular avenue, from Shakespeare to Tennyson, as if it were the Tottenham Court Road' (hol. 377). The excitement this sort of conversation engendered can be sensed in the memories of a character in 'The Pargiters':

Among the things they used to talk about before . . . was the possibility of unravelling a whole play or poem from one word . . . He could remember ringing her up at two in the morning simply because he had discovered something about King Lear. The whole truth, which nobody except themselves, had ever yet been able to say. (vi. 111–12)

The diaries and letters are replete with allusions to such conversations with Leonard, with Vanessa's children, and with various friends—Clive Bell, Roger Fry, Katherine Mansfield, Desmond and Molly MacCarthy, Janet Case, Lytton Strachey, Vita Sackville-West, Ethel Smyth, T. S. Eliot, and so on.[1]

The first fruits of her reading and her conversations are evident in Woolf's second novel, *Night and Day* (1919), which frequently mentions Shakespeare, and, according to a number of critics, treats its characters and structure after the manner of a Shakespearian comedy. Josephine O'Brien Schaefer in her fine pioneering study (51) was the first to point out resemblances to *Twelfth Night*:

[1] Woolf was at times more knowledgeable than her friends. Late in life she was able to point out to T. S. Eliot that Shakespeare used the phrase 'hollow men' in *Julius Caesar* (letter 3367a in Banks 198).

The humor of shifts and devices by which the couples are realigned is similar: the plight of Rodney courting Cassandra under the cloak of his engagement to Katharine resembles the situation of Olivia trying to woo Viola while she is an ambassador from Orsino . . . Virgina Woolf approximates the Viola–Sebastian relation to Olivia very effectively in the Katharine–Cassandra relation to Rodney.

This last point is especially persuasive since Schaefer demonstrates that both Mrs Hilbery and William Rodney 'find' Cassandra when they believe they have been looking for Katharine. Just as Olivia seeks in 'Cesario'–Viola what she finally finds in Sebastian, certain qualities in someone who is a man, so Rodney 'has really been seeking in [Katharine] what he finds in Cassandra: the charm, the compassion, the attentiveness of the thoroughly conventional woman'.

Several critics have followed Schaefer's lead in finding Shakespearian echoes in *Night and Day*. Fleishman, in pointing out a host of parallels, contends that 'the winey spirit that pervades its lovers' illusions and transformations resembles that of the early comedies, while the mystic aura of its denouement is that of the late romances' (22). Although Fleishman demonstrates links with *As You Like It*, *The Tempest*, and *A Midsummer Night's Dream*, the very multiplicity of plays persuades him that 'no one Shakespearian element is allowed to predominate . . .' (24). Margaret Comstock develops some of the parallels, especially those with *As You Like It*. She shows that Katharine's assumption of a Rosalindish stance 'helps her resist the alienation that would result if she slipped into the kind of marriage normal in her society'; that Ralph Denham, like Orlando, can profit from the resistance of his beloved; and that Mary Datchet functions much as Jaques does, to suggest the possibilities of a happy life without comedy's more usual marriage at the end (160–3).

The parallels cited by these critics make a great deal of sense. *Night and Day* does indeed subject to typically Shakespearian complications five young people who themselves resemble from time to time some particular hero or heroine of the festive comedies. Yet these complications of the plot are only the skeleton of the book: while they may determine its shape, they are not its flesh and blood, and they are not its clothing—all of which, finally, make for the peculiarly mixed genre of Woolf's second novel. I am referring to two elements that add to the distinctiveness of *Night and Day*: its debt to problem comedy, and its use of the Shakespearian Fool, a kind of character who is as much at home in tragedy as in comedy.

There is no missing the point that Woolf wanted the reader to think of Mrs Hilbery as the Shakespearian Fool, for she actually says to Katharine: 'I'm quite a large bit of the fool, but the fools in Shakespeare say all the clever things' (306). Her appearance too is suggestive of a fool, her large eyes, 'at once sagacious and innocent' (21), and Woolf gives Mrs Hilbery a large measure of inconsequential action and dialogue. She hurries off to Stratford at a seemingly inopportune time, just when her daughter Katharine's life is most complicated—and yet as it turns out Katharine needed to be on her own for that period. She offers up a comment of Browning's on the Jewish blood in every great man—as a way of unruffling the family feathers over the illegitimate births that seem to have been proceeding from Cyril Alardyce (123). She feigns approval of Katharine's engagement to William Rodney, when all the time she is monitoring the progress of the growing love of her daughter for Ralph Denham. Scatterbrained though she seems, she does indeed 'say all the clever things', and has that same awareness of the void that characterizes both Feste and Lear's Fool. When she finally talks most seriously with her daughter, 'She cast a lightning glance into the depths of disillusionment which were, perhaps, not altogether unknown to her' (484–5).

In her expansive way she dreams of a playhouse where all of her family and their friends would play Shakespearian roles. She tells Katharine 'you'd be Rosalind—but you've a dash of the old nurse in you. Your father's Hamlet, come to years of discretion; and I'm—well, I'm a bit of them all . . .' (306). If her reach here exceeds her grasp, that's what a Shakespeare's for. It is generally thought that Woolf modelled Mrs Hilbery primarily on Anne Thackeray Ritchie; but significantly she shifted her character's literary taste from Aunt Anny's favourites, later English writers (Boyd 91), to writers of the Elizabethan age. In so doing she gave the character a background, as it were, for her Shakespearian role as Fool. As with the Fool's ministrations to Lear, Mrs Hilbery stage-manages her daughter's relationships with men so unobtrusively that Katharine is unaware of her mother's subtle machinations. Only when Mrs Hilbery arrives back at the house, carrying boughs and flowers from Shakespeare's tomb (sic; or perhaps from some London florist), does she speak unequivocally, and then she gives voice to the comic spirit which asserts that great poets approve of love; that 'it's what we feel that's everything'; that there are many different ways of loving; that 'we have to have faith in our vision' (480–4). It is finally time for her to make the choric comment that

Woolf was beginning to sense in the dialogue of Shakespeare's fools, sometimes in agreement with the prevailing attitudes of a given work, sometimes in contrast.

There is need for such commentary in *Night and Day*, for, although it is a comic novel, its tone is remarkably serious. If it is true that the course of true love never did run smooth, the course of Katharine and Ralph's love for large stretches of the novel seems barely to run at all. Festive comedies do not for a minute raise a question about the nature of the feeling of even the most inconstant characters: it is unequivocally love. Certainly in the two plays most consistently suggested as parallels to the novel, *Twelfth Night* and *As You Like It*, one never questions the love of Viola for Orsino, or of Rosalind for Orlando; although Orsino believes that he loves Olivia, Shakespeare reveals his affection and growing love for Viola; and there is never a doubt about Orlando's feeling for Rosalind. Here is the most basic discrepancy between *Night and Day* and Shakespeare's festive comedies. Indeed, if seeking a more exact parallel, one would have to go to Shakespeare's problem comedies for the same analytic tone; and if for the disposition of the love matches in *Night and Day*, a particular problem comedy would immediately suggest itself—*Measure for Measure*.

Measure for Measure is the only play from which Woolf actually quotes in *Night and Day* (155). It is one of Shakespeare's thorniest comedies: there is absolutely no sense of inevitability about the love matches; it scrutinizes the relationship between the sexes; and it places the action in an atmosphere of corruption and depravity. The action of Shakespeare's play centres primarily on Isabella, a young woman intent on entering a strict order of nuns at the outset of the play. But because Isabella's brother Claudio is facing death for having got his fiancée Juliet with child, Isabella returns to the world to beg mercy from Angelo, who promptly wants to sleep with her. The Claudio–Juliet problem serves the purpose of introducing the fact of sexual freedom in *Measure for Measure*, much as does Woolf's mention of Cyril Alardyce in *Night and Day*; and this first 'match'—Angelo's attempted wooing of the cold and 'enskied' Isabella—structurally parallels William Rodney's wooing of Katharine. Ultimately Isabella, with the help of the Duke, promotes Angelo's marriage to Mariana, a young woman who loves him and lives in the country (at the 'moated grange'). Obviously Katharine, assisted by Ralph, accomplishes the same feat for the rural and infatuated Cassandra, and by seeming to go along with a man in whom she is not interested (Katharine's false engagement paralleling Isabella's seeming acquiescence). And again, the marriage is to the man who was at first interested in the matchmaker. Finally, the suggested marriage between Isabella and the Duke at the end of *Measure* bears some resemblance to the projected marriage of Katharine and Ralph at the conclusion of *Night and Day*. Needless to say, the plots of the two works are far from identical, and there is no Mary Datchet in *Measure for Measure*. But there is much the same tone, a quiet brooding over the nature of love, and its place in a difficult world. Like *Measure for Measure*, *Night and Day* (as even its name suggests) can be considered a problem comedy.

Characteristically, both works signal a disconcent in their authors with the limitations of a genre—said of Shakespeare, and proved in the event with both. Woolf's next novel, *Jacob's Room*, begun in April 1920, was the first of her experimental books; and during its composition Woolf took the first major step from being a reviewer to being a critic. The book of criticism she then planned, 'Reading', was published as *The Common Reader* in 1925.

As nearly as I can tell, the first of Shakespeare's plays that Woolf read specifically for 'Reading' was the one that had figured so importantly in *Night and Day*, *Measure for Measure*. It was her third reading of the play. She had read it in 1916 and again in 1918, an experience of 'ecstasy' (*N&D* hol. 6 Oct. 1916–5 Jan. 1917; *L*. 910, 25 Feb. 1918; *D*. 2 Mar. 1918). In June of 1921 she re-read the play, this time with pen in hand. She knew from earlier readings that it is difficult and that the dialogue requires study if one is to glean the motives of opaque characters (MHP/B2d, 40). Thus putting aside her annoyance with critics she enlisted the help of a couple: one found in her father's library, George Brandes; and later, when she tried to write something about the play, she also consulted Coleridge. Brandes proved to be less than helpful despite the scholarship that informed his critical pronouncements. He believed that Shakespeare dwelled in *Measure for Measure* on 'baseless criticism by subjects' in order to show 'how apt princes and rulers are to be misjudged' (ii. 79). Brandes envisaged a sycophantic playwright, a man who punished the character Lucio severely for slandering the Duke because he was more interested in royal favour than in dramatic appropriateness. Today, however, many readers are convinced that the harsh judgement suggests not the baseness of the malefactor but rather the inequity of the judge. This more modern view was the one Woolf took, in defiance of Brandes: 'I suspect that Shre meant to poke fun at the Duke, only didnt take the trouble to work this out' (MHP/B2d, 39). Her interpretation reflects her understanding of the subtle means a writer can employ to question highly placed characters.

Woolf was fascinated by the complexity of the Duke, especially his earlier 'impotency of will' in enforcing the law, which she finally attributed to his introspective and philosophical temperament. There is ample justification for this somewhat eccentric view, and Woolf found a striking parallel in the characterization of Claudio, whose 'expansion of the imagination . . . seems to paralyse action' (40). Claudio tells his sister Isabella that 'death is a fearful thing', and elaborates thus:

> . . . to die, and go we know not where;
> To lie in cold obstruction, and to rot;
> This sensible warm motion to become
> A kneaded clod; and the delighted spirit
> To bathe in fiery floods, or to reside
> In thrilling region of thick-ribbed ice;
> To be imprison'd in the viewless winds
> And blown with restless violence round about
> The pendant world . . .

As was true in her judgement of *Hamlet*, she found more to praise in an expansive imagination than to blame in inaction. So impressed with Claudio's vision of death was Woolf that she made use of it in two of her novels. She quoted the last several lines in *Night and Day* (155), associating them with Ralph Denham when he hears that Katharine has become engaged to William Rodney. Mrs Cosham asks Ralph to explain the obscure lines, but he is 'so much distracted' that 'his eye could hardly follow the words on the paper. A moment later he heard them speak distinctly of an engagement ring.' The irony of Katharine's being engaged to William Rodney is underscored by the lines from *Measure for Measure*: placing the speaker beyond human confines of time and space, they suggest that Ralph (rather than her fiancé) has much in common with Katharine, whose flights from the here and now are repeatedly established. But he cannot communicate with Katharine any more than he can change his unsatisfactory profession, living more the life of imagination than of action.

As Ralph walks along the Embankment after this scene, 'the pain spreads all through him' and he becomes like the dead body Claudio describes:

The world had him at its mercy. He made no pattern out of the sights he saw. He felt himself now . . . adrift on the stream, and far removed from control of it, a man with no grasp upon circumstances any longer. Old battered men loafing at the doors of public-houses now seemed to be his fellows. . . . They, too, saw things very thin and shadowy, and were wafted about by the lightest breath of wind. (157).

The passage from *Measure for Measure* that inspired this description is also echoed in Isa Oliver's vision of death in *Between the Acts*: 'Where do I wander? . . . Down what draughty tunnels? Where the eyeless wind blows? And there grows nothing for the eye. No rose. To issue where? In some harvestless dim field where no evening lets fall her mantle; nor sun rises' (154–5). The imagery is similar to Shakespeare's, and the 'eyeless wind' recalls the 'viewless winds' in Claudio's speech. The parallel with Claudio reinforces the point that Isa's romantic imaginativeness, frittered out in verse-making and abstractedness, makes of her an 'abortive' person (15). As sometimes happened in Woolf's reading of Shakespeare, her ability to understand his characterization contributed to her conceptions of character in her own writing.

The heroine of *Measure for Measure*, Isabella (who may have contributed her name to Woolf's related character in *Between the Acts*), presented greater demands on her critical powers than had Claudio or the Duke. Here was a situation of great interest: a young woman, who at the play's outset intends to become a nun, must turn her attention to winning her brother's freedom; and she eventually manages, with the help of the Duke, to circumvent the one preferred means of winning it, losing her chastity to the Duke's deputy, Angelo. In spite of the many vicissitudes involved in the working out of these problems, Brandes had very little to say about Isabella beyond calling her 'young, charming, and intelligent' (ii. 75), so Woolf proceeded on her own to form a coherent picture. There were real difficulties because of Isabella's seeming inconsistencies. She is 'fiery & quick witted' when Angelo asks her what she would do if someone offered to save her brother only if she gave the treasures of her body. She replies:

> The impression of keen whips I'ld wear as rubies
> And strip myself to death, as to a bed
> That longing have been sick for, ere I'ld yield
> My body up to shame.

'Now that's vehement,' Woolf exclaimed. But then, when Isabella says in her soliloquy following Angelo's proposition,

> Then, Isabel, live chaste, and brother, die;
> More than our brother is our chastity

the words struck Woolf as 'unreal'. 'Would she not have kept at that heat?—Then, possibly swung round? Its the coldness that is odious . . .' (MHP/B2d, 43). But eventually she had to admit that the 'religious sanctimonious hardness' she found in Isabella's treatment of her brother in prison at least had the warrant of consistency of characterization: 'I think Isab. *is* consistent—a *religious* woman all through. Her argument that her brother deserved death because he had actually . . . *done* evil, while Angelo had only intended it is in keeping with her clearheaded coldness' (44). This rather unattractive young woman represented an important approach to the theme of chastity that Shakespeare also explored by means of the Duke's inability to enforce his state's laws on fornication, and the untested Puritan Angelo's enforcing them only to fall prey to lust himself. 'Clearly,' said Woolf, 'Shre wished to argue the question of chastity himself. I mean there is a brooding & question behind it all.'

Nine months later when writing 'Byron and Mr. Briggs' Woolf needed some examples of what precisely might be gained from critics and read Coleridge's comments on *Measure for Measure* for the first time. They did not square with her own perceptions of the play: to Coleridge the play was 'painful'; and the pardon and marriage of Angelo was unjust, and 'likewise degrading to the character of woman'. 'Painful' is hardly what Woolf would call this interesting play. Despite Isabella's coldness and the duke's 'impotency', both grappled with difficult ethical issues and emerged in Woolf's view with their integrity intact. Nor did Woolf agree about Angelo. No, Woolf could not trust even Coleridge to do her reading for her. The next time that her common reader, Mr Briggs, read the play, 'he had forgotten what Coleridge said; or his own ideas seemed fresher . . .' (329–30). When she ventured, some six years later, to comment on *Measure for Measure*, like Mr Briggs she seems to have forgotten what Coleridge said and to have reaffirmed her own earlier views: in *Measure* 'passages of extreme psychological subtlety are mingled with profound reflections, tremendous imaginations' (*CE* ii. 225). The former would be Shakespeare's probing of the question of chastity, and the 'reflections' are to be found in the speeches of Claudio, Isabella, and the Duke. In these Shakespeare revealed his capacity to deal with large issues rather than ephemeral personal and topical concerns, and that Woolf found commendable.

It is somewhat surprising that Woolf chose to read Shakespeare's history plays, but read them she did. Their world is familiar to anyone growing up in England, performances of the *Henry IV* plays and *Henry V* extremely common, and *Richard II* and *Richard III* done almost as frequently. Woolf mentioned Falstaff (who dominates the *Henry IV* plays) in the same breath with Lear and Hamlet and Cleopatra to illustrate Shakespeare's ability to create character (*CE* i, 8; *CE* ii. 190, 193; 'Anon.' 422 n). He was the great ancestor of all British comic characters (*CE* i. 312) and the most 'human' of Shakespeare's creations ('Byron and Mr. Briggs' 340). When Woolf wanted an example of Shakespeare's ability to confer immortality on a character, an example of the superiority of literature to biography, she naturally thought of Falstaff: 'Even Dr. Johnson as created by Boswell will not live as long . . .' (*CE* iv. 227). And yet one suspects that her appreciation of Falstaff derived more from seeing performances than from reading the plays, for she seems to think that he speaks in blank verse (*L.* 2634, 12 Sept. 1932)—a matter that the recorded reading in 1933 would have set straight (*D.* 26 June), she badly misses the point of Sir Walter Blunt's dressing as the king at Shrewsbury (*CE* ii. 266), and she rarely alludes to the plays (*CE* iii. 45; *D.* 30 Sept. 1938). The allusions would of course have been part of the fabric of Woolf's life. As for *Henry V*, the chauvinism and bellicosity of the play would seem to have alienated Woolf to such an extent that she uses a preference for it to satirize two characters in her first novel, Clarissa Dalloway and Mr Grice. Grice finds Henry 'the model of an English gentleman' (*VO* 54).

Woolf would probably not have gone on to read the history plays with care had she not made a concerted effort in the 1920s to fill in the gaps in her education (the notes date from the spring and summer of 1924). She used Sir Sidney Lee's speculative chronology of Shakespeare's works in the *DNB* (MHP/B2o, 47–8) and set about reading some history plays, beginning with *Richard III*, then *King John*, and finally *Richard II*, the order in which they were written. She did not include the earliest plays—the three parts of *Henry VI*—but the ones she selected, read in this order, would have given her a fair idea of Shakespeare's early development in the genre.

Her assumption would seem to have been that even in the first half of the 1590s Shakespeare had the capacity to do just about whatever he wanted to do. A rapid reading of *Richard II* a year earlier convinced her that even in the early plays Shakespeare was capable of writing 'great poetic passages' even if he did not prepare sufficiently for them (xxv. 27); the second reading convinced her that there seemed to be 'a flood of poetry trying to burst through in these early plays & sometimes getting its way'. The resources of the language were at Shakespeare's command. He could coin words, '[mould] them on his tongue', and used adjectives to 'paint nouns' (MHP/B2o, 52, 56). He could make vivid the simplest colours of his palette, and the most commonplace creatures and activities were the vehicle for remarkable figures of speech. Richard III is 'that bottled spider' and 'hunch backed toad'. In *King John*, 'Life is as tedious as a twice-told tale | Vexing the dull ear of a drowsy man'; and the Bastard refers to 'Old Time the clock-setter, that bald sexton Time!' But even in Shakespeare's non-figurative language Woolf recognized his 'prodigality', as in Richard's description of Bolingbroke's 'courtship of the common people':

> Off goes his bonnet to an oyster-wench,
> A brace of draymen bid God speed him well,
> And had the tribute of his supple knee.

Shakespeare was able to 'make brilliant what cd. have been left dim' (52).

But Woolf seems to have thought that he had little control of his great talents. She tried to determine the extent to which Shakespeare responded to the presumed demands of his audience. Whenever she found either exaggerated and wildly extravagant speeches which were out of keeping with requirements of the drama, or speeches which were jingoistic, she labelled them 'gallery speech'. It seemed odd to her that in the scene of Richard's banishing Bolingbroke, for example, there should be on the one hand 'psychological subtlety' but, on the other hand, the chauvinism of 'boast of this I can, | Though banish'd, yet a true-born Englishman' (52). She concluded that the audience 'pulled' the earlier plays out of Shakespeare, unduly influencing him to include entirely too much 'gallery speech' (53).

But the worst of the three in this respect was *Richard II*. Woolf alludes briefly to the play in *Mrs. Dalloway*, the novel she was concurrently writing. The mildly satiric portrait of Millicent Bruton draws on Shakespeare's characterization and dialogue of John of Gaunt, an old man whose days of power are long since past. In old Lady Bruton's case it was her sex that kept her from the corridors of power, but 'she had the thought of Empire always at hand . . . one could not figure her even in death parted from the earth or roaming territories over which, in some spiritual shape, the Union Jack had ceased to fly. To be not English even among the dead—no, no!' (275). This is reminiscent of John of Gaunt's urging his son to imagine his exile in France as simply another version of England. And Lady Bruton 'never spoke of England, but this isle of men, this dear, dear land, was in her blood (without reading Shakespeare) . . .' (274)—she is slightly mis-quoting John of Gaunt's great speech on 'This royal throne of kings'. The jingoism of the speech suits Lady Bruton admirably.

Like *Richard II*, *Richard III* would play a role in Woolf's fiction, specifically in *The Years*. Unlike *Richard II*, both *Richard III* and *King John* achieved a better balance between crowd-pleasing rhetoric and psychological subtlety. While to Woolf much of the dialogue in *Richard III* was mere 'mouthing', much had 'passion & quickness' (MHP/B2o, 55), a prime example of the latter being Richard's question, 'Was ever woman in this humour wooed | Was ever woman in this humour won?' But when one of their murderers says of the princes, 'Their lips were four red roses on a stalk, | Which in their summer beauty kiss'd each other,' Woolf condemned the 'out of place evanescent poetry' (50). Similarly, she criticized Anne's ranting about her dead husband's bleeding wounds, but recognized that it would be hard to beat the effectiveness of her simple description of sleepless nights in Richard's bed:

> For never yet one hour in his bed
> Did I enjoy the golden dew of sleep,
> But with his timorous dreams was still awak'd.

His 'terrific villainy', at times 'scarcely credible', was a bit easier to take because of the bad dreams and his haunted conscience on the eve of the final battle. And his soliloquies, even if aimed at the gallery, were at least 'very quick going rant' and often showed 'the beginning of analysis' (57). Finally, some scenes had the ring of truth, for example, the one in which Richard allows himself to be forced to take the crown, having set up the entire scenario himself. When the wildly malignant Richard says 'O, do not swear, my Lord of Buckingham', Woolf rightly observed that Shakespeare 'could make his lines go in & out of peoples minds' (56).

King John elicited much the same response as *Richard III*: some annoyance over Shakespeare's lavishing the most extravagant imagery on totally inappropriate scenes and characters, but enough pleasure from his superb use of language in the Bastard to counterbalance a whole parliament of gallery speech. It was 'in the Bastards character' to use proverb, 'country speech', and slang, for he had 'no patience with the high flown' (MHP/B2o, 49). In one of his many speeches that Woolf recorded, he tells his mother that he is not Sir Robert's son: 'Sir Robert might have eat his part in me | Upon Good Friday and ne'er broke his fast.' She was also delighted to find in the Bastard 'outbreaks of meditation comment', as in the soliloquy on self-interest, 'Mad world, mad kings'. Half-way through the play Woolf commented that 'it lights me as I walk to think I have 2 acts of King John tonight' (*D.* 15 Aug. 1924). So impressed by the play was she that some fifteen years later she remembered a line from it with almost complete accuracy: she was describing Leslie Stephen after his wife's death, sitting 'like the Queen in Shakespeare—"here I and sorrow sit" . . .' ('Sketch', *MB* 94). A more apposite allusion would be hard to imagine, for the speaker, Constance, says she will not move, her grief is so great, but that kings should come to her; and Leslie did the same, receiving visits from 'sympathetic women, old friends'.

Woolf aimed at a certain variety in her reading of Shakespeare in the 1920s, sampling genres she was not accustomed to reading, comedy and satire as well as the history play. But she did return to her favourite genre, tragedy, during the 1924 readings for a play with which she had long been familiar—*Antony and Cleopatra*. She also ready Dryden's *All for Love*, but, while there was much to admire in his version, a comparison of the barge scenes convinced Woolf that he 'takes the glow out of Cleopatra', and his Cleopatra is less sumptuous and subtle than Shakespeare's, her ways with Antony less imaginative. Shakespeare's language seemed difficult, but, because *Antony and Cleopatra* was 'the most extravagantly languaged of the plays', its 'pelt of ideas & words' was worth some effort (MHP/B2o, 2–4). The combination of rich language and a tragic heroine was irresistible.

So excited was Woolf by this reading of the play that her commentary spilled over into the draft of *Mrs. Dalloway*. Septimus Smith discovers that only in *Antony and Cleopatra* can he find expression for the anguished love he feels for Miss Isabel Pole. The play with its 'other tortured souls' in his mind as he walks down the street 'raises powerful spirits', makes 'surge up visions, rhapsodies . . .'. But at the same time the grandeur of Antony and Cleopatra's love makes him sadly aware of the disparity between 'what one says & does, [and] what one is capable of doing' (MS 51,044, 104–5).

The published novel does not include this passage, a reasonable view of the function of art in embodying or articulating an ideal. Probably stress, by her use of Septimus, a badly distorted view. ... *Dalloway* she characterizes Septimus's earlier reaction to ... t boy's business of the intoxication of language' but then ... shrivelled utterly' (133). After he has returned from the ... ocked, desperately unhappy, mentally ill, his wife Rezia says s... ust have children. They had been married five years', but Septimus knows that 'one cannot bring children into a world like this'. Besides, he has it on good authority that 'copulation was filth' to Shakespeare 'before the end' (134–5). The revelation was right there for him in *Antony and Cleopatra*: 'How Shakespeare loathed humanity—the putting on of clothes, the getting of children, the sordidity of the mouth and the belly!' (133–4).

Woolf herself had almost no fault to find with *Antony and Cleopatra*. She could not sufficiently praise the language of the play, mystical, extravagant, splendid; in spite of all our study of language, we have not appreciably improved on it (*CE* ii. 151, 250; *CE* iv. 200). Favourite though it was, however, *Antony and Cleopatra* was not as much a fixture of her mind as *Hamlet* or *Lear*, judging from the infrequency of allusion to it in letters or diary. The few are to the suicide scene, and all joke about the asp (*L.* 1864 (1928), 2262, 2264 (1930), 3084 (1935)), per-haps another sign of discomfort with the death wish. But, additionally, Cleopatra is not seen in her full humanity as Hamlet or Lear is, for Shakespeare focused almost exclusively on Cleopatra as lover, on what Antony called his 'serpent of old Nile'. In *A Room of One's Own* Woolf contends that, if Shakespeare were to have been under the same constraint in his depiction of males as of females, to see them as lovers, there would have been 'no Caesar, no Brutus, no Hamlet, no Lear, no Jaques—literature would be incredibly impoverished . . .' (145). But, if Shakespeare could think of Cleopatra only as lover, he none the less created in her a real woman, as he had not fully succeeded in doing with Lady Macbeth, Cordelia, and Ophelia.

In Woolf's last novel Mrs Swithin says to the writer of the pageant, Miss La Trobe, 'What a small part I've had to play! But you've made me feel I could have played . . . Cleopatra!' (*BA* 153). Yet Mrs Swithin all her life had been the antithesis of Shakespeare's queen, vacillating and of no particular importance. A sweet old woman, comic in her wandering dialogue, whom people call 'Batty' and 'Flimsy', she is somewhat reminiscent of Mrs Hilbery in *Night and Day*. In Woolf's 1924 reading of *Antony and Cleopatra* she had been especially struck by the richness of Cleopatra's 'method of baiting Antony' (MHP/B2o, 4).

Between the Acts's 'Cleopatra' is the object of her brother's incessant baiting. Her mildness in the face of his exasperation does not suggest that her relationship with her now-dead husband was tempestuous, but rather that she maintained harmony by a selfless adaptation to the needs of her family. But she is not intimidated really by anyone, though her brother Bart does not miss a chance of vaunting his superior education. If her 'one-making' seems a bit facile and her religion almost ludicrous, Woolf never shows Mrs Swithin engaged in any activities which cause discomfort to others. In fact, there is in Mrs Swithin evidence of something which for want of a better word one might call grandeur, glimpsed in such actions as her immediate acceptance of William Dodge, or in her lively intelligence and considerable power of imagination. Thus her telling Miss La Trobe that she might have been a Cleopatra is not preposterous. It was by her choice, albeit a limited Victorian one, that she was 'flimsy'. Woolf honours this woman who opted for a lesser role, though she herself would have chosen Cleopatra's (her persona late in life for a masquerade (*L.* 3483, 29 Jan. 1939)). Perhaps that is why she allows Mrs Swithin to have it both ways: after the pageant, when Lucy enters into a 'great picture of Venice—school of Canaletto', art and nature conspire to effect a change: 'The sun made each pane of her glasses shine red. Silver sparkled on her black shawl. For a moment she looked like a tragic figure from another play' (*BA* 214).

That *Antony and Cleopatra* plays this role, small but significant, in Woolf's last novel is to be expected, for it inspired in her the veneration she felt for the greatest of the tragedies, for *Hamlet, Othello, Macbeth,* and *King Lear.* These were the plays that echoed in her mind and entered most frequently into her own fiction. The three last novels hark back to them through frequent allusion and in a variety of other ways. The 1930s were a time ripe for Shakespearian tragedy, with on the one hand its assumption of the perilousness of the human condition and the inadequacies of social institutions, and, on the other, its quiet insistence on human grandeur. Of course Woolf thought of the comedies, but the tragedies dominated her thinking, and that with increasing power from *The Waves* onwards.

It is possible to trace Woolf's steps in composing *The Waves*, thanks to John Graham's edition of the two holograph drafts, and to discern therein two unmistakable patterns. The first is a slight increase overall in allusion from draft one to draft two to published novel. The second is the assignment of virtually all Shakespearian allusions to Bernard. The handling of *A Midsummer Night's Dream* is a case in point. Early on an unidentified speaker, possibly a narrator, mentions that at graduation the girls had put on a performance of the play (*Waves Hol.* 1. 137). The play surfaces again when Bernard describes the pregnant Susan recalling the 'vot'ress' of Titania's order, who imitated big-bellied sails that conceived by the wanton wind: she swayed down the terrace 'with the lazy movement of a half filled sail' (1. 375)—an image that carries over into the novel (268). Apparently Woolf thought it appropriate for a novelist to have learned the image from reading or seeing Shakespeare. It would not be appropriate for Rhoda: when she hears of Percival's death, quoting the pathetically disillusioned Gloucester, she says of the gods, 'They kill us for their sport' (1. 251). But Woolf immediately deleted the quotation, and in the novel Rhoda at the same juncture merely observes that she is alone in a hostile world (159).

Thereafter, with only one exception, all allusions to Shakespeare are put in the mouth of Bernard. The typically Shakespearian 'See where he comes!' or 'Look where she comes!', originally assigned to Neville, in the novel is Bernard's.[2] But the exception, from the first draft to the novel, also involves Neville, who equates ordinary people on a busy London thoroughfare with Shakespearian types and characters: 'Here's the fool, here's the villain, here in a car comes Cleopatra, burning on her barge' (196). Neville brags convincingly about his maturity, his newfound ability to see the impersonal behind the personal and therefore not to insist irritably on changes in anyone's character. But in giving the remainder of the Shakespeare allusions in *The Waves* to Bernard, Woolf was attempting to do more, to gain for his voice the resonance of the plays to which he alludes.

But Woolf had to work her way slowly towards that result. At first she scattered the allusions almost indiscriminately, as when, for example, Bernard sees that conventional language, however insincere and cliché-ridden, is necessary; without it, he says,

life would be, even more than it is, a litter of nursery rhymes . . . Pillicock sat on Pillicock hill [*Lear* III. iv. 76] . . . & fragments of half remembered songs . . . Sigh no more ladies, ladies sigh no more [*Much Ado* II. iii. 62], Come away Come away death [*Twelfth Night* II. iv. 51], Let us not upon the rack of this

---

[2] Graham ('Manuscript' 323) points out that the image is associated with Percival, and that the revisions 'help to consolidate the particular heroic significance of Percival . . .'. They do the same for the speaker, Bernard. Furthermore, Woolf's addition to Bernard's soliloquies of allusions to the great tragic heroes, documented in my text, lends credence to Graham's contention (*passim*) that Woolf's revisions were intended to develop the novel's 'heroic theme'.

tough world [*Lear* v. iii. 315] Let me not to the marriage of true minds [Sonnet 116]—It was a lover & his lass [*As You Like It* v. iii. 16]. (1. 368)

It amounted to no more than a flexing of literary muscles, from which exercise only three passages survived in the published novel. One was the song North would also allude to (in *The Years*), 'Come away, come away death,' twice representing in Bernard's mind the seething life of the imagination (259, 282). The quotation from sonnet 116 is linked with this song from *Twelfth Night* (259) as is the 'nonsense' from *Lear* (282), perhaps because both can touch what is unaccustomed, the idealistic or the perverse. Bernard envisages existence as a system of checks and balances, the prose of everyday life and the poetry of literature serving as useful correctives to each other.

Thereafter Woolf held to a sure course in the development of Bernard's characterization by means of allusion, introducing into the second draft allusions entirely absent from the first, and retained them for publication. Bernard acknowledges his friendship with Neville by saying, 'I too will press flowers between the pages of Shakespeares sonnets' (2. 492; *Waves* 88); and he remembers his first love, Susan, with an allusion to Othello's love for Desdemona: 'If it were now to die, twere now to be most happy' (2. 669). The allusions contribute to the complexity of this characterization, suggesting at the same time the intensity of his feelings for others and his equally strong tendency to step back, analyse, and even dramatize feeling. Given such complexities, the range and depth of tragic heroes must have struck Woolf as most fitting for the character who emerges gradually as central. The increasing centrality of Bernard is achieved mostly by the domination of his monologue at novel's end, a spot that could only be enhanced by reference to the major Shakespearian tragedies. In his summing-up, allusions to both *Hamlet* and *King Lear* abound.

Bernard knows what it takes King Lear total dislocation to learn, that within each human being is an aboriginal self, 'guttural, visceral . . . He now washes his hands before dinner, & puts on a tail coat, to impress the waiter; but he is naked hairy within me . . . He perpetually mops & mows with his half idiot gestures . . . pointing greed & desire' (2. 728). The revision of this passage in *The Waves* merely intensifies Bernard's depiction of the 'savage' who 'squats in me . . . He buttons on trousers and waistcoats, but they contain the same organs' (289–90).[3] Here are

---

[3] Schlack (*Continuing* 122–3) finds parallels in language, 'stormy', 'sulphurous', and 'howl' (*Waves* 239, 295).

the kinds of things that Lear discovers: that women are centaurs 'down from the waist'; that even a king's hand 'smells of mortality'; that robes and gowns of office hide vices; that 'unaccommodated' man is an animal. Here too is Edgar's fiend 'of mopping and mowing, who since possesses chambermaids and waiting-women'.

But Bernard is able to transcend the vision of the sulphurous pit when he dissociates himself from selfhood, as Lear also does when, chastened by neglect and madness, he is cleansed of ego. Lear hopes to take on with Cordelia 'the mystery of things | As if we were God's spies'. Bernard echoes his words: 'So now, taking upon me the mystery of things, I could go like a spy without leaving this place . . .' (291; see *Waves Hol.* 2. 730). Also like Lear, who finally admits to being a foolish old man and who acknowledges his own share in his downfall, Bernard can say,

I, who had been thinking myself so vast . . . a whole universe, unconfined and capable of being everywhere on the verge of things and here too, am now nothing but what you see—an elderly man, rather heavy, grey above the ears . . . I have made an awful ass of myself and am justly laughed at by any passer-by. (292)

Bernard's insights into his universe and his moments of grandeur alternate with that concern for self which is characteristic of the great tragic heroes. Even though Woolf felt that the writing of poetic plays had become impossible after Shakespeare (*L.* 1980, 8 Jan. 1929), she in fact conceived of *The Waves* as 'a novel & a play' (*D.* 21 Feb. 1927), as a 'playpoem' (*D.* 7 Nov. 1928) in which she could capture 'a mind thinking' (*D.* 28 May 1929). Finally she acknowledged that *The Waves* was becoming 'a series of dramatic soliloquies' (*D.* 20 Aug. 1930). And that is what the bulk of the novel is, a play without dialogue, a play with everything left out but the soliloquies. These take much from Shakespeare's: all six characters examine their lives, relive and reinterpret the past, capture meaning in recurrent images and metaphors, and in general touch upon internal reality before being impelled back into an external reality now more meaningful for their having made that excursion.[4] It is this concentration on the dramatic soliloquy that makes *The Waves* Woolf's most Elizabethan book in form.

---

[4] Albright (104) rightly contends that 'the technique of the soliloquy . . . permits distinctness, pointedness of internal characterization beyond the previous usage of novelists . . .'.

Woolf read a lot of Shakespeare immediately after finishing writing, 'when my mind is agape & red & hot. Then it is astonishing' (*D.* 13 Apr. 1930). She saw performances of both *Hamlet* and *Othello* (*L.* 2185, 2 June 1930; 11 June 1930), the sources of the greatest of the soliloquies. Of all the minds Shakespeare reveals in the solitude of the soliloquy, it is Hamlet's that most resembles Bernard's. In the second draft Bernard talks about Shakespeare in general with his friends (2. 679), but this is particularized to *Hamlet* in the novel (256). The revision alerts the reader to the import of a passage in which Bernard behaves like Hamlet overreacting to Gertrude's marriage. Bernard feels nothing but disgust at Susan's marriage to a boorish country squire:

A man in gaiters, a man with a whip, a man who made speeches about fat oxen at dinner—I exclaimed derisively and looked at the racing clouds, and felt my own failure; my desire to be free; to escape; to be bound; to make an end; to continue; to be Louis; to be myself; and walked out in my mackintosh alone, and felt grumpy under the eternal hills and not in the least sublime . . . (257)

It is an anthology of Hamlet's ideas, his horror at the marriage, his attitude in the clouds' scene with Polonius, and all the contradictions voiced in the soliloquies, with enough verbal echoes to reinforce the parallel (for example, 'I could be bounded in a nutshell, and count myself a king of infinite space'). And just as Hamlet faces death personified ('this fell sergeant death is strict in his arrest')—to Woolf a peculiarly Elizabethan idea—so Bernard perceives death as an enemy advancing against him. Like Hamlet (though the words are his own) he goes to meet the enemy 'unvanquished and unyielding' (297).

In an essay written in 1927, a couple of years before she actually began *The Waves*, Woolf predicted that there would be a new sort of novel, having 'something of the exaltation of poetry, but much of the ordinariness of prose. It will be dramatic, and yet not a play' (*CE* ii. 224). The novel would be less interested in recording facts than in giving 'the relation of the mind to general ideas and its soliloquy in solitude'. The need 'for ideas, for dreams, for imaginations, for poetry' was not then met by the novel, but 'it is one of the glories of the Elizabethan dramatists that they give us this' (225). Although 'the older forms of literature' such as the epic or the verse drama had already 'hardened and set' before women could shape them (*Room* 134), a return to the Elizabethan drama, shorn of the plot, proved that something was salvageable. Woolf selected as a model for her hero the most introspective of Shakespeare's heroes, Hamlet; and selected the

most introspective element of Shakespearian drama, the soliloquy, as
the model for her form. The old form took on her own mould, and
produced an entirely internalized drama.

I have discussed quite a few of Shakespeare's tragedies because it is they
rather than comedy that appealed to Woolf. When she did read the
latter, the so-called festive comedies were less likely to inspire note-
taking than either problem comedy (*Measure for Measure*) or satire
(*Troilus and Cressida*). *Twelfth Night* seems to be an exception to this
rule, for Woolf did take notes when she read it in 1924; but they are
really minimal (she skimmed the play, read a bit that a critic said about
it, and noted the speech that originally had attracted her years earlier
('Sketch', *MB* 119), Orsino's 'If music be the food of love' (xix. 20)).
She would probably not have returned to the play had she not been
obliged, awkwardly enough, to write a review of Tyrone Guthrie's 1933
production, which featured Lydia Lopokova as Olivia (*D*. 10 Sept.
1933): 'the only possible line to take is how very exciting it is to see
Shakespr [*sic*] mauled . . .' (*L*. 2795, 19 Sept. 1933).

But the review is tactful, criticizing the scenery, with which
Lopokova obviously was not involved, and making her failure as an
actress into a sort of triumph for a sunny personality. Beyond the
personal question, the review is valuable in that it was the occasion for a
sustained though brief piece of criticism of a Shakespeare play (*CE* i.
28–31). Two matters interest Woolf, and not unexpectedly they are
language and characterization. On both topics she speaks sensibly and
convincingly. Although it is clear that she disapproves of the particular
bodies chosen to represent Shakespeare's characters, she suggests that
what is involved is merely two different 'versions' of character, the one
she happens to envisage when reading, and the one the actors convey at
the Old Vic. (29–30). She even finds the acted version superior in one
respect, although amusingly enough the superiority is based on the
actors' ability to be silent (29). In criticizing the mildness of the
production's Malvolio—'a splendid gentleman . . . who has no quarrel
with the world'—and the gaiety of Lopokova's Olivia, Woolf must
articulate her own conceptions arrived at in reading, to wit: Malvolio is
'a fantastic complex creature, twitching with vanity, tortured by
ambition', while Olivia is 'a stately lady; of sombre complexion, slow-
moving and of few sympathies' (30).

By the 1930s Woolf was an attentive reader, and unlikely to be
persuaded by a production, even one with the best credentials. She was

happy to spend the time necessary to 'unfold the implications' of Shakespeare's dense language (28). Words 'rush and leap out with a whole character packed in a little phrase. When Sir Andrew says "I was adored once", we feel that we hold him in the hollow of our hands; a novelist would have taken three volumes to bring us to that pitch of intimacy.' The contrast between the play she had read and the play she saw at the Old Vic. was striking. In production, Shakespeare's poetry was not audible, 'for when he wrote as a poet he was apt to write too quick for the human tongue', with the result that 'the speaking voice falters in the middle'. But the eye can rapidly send to the brain 'the prodigality of his metaphors' (30–1). From her reading she identified something peculiar in the the first few scenes: 'From the echo of one word is born another word' (e.g. from 'live in her' to 'liver'; from 'Illyria' to 'Elysium'). It did not seem to matter to Shakespeare that the first example was dreadful, the second beautiful, since both made for the peculiarly musical quality of the play.

Accustomed to Woolf's practice in novels and essays written through, say, the late 1920s, one would conclude that her reading of Shakespeare generally bore fruit visible in allusion and/or structure. Her reading in the 1930s, however, did not in general follow this pattern. If she were reading a play for the first time, it seems not to have occupied her mind after she put it down, even if the experience was enjoyable. Only if she had read the play previously did the re-reading make enough of an impression for it to enter into her fiction. In the 1930s Woolf's reading of Shakespeare was more of a hodgepodge than her earlier reading had been. She read comedy, tragedy, and dramatic romance; the plays were drawn from Shakespeare's early, middle, and late periods; some she had read before, while others were new acquaintances; some were well known, others among the lesser works. In addition to *Twelfth Night* she also read again both *Troilus and Cressida* and *Cymbeline*. *Titus Andronicus* and *The Taming of the Shrew* extended her acquaintance with the early plays, which had been represented thus far only by the history plays; and *Timon of Athens*, *Pericles*, and *Coriolanus* did the same for the later canon. She wrote a critical essay only about *Twelfth Night*, but took notes when reading the other plays.

The one that fares best of all is *Troilus and Cressida*, perhaps because of its intrinsic merit, but also because the 1934 reading was a return to a play read before (*L*. 1221, 25 Feb. 1922). She had been sufficiently caught up to 'take sides for and against' the great men who people the play, and she was wild about Shakespeare's extravagant language. But the special attraction was his ability to make big ideas absolutely real: war emerges vividly in the violent metaphor of 'hot digestion of this cormorant war'; and Shakespeare is able to 'coin full blooded images where we have only the ghosts of ideas', as in Ulysses' speech on time putting 'alms for oblivion' in his wallet (MHP/B2q, 60–1). Her only strictures against the play in 1922 had to do with what she took to be a basic 'failure of construction', the last act not providing 'the inevitable catastrophe' ('Byron and Mr. Briggs' 347).

By 1934 she was ready for satire, and it was the very 'unfinished' character of the play that most attracted her. Hector is killed at the end, not Troilus, who in fact goes off without Cressida. Nor are the final words of the play 'Now is acted our drama—but an obscene scoff of Pandarus. And Cressida's state of mind unfinished too.' Shakespeare's allowing a characterization to emerge 'from reflection all round' naturally appealed to a writer who had attempted much the same thing in her novels in the 1920s, from *Jacob's Room* onwards (xxvi. 53–4).

Lines from this play provided a handy commentary on Woolf's life. Cressida's cynical belief about love, that 'Things won are done; joy's soul lies in the doing', Woolf would quote to convey what she felt about writing, the excitement to be found in 'the writing, not the being read' (*D*. 27 Oct. 1928). In 1922 she had praised the description of Achilles: 'The large Achilles, on his pressed bed lolling | From his deep chest laughs out a loud applause.' Years later, in 1939, Woolf quoted the lines in a reminiscence of her cousin J. K. Stephen, whose power and erratic behaviour brought Achilles to her mind ('Sketch', *MB* 99). The play met Woolf's needs in the turbulent 1930s: at one point, after a retreat to Rodmell during increasing preparations in England for the imminent war with Hitler, she chose to read it again (*L*. 3448, 3 Oct. 1938). And some striking images from the play would appear in her last novel as a comment on the effects of that war.

Woolf's growing appreciation for *Troilus and Cressida* illustrates her developing capacity to grasp something other than tragedy, rather than some slavish love of Shakespeare qua Shakespeare. Actually, in the 1930s she was no longer intimidated by his greatness. Although she was fond of saying that Shakespeare 'surpasses "writing" ' (*D*. 20 Aug. 1930), she could entertain the notion that he was capable of writing poorly. In her reading of several plays in July of 1934, including *Timon of Athens*, *Titus Andronicus*, *Pericles*, and *Coriolanus*, she was quite discriminating. Very little in *Pericles* attracted her beyond the magnificent vision of Thaisa drowned at sea ('And humming water must o'erwhelm thy corpse, | Lying with simple shells'), and the circumstance that, against all odds, she is later found alive (that gave Woolf, she said, 'a little genuine start' (xxvi. 59)). *Titus Andronicus* was 'a far worse play than Pericles. Still wooden: a machine,' the 'piled up physical horrors' relieved by neither especially noteworthy poetry nor convincing characters (60). She had once stumbled on a beautiful line from *Titus*, 'Upon a gather'd lily almost wither'd', but it merely proved that even in the 'less known & worser plays' Shakespeare's remarkable fecundity 'lets fall a shower of such unregarded flowers' (*D.* 13 Apr. 1930). When she finally read the play in its entirety, although she again noticed the line, it did not cast an aura of beauty over the rest.

By October of 1934 she had also read *Troilus and Cressida, Cymbeline,* and *The Taming of the Shrew,* all with considerably more pleasure. But she was disinclined to applaud everything that Shakespeare wrote. She criticized the attitudes embraced at the end of *The Taming of the Shrew* as 'anti-feminist'. Katherina tells the other newly married women that 'thy husband is thy lord, thy life, thy keeper', and reminds them that husbands labour out in the world while wives lie 'warm at home, secure & safe'. Woolf commented that this is 'scarcely an accurate account of an Elizabethan womans life; or of our own'. And as for Petruchio's wanting 'obedience'—no, that wasn't so either: 'in fact, Pet. craved lies' (xxvi. 56). Shakespeare must have been 'working on something that did not greatly interest him . . .' (55).

Woolf did not carp unreasonably, but when, for a variety of reasons, Shakespeare failed in conception or execution, she was comfortable enough to say so, but still sufficiently fascinated by the writing problems involved to give the plays some thought. When, on the other hand, she found merit in a play, she happily acknowledged it. The contrast can be observed in her reactions to two of the later works which she read at this time, *Timon of Athens* and *Coriolanus,* both read in the same month, July of 1934.

The story of *Coriolanus,* although apparently difficult for Woolf to follow with its 'stir & chop & change of action', was, she said, 'magnificent'; it considered the effect of argument on the masses and on individuals (a topic of great interest in the mid-1930s) and it ended absolutely rightly. The hero was very much to her tastes, 'overblown, insolent, blind, tremendous'. But *Coriolanus* was no *Lear* or *Hamlet,* for its difficulties arose from 'the hurry of action, not from the difficulty of the thought as in the [high] tragedies' (xxvi. 63). She regretted as well that there was 'very little contemplation: therefore very little poetry'

play was none the less worth close study because of
_re_'s solutions to problems that every writer encounters. She
that he managed a long speech by interspersing brief
inte.._. tions; that his obscurity might have been a way of showing 'the
pressure of excitement'; and that he probably left out transitions in
order to achieve a vigorous effect, to reveal for example the 'pent up
energy' of the hero. These observations have a distinctly modernist cast,
and betray the special interest a twentieth-century novelist might take in
the experiments of Shakespeare's later career.

The play was one Woolf found especially attractive late in her own
career, the 1934 reading undertaken when she was completing *The
Years*, and another, in 1940, when she was writing *Between the Acts*.
Her later reactions to *Coriolanus* bear out the truth that, as one's
experiences become more comprehensive, one's ability to respond to
Shakespeare also grows. In 1940, the Second World War impinging
daily on Woolf's life, she came to see that the peculiar language of the
play ('rugged, turbid: broken: violent') reflects 'the physical effect of
fighting' on Coriolanus (MHP/B2c, 14). At times the language is
difficult because it is so highly compressed, but at times it is pellucid in
its simplicity, in either case its spareness appropriate to the military
experience of Coriolanus. Even the speech of others takes colour from
the hero, the crabbedness and impatience, the 'mixture of high blown
conceits & crude language of a piece with C.' Also reflecting the effect
of fighting are the 'contortions by which a scene changes'. In *Between
the Acts*, set just before England's declaration of war against Germany,
Woolf seems to have applied the lessons she learnt from reading
Coriolanus. It is certainly clear that the play was much in her mind at
this time. In one remarkable scene, right after he has been banished by
an ungrateful populace, Coriolanus says the simple but intense words,
'There is a world elsewhere.' Once during the war, when reading a
friend's autobiography, Woolf enjoyed the brief respite, 'three hours
of continuous illusion—and if one can get that still, there's a
world—what's the quotation?—there's a world outside' (*D*. 9 Feb.
1940).

Woolf read *Timon of Athens* directly after she had finished *Coriolanus*
in 1934. Despite the fact that neither play was rich in poetry, she was
surprised that *Timon* 'is the same time as Coriolanus!' (64), for
Coriolanus is clearly the superior play—though for that very reason she
was especially interested in *Timon*. She had criticized the intrusion of
'personality' into literary creation several years earlier in *A Room of*

One's Own. Now she found fault with Shakespeare for allowing his own emotion into _Timon_: the play 'almost reads like a voiding of Shakespeare's rage: the motive to disburden himself of hate of men'. True, by the end of the play she had found 'a few single contemplative lines' to record, but she also noted terrific obscurities which she attributed to Shakespeare's emotional involvement with the material. She questioned, she said, 'if the greatest poetry can be written in this rage' (xxvi. 65). In _Coriolanus_ the language is appropriate to the character who speaks it but not in _Timon_.

These then are the plays on which Woolf made notes in the 1930s. Of them, only _Titus Andronicus_ and _Timon of Athens_ made an appearance in the novel she was then writing, _The Years_. _Timon of Athens_, in spite of its imperfections, may have provided in its misanthropic hero a perfect model for the younger daughter of Eugenie and Digby Pargiter. For Woolf at first conceived of Elvira (later renamed Sara) as a biting satirist and misanthrope; and of all Shakespeare's characters, Timon is (with the possible exception of Thersites) the best model. In what appears to be Woolf's first version of the scene in the 1907 chapter in which Sara is alone in her bedroom on Browne Street (cf. _Years_ 132 ff.), one of her books is _Timon of Athens_ (_Years_ hol. iii. 114). But while a shred of _Timon_ survived from 'The Pargiters' into _The Years_, a few allusions did not. In almost every case allusions to that play and others by Shakespeare were voiced in the drafts by Elvira. Their early inclusion, and subsequent deletion, are both contingent on the nature and function of Elvira/Sara. Elvira differs from Sara in several significant ways, not the least of which are her more heavily stressed deformity and her greater tendency to preach. Ideas that would later appear in the openly didactic _Three Guineas_ are only thinly disguised as dialogue. At every opportunity Elvira lectures the members of her family rather than talking to them naturally. The only real compression in her dialogue occurs in the frequent literary allusions which sprinkle her speech. These comprise a little anthology of Elizabethan literature, and reveal those plays of Shakespeare that were of greatest significance to Woolf.

Elvira quotes Shakespeare throughout 'The Pargiters'; and she restates Woolf's own ideas as well. Thus equipped, she speaks 'the truth', as her name suggests; and even her family nickname, 'Hunch', although a playful allusion to her deformity, just might imply that her truths proceed from intuition. She is distinguished from those who resort to lies when they find the truth too discomfiting. For example, in a scene similar to one in *The Years*, when Rose Pargiter visits her cousins Elvira and Maggie, she annoys Elvira by denying the obvious hatred both felt for their fathers. Elvira immediately retreats to a book—as she does to allusion—her antidote against the lies of life.

These allusions come easily to Elvira's lips, for they are the link between the two realities in which she exists. Her cousin George (North in the novel) analyses her eccentric manner of speaking:

> The words ran themselves into a kind of rhythm. It was an old habit, when they were alone; he remembered it; & in spite of the exaggeration . . . the piling up & the arbitrary skips & jumps, it seemed to him that she was never more natural or at her ease than when she used language which to anyone coming in suddenly would have seemed silly, highpitched; so that perhaps the ordinary talk of people is . . . after all nothing but a ready made . . . reach me down stuff. (vi. 119–20).

George's contention that Elriva's language is a truer and more intense vehicle than the second-hand prose of others resembles Woolf's analysis of Shakespeare's language in *Julius Caesar*, *Coriolanus*, and especially *Timon of Athens*. Like poetry, Elvira's words exaggerate; like poetry, they often omit transitions; and like poetry, they 'pile up' images. From the drama of the Elizabethan age she developed a characteristically poetic way of structuring her thought.

Woolf underlines this eccentricity of speech by Elvira's being a bit deformed, one shoulder higher than the other, so that her 'movements were always abrupt & sidelong' (iii. 101; cf. *Years* 122). She skips rather than runs, and is always jumping up and whirling about. There is something eerie about her, part witch, part fool, part 'touched' poet. At one point Elvira astounds her cousin Eleanor with her prior knowledge of Abel Pargiter's having had a mistress. And how did Elvira know this? 'By the pricking in my thumbs,' she says (v. 122), the witch's knowledge in *Macbeth* that something wicked this way comes. Woolf felt that the intuition of the witch had the same imaginative source as that of the woman who, in earlier times, unable to be a poet, 'mopped and mowed about the highways crazed with the torture that her gift had put her to' (*Room* 84–5). In a sense Elvira is the forerunner of Albert, the village idiot in *Between the Acts*, who skips and ambles across the lawn, 'mopping and mowing' (86), and in general acts the role of fool or court jester. The scene in which Elvira and her cousin prepare for the family party at Delia's, also found in the novel (338 ff.), but more fully elaborated in the draft, leaves no doubt as to her function. After Elvira and George read bits of *The Tempest*, she says they should 'dress up &

go to the party' where they will 'act another play', with George taking the role of 'returned wanderer' and Elvira 'the part of zany fool buffoon . . .' (vi. 113–14). She even dresses the part, going to the party in unmatched stockings, a detail kept in *The Years* (370). As Radin maintains (99), 'dressed as a fool, she retains her right to ridicule and mock, to be different'. Albert's mockery in *Between the Acts*, and Elvira's in 'The Pargiters', suggest that both characters satisfied Woolf's need for choric expression of a particular view, and that was one of scorn. Soon after beginning Part Two, Woolf saw Elvira's role in terms of a visionary chorus or fool, for she needed to provide some comment 'while keeping the march of events. The figure of Elvira is the difficulty. She may become too dominant. She is to be seen only in relation to other things', thereby giving 'a great edge to both of the realities—this contrast' (*D*. 25 Apr. 1933).

Woolf went on to say that the book should include a variety of genres, with possibly 'a play, letters, poems' to 'hold them all together'. The play waited for *Between the Acts*, letters for *Three Guineas*. Poetry, Elvira's quotations of poetry to be exact, was one of the things holding the parts together, and another was the total characterization of Elvira, in which these quotations play a large part. She comments on every major idea presented in 'The Pargiters', from Part Two through to the end of the novel, speaking either directly to the point or satirically about it.

Occasionally Woolf makes some use of specific Shakespearian characters or situations without actual quotation, as for example in Elvira's statement: 'Naturally, Aunt Isabella spent the finest . . . days of the year sitting in the drawing room waiting for the maid lest she should be—what was the word—assaulted, accosted, insulted?' By showing here that around the turn of the century women were limited even in their ability to venture outside their houses, to give the reader some sense of the absurdity of 'Aunt Isabella's' predicament, Woolf has Elvira say, 'That's *Measure for Measure* (v. 136), reminding readers that contemporary mores are often dangerously antediluvian. Shakespeare had created a character whose 'religious sanctimonious hardness' was even then destructive. To see a Shakespearian situation as 'old fashioned', while not Woolf's usual tack, was useful from time to time.

More frequently the primary vehicle for Elvira's satiric comment is direct quotation of Renaissance texts, and particularly of Shakespeare, thus bringing to bear directly in the novel the ideas of the source. The scene in Elvira's bedroom, where Woolf includes *Timon of Athens*

among her books, examines in great detail the character of Elvira and
her relationships with her immediate family. She is discontent,
irascible, even rather violent. She disdains her much-honoured father,
Digby, who like other men of the Pargiter family 'had Latin read over
him' at Oxford (iii. 121) in spite of the fact that he was 'a shell; corrupt;
light, like a tree eaten out by fungus' (149). The image sounds like
Timon speaking to prostitutes of the physical effects of syphilis,
'Consumptions sow | In hollow bones of man,' lines from Woolf's
favourite scene in that play. Later Elvira tells Maggie that the future
will have nothing but disdain for twentieth-century man, who will seem
savage, barbarous: '. . . a man, by looking in at this window into this
den, this cave . . . will hold his nose & say Pah they stink' (iv. 65).
Woolf's addition of the den, the cave, recalls *Timon*; the stench, the
graveyard scene in *Hamlet*, when the hero curiously considers the
history of great men 'turn'd to clay': he picks up a skull, asks Horatio if
even Alexander looked so in the earth, 'And smelt so? pah!' To Woolf,
'pah' was a word 'people say in Shakespeare' (*D.* 1 July 1931)—in both
Hamlet and *King Lear*. When Lear realizes that civilization cannot
change human beings, he says that from the waist down women belong
to the devil:

> there's a hell, there's darkness,
> There is the sulphurous pit, burning, scalding,
> Stench, consumption. Fie, fie, fie! pah, pah!

In *Hamlet* and *Lear* mankind, dead or alive, elicits the overwhelming
revulsion Elvira herself feels.

The scene is one that Woolf retained in the '1910' chapter of *The
Years*, and not only retained, but elaborated. When Sara says, 'Pah!
They stink,' her sister sees her momentarily as one of the beasts Sara
imagines:

Curled round, with her hair falling over her face and her hands screwed
together she looked like some great ape, crouching there in a little cave of mud
and dung. 'Pah!' Maggie repeated to herself, 'They stink' . . . She drove her
needle through the stuff in a spasm of disgust. It was true, she thought; they
were nasty little creatures, driven by uncontrollable lusts. (189)

Maggie, of course, tempers her disgust with a recognition of the 'beauty
and joy' of which mankind is also capable. But Sara repeats the phrase,
'this cave of mud and dung' when they have all retreated to the cellar
during an air raid in '1917' (293), the words and circumstances making

Maggie's earlier hope seem rather naïve. And Lear's and Hamlet's vision of the stench of humanity is validated by the remainder of the '1910' scene, one of brutality and death.

In the draft of this scene, the stench of humanity actually makes Elvira sneeze, thereby providing a transition of sorts to another allusion to Shakespearian tragedy. When Iago taunts Othello about the handkerchief, Othello becomes more and more distraught until he falls into a trance with the words, 'Pish! Noses, ears, and lips, Is't possible? Confess? Handkerchief? O devil!' Elvira remembers the heart-rending speech, but focuses on a more pervasive disgust with the body. The man of the future looking into the window of their 'cave' will say that ' "To blow one's nose in a pocket handkerchief . . . is an impossible outrage upon the decencies of [civilisation] humanity . . . Nasty things, [noses] ears, hands, finger nails.' She held up her hand & looked at it (iv. 65). It is as if mankind is trapped, not only by a propensity to lust, but also by being tied to a physical body whatever its demands.

Whereas in *The Years* Maggie can somewhat mitigate her sister's disgust, in 'The Pargiters' it is Elvira's view that predominates. Although she is allowed great sensitivity to beauty, she sees man as doomed. He is alone in a meaningless universe, as a further allusion to a Shakespearian tragedy makes clear. Immediately following her outburst, Elvira sneers at her sister for making a dress for a party tomorrow: 'Tomorrow, & tomorrow, & tomorrow' (iv. 65). Woolf here recalls the scene she had singled out in her first reading of *Macbeth*, when the beleaguered king learns that his wife is dead, and life is merely 'a tale' | Told by an idiot, full of sound and fury, | Signifying nothing'. Man alive is as meaningless as man dead, the lines in *Macbeth* cited almost as a counterpart to the lines from *Hamlet*. Alexander the Great and imperious Caesar, dead and turned to clay, might stop a hole to keep the wind away; all our yesterdays lead only to dusty death.

Woolf's book was designed to hold 'millions of ideas [on] history, politics, feminism, art, literature—in short a summing up of all I know, feel, laugh at, despise, like, admire hate & so on' (*D.* 25 Apr. 1933). The side facing the reader most of the time is life as lived by men and women who subscribe to patriarchal concepts. Woolf's mouthpiece for the 'other side' of this world is Elvira, who with her sister has been uncorrupted by it. Elvira's meticulous weapon of scornful literary allusion is turned on some unexpected targets, for example activist women who attack some evils while allowing or encouraging other evils to thrive. There is something incongruous in Kitty's appearance that matches the ineffectiveness and vagueness of her aristocrat's desire to do some good for women at a women's suffrage group. In order to convey her criticism, Woolf chose for Elvira Volpone's seduction speech to Celia, to whom he offers 'A diamond would have bought Lollia Paulina | When she came in like star-light, hid with jewels.' In an early draft Elvira describes Kitty entering the meeting 'robed in jewels dressed in starlight . . . Only I havent got the quotation right' (iv. 56). She does get it right eventually, and Elvira again recalls the image when she sees Kitty at Delia's party years later (vii. 119). This allusion suggests that Kitty has sold herself to a wealthy man (to whom clings the repulsiveness of Volpone), and that to enjoy his wealth she lives a life at variance with her political convictions (cf. *Years* 187, 392).

Another activist who is the butt of Elvira's satiric allusions is Rose Pargiter, whose work as a suffragette does not prevent her from joining the patriarchal establishment in wartime. The energies that Rose might devote to doing something about the more basic corruptions of society are always displaced: '. . . the dog dies for instance, & Rose, who is desolated by the death of a dog, her life has been largely spent in tending animals of one kind & another, buys a little plot, Maggie, in the dogs cemetery: a little grave—a little, little grave' (iv. 13). The allusion is of course to Richard II's self-pitying deposition speech in which he expresses his willingness to exchange his 'large kingdom for a little grave, | A little little grave, an obscure grave'. Richard is so fascinated by the thought, that he plays into the hands of the very man who will usurp his throne, the politically canny Bolingbroke. No more far-seeing is Rose. Although a feminist she is not a pacifist.

Elvira's feminism, like Woolf's, is primarily an attack on the predominantly masculine penchant for aggressiveness in all its forms. She alludes to two Shakespearian plays in support of that view, one of them *The Tempest*, which she discusses with George prior to their going to Delia's party. Woolf's choice of the play is a logical one given Elvira's conception of the masculine world. The play for her is not a paean to reconciliation and forgiveness, but rather a proof of masculine brutality. When Elvira tries to imagine the opening scene, she does not sense the humour but rather the horror of the man-invoked tempest for those on board the ship. 'The play begins, she said, like this . . . She wailed' (iv. 112). In discussing with George the decline in writing since Shakespeare, Elvira blames the hierarchical scheme found wherever one looks in society today—in the universities, in organized religion, in the government. She compares present-day disrespect for authority with a case found in *The Tempest* by showing George a picture of a man in uniform, looking for all the world like

the great baboon at the zoo who sucks a paper in which sweets have been wrapped—

> Ban, ban, Caliban,
> I'll be the master, you'll be the man.

The incorrect rendition of Caliban's disdain for Prospero ('Has a new master, get a new man') suggests that, when once a man has won freedom, he cannot wait to enslave another. The baboon-like military man is no better, and Elvira concludes that this 'type of masculinity' is not 'one that commands the knees of my soul to reverence' (vii. 12).

In *The Tempest* Elvira finds, then, the atmosphere of hatred, revenge, and disregard for one's fellow man that she dislikes in present-day society. But *Othello* supplies the prototype for the more active aggressiveness that is at the heart of her argument against the male establishment. When Othello bemoans the loss of his 'occupation', he is speaking of grace and honour, brilliance and command, of his *raison d'être*. Woolf feared that no lasting peace would be possible following the Second World War because of the attractions of a military life. Elvira's uncle, Colonel Abel Pargiter, is of that persuasion. Elvira remembers the early days at Abercorn Terrace, when 'Uncle Abel came in, with his horrid little shiny knuckles . . . where he'd cut off the head of a blaspheming & Turk' (*sic*; v. 119)—another conflation of words and ideas from Othello's final speech.

Elvira's feelings about aggressiveness make her sensitive to related patterns of behaviour such as disregard of feelings, overemphasis on money, difficulty of relations between the sexes. And in these areas too she harks back to *Othello*, as well as to other Shakespearian plays, for phrases expressive of her condemnation. A woman, she has been denied access to productive employment, despite the fact that her family was not able to leave her financially independent. The Digby Pargiters educated their three sons, not their two daughters. She thus knows full well that her own inability to support herself can be laid at the door of a society which fails to equip women for work, on the assumption that their task in life is marriage—and yet, in her case, will not consider her marriageable because of her physical defect. Elvira's options for employment are extremely limited: like Woolf, she accepts a job as book-reviewer for a newspaper but disdains it and herself for commercialism. As is her wont, Elvira sharpens her attack by means of allusion. Her editor would disapprove of Woolf's favourite line from the otherwise-neglected *Titus Andronicus*, 'Upon a gather'd lily almost withered.' 'Gather'd would be deleted as 'a superfluous epithet' (vii. 11). Why then does Elvira write for the paper? Woolf first wrote the phrase 'To make money', but substituted the words 'Put money in your purse' (vii. 33–4), an exact quotation of Iago's advice to his gull Roderigo. The revision changes a rather normal activity, self-support, into a sinister acquisition of money by sordid means. In a corrupt society, where newspaper editors are like the 'consistent devil' Iago, all are corrupted.

Elvira is given another of Iago's lines, one of his most sneering, bragging of his ability to seem to serve Othello when he in fact serves only his own interests. If ever his outward appearance fails to conceal what is in his heart, he says, ' 'tis not long after | But I will wear my heart upon my sleeve | For daws to peck at'. So Peggy, the physician sister of George, 'has something formidable; she doesn't coin her soul for the birds to peck at: coming out of a sick room' (vi. 102). She objects to Peggy's scientific orientation, to her treating her patients as problems to be solved rather than as human beings.

Woolf obviously was carrying Elvira's biting satire to inappropriate lengths. Suggestions of the cold calculation of an Iago should be reserved for villains, not used with people who happen to be members of a profession that one dislikes and distrusts. She probably understood the lines she selected, and, even if they were inappropriate as applied to Peggy Pargiter, their being spoken by Elvira was certainly consistent with her characterization as biting satirist. All of Elvira's uses of Shakespearian drama (and of *Volpone* as well)—the role of Fool, the evocation of setting and theme, and all allusions save those to *Othello*—were in keeping with other requirements of the fiction. Together the contributions of *The Tempest* and *Measure for Measure*, of *Richard II*, of *Timon of Athens*, *Titus Andronicus*, *Hamlet*, *King Lear*, and *Macbeth*, and even much of what Woolf took from *Othello* create a rich novel grounded in a literary tradition of social criticism.

Quotations from Shakespeare, often showing the marks of imperfect memory rather than recent reading, flowed from Woolf's pen rapidly. Perhaps the allusions were as much a voiding of Woolf's rage over social injustice as the claimed *Timon* was of Shakespeare's misanthropy. The difference is that Woolf went on to revise 'The Pargiters' and to make of it *The Years*. Her fear that Elvira might become too dominant was more than justified. In addition, Woolf seems to have originally intended Elvira to be a writer; a change in that conception would have suggested 'that most of her literary comments would have to be deleted from the published novel' (Radin 44-5). Some of the quotations were dropped, some of Elvira's criticism was toned down, and in *The Years* Sara's propensity for Shakespearian allusion is shared to some extent with North Pargiter.

Woolf also introduced materials from a couple of plays not brought into 'The Pargiters', *Richard III* and *Twelfth Night*. Woolf read *Richard III* in 1924. While it contained too much 'gallery speech' for her taste, she preferred it to both *King John* and *Richard II*, for the hero was at times believable and the dialogue often compelling. She had shown some interest in King Edward's compunction over the murder of his brother the Duke of Clarence, and had copied into her reading notes some of Clarence's speech about his 'fearful dreams' to the jailer in the Tower before his murder. He was drowning, and he saw 'sights of ugly death'—wrecked ships, 'a thousand men that fishes gnaw'd upon', gold, anchors, precious stones and jewels. Some memory of these lines seems to have combined with the coral of 'Full Fathom Five' (Albright 114) for Sara's account of standing with Rose on a bridge, looking into the water: 'Running water; flowing water. May my bones turn to coral; and fish light their lanthorns; fish light their green lanthorns in my eyes' (186). Sara may be thinking of Clarence, a man whose brother is about to have him killed by drowning, because of her hard feelings over Maggie's impending marriage and her consequent desertion. If one can make allowances for Sara's characteristic exaggeration, the beautiful images have an uncanny rightness.

Clarence's speech to the jailer about his dream also contains a description of the ghost of his nephew Edward, whom he had killed and now meets in the underworld:

> Then came wand'ring by
> A shadow like an angel, with bright hair
> Dabbled in blood . . .

In *The Years* someone actually reads this passage—not Sara but 'Eleanor's nephew, North' (284-5). I have mentioned earlier North's visit to Sara, his saying aloud Marvell's 'The Garden', with its praise of solitude, in effect a cut at Sara. Before North left England she had criticized him for being a soldier, and when he reminds her of an angry letter she wrote to him in Africa, Sara 'lifted her lip like a horse that is going to bite' (321). When Sara leaves the room, North feels deserted and stumbles on a line from a play completely at random: 'A shadow like an angel with bright hair . . .' (318). The vision of a nephew's return to haunt his uncle casts Sara in the role of Clarence, an elaborate and perhaps oversubtle use of allusion to suggest the difficulties created for the younger man by the unfairness of his cousin's criticism.

And it is unfair, for North has recognized his mistake and made the move that Woolf approved, away from army and empire. In fact, his having served the empire gives him a bit of the aura Woolf painted around Percival (and others representing traditional values (Graham, 'Manuscript' 314)). She certainly treats him with gentleness, almost mellowness, a man who has joined the ranks of those 'Shakespeare would have approved of'. As if in approbation of his views, Woolf allows North his share of Shakespearian allusions. Not only does he read the line from *Richard III*, but he also discusses Shakespeare with Sara, commenting on the Porter scene in *Macbeth* (the rightness of comedy following the murder of the king) and on the opening of *The Tempest* (345–6). Just as Elvira/Sara recalls the exclamation of disgust, 'Pah!', that Woolf saw as typically Shakespearian, so North's reaction to the thought of 'other people's hairs' left in the bath is a resounding 'Pah!' (340).

In addition, he invokes another of the plays Woolf read in 1924, *Twelfth Night*, of which she had reviewed the 1933 production at the Old Vic. She notices in that review the musical quality of the play, and quotes Orsino's request that Feste repeat the song he had sung the previous night (*CE* i. 28), chanted by 'The spinsters and the knitters in the sun'. This 'old and plain' song, which 'dallies with the innocence of love' as in the good old days, is in North's thoughts when he looks over at his Aunt Eleanor and Uncle Edward, who are having a marvellous time talking about everyone at Delia's party: 'They chatted, basking there at their ease. Spinners and sitters in the sun, North thought, taking their ease when the day's work is over . . .' (409). This is North's benediction on an age that is rapidly fading now, for he finds much to commend in their 'tolerant, assured' manner, which creates a beauty all its own. 'For them it's all right, he thought; they've had their day: but not for him, not for his generation' (409–10). North knows that the good old days have been defeated by the urgencies of the modern age, that the liberalism of his father's brothers and sisters will be ineffective in the combat with mob psychology. The distance between the needs of the present and, as he sees it, the comforts of the past can be measured by his thinking of the nostalgic Orsino.

North's reading of the damaging line from *Richard III*, on the other hand, is a matter of chance (he picks up the book which opens at the passage). The passage reminds the reader of the family tensions reflected in that play, while North's merely stumbling upon it keeps his hands clean as it were. He is no carping critic and no misanthrope. His benign reference to *Twelfth Night* adds to the positive picture. In handling North's allusions to Shakespeare in this way, Woolf gives him precisely what he wants, both one of the 'emblems and tokens' by which he can be identified as himself, and, somewhat paradoxically, through the community which those familiar with Shakespeare are part of, a way of uniting himself with others (410).

And that, finally, is what most of Woolf's use of Shakespeare depends on and capitalizes on. What we share is Shakespeare. Readers of English are at home with his works, and discover that at the least they have in common their love for him. There develops a special sort of contact with Shakespeare and with each other when we 'read collectively, learned side by side with the unlearned, for generations . . .' (*CE* ii. 275). Thus, when each of Woolf's novels brings Shakespeare into its fabric, his characters and their words enrich the reader's experience. And that is most intimately true in *Between the Acts*, where Woolf alludes to Shakespeare as a virtuoso plays a very fine instrument, with sure expressiveness and a remarkable range of tone.

An 'Elizabethan' play makes up part of the pageant. Woolf includes in it for the sake of authenticity a couple of quotations that have an unmistakable period air—witness Elizabeth's line '*Play out the play*' from *Henry IV, Part I* (88) and Ferdinando's '*Look where she comes*!' a common exclamation throughout the drama of the period, though Woolf probably knew it from *Othello* (91). The audience also contributes to the Elizabethan atmosphere, Giles with 'Loud laughter' from *A Midsummer Night's Dream* (85), Isa with her paraphrase of one of Romeo's lines (91), and Mrs Swithin with her 'unacted part' of Cleopatra.

Authenticity of another sort is achieved by three allusions to Shakespeare within the Restoration play, for the playwrights of the time were fond of quoting him. In every case Woolf takes a seriously meant passage that everyone knows well and puts it in a ludicrous context. What was dead serious in *The Years* is turned on end when Sir Spaniel Lilyliver kisses the superannuated Lady Harpy Harraden and gasps out, '*Pah! she stinks!*' (133). Finally Lady H. H. is deserted by everyone, even her maid Deborah (whose note quotes the Jacobean ballad, '*What care I for your goose-feather bed? I'm off with the raggle-taggle gipsies, O!*'), and she feels forsaken: '*O ingratitude, thy name is Deborah!*' (148). Hamlet again, this time in soliloquy over what Woolf believed to be the initial cause of his depression, his mother's hasty remarriage. Woolf shifts mood just slightly as Lady H. H. alludes to Jaques's seven ages of man speech from *As You Like It*, with '*I'm alone then. Sans niece, sans lover; and sans maid*' (148). The fun of the entire speech is in the incongruity of the allusions. In a way Sir Spaniel and Lady Harpy were made for each other. At any rate, the allusions to Shakespeare work with characterization and plot to produce a convincing Restoration play.

The 'Elizabethan' play, presented via a couple of key scenes and a summary of the plot, is equally convincing. The plot is meant to be representative of the convolutions typical of the Elizabethan play in general, but it actually derives quite specifically from Shakespeare. A couple of the details bring to mind *As You Like It*, the false Duke undoubtedly suggested by Duke Frederick, and the princess disguised as a boy very possibly by Rosalind. But the latter detail could as easily be taken from *Cymbeline*, for the play was an old favourite of Woolf's and the dirge in it that is sung over the disguised princess is used extensively in *Mrs. Dalloway*. The provenance of the remainder of the plot is unquestionable: it is *Cymbeline*.

In *Cymbeline* Imogen plays the role of the boy Fidele and lives with her unrecognized brothers in a cave; in Woolf the parallel figure, Carinthia, was lost in a cave. In *Cymbeline* the heir to the throne and his brother were stolen from the court by their nurse, and the heir is recognized twenty years later by a mole on his neck; in Woolf the heir, Ferdinando, was 'put into a basket as a baby by an aged crone' about twenty years ago, and is now recognized by the mole on his arm (88–91). In *Cymbeline*, when the old retainer who raised the king's sons returns them to their father, he blesses them with these words: 'The benediction of these covering heavens | Fall on their heads like dew!' In Woolf a priest blesses Carinthia and Ferdinando: 'Let Heaven rain benediction!' (92). The echo ensures the positive air of dramatic romance that Woolf aimed at in the 'Elizabethan' play, and the entire plot is skilfully contrived to that end.

The atmosphere of *Between the Acts* shifts frequently, at times light-hearted and good-humoured, as in the upbeat ending of the Elizabethan play, at times quite the reverse. The many parallels with *Cymbeline* might be extrapolated to the novel as a whole. Giles and Isa Oliver like

Posthumus and Imogen are estranged through most of the two works, and perhaps there clings to the modern pair something of the fruitfulness promised the earlier pair. The parallel between the novel and the play to which Woolf frequently alludes lends some support to that hope.

But allusions to two other Shakespeare plays are certainly anything but positive, and they are to be found in the twentieth-century part of the pageant, the 'ten mins. of present time' (179). The setting for them is equivocal, a rain dispelling the aridity of our wasteland, but Isa is obsessed with suicidal thoughts. The question that Woolf asks is whether mankind will be able to rebuild civilization after the devastation of the Second World War. The nursery rhyme of the king in his counting house betokens prosperity, and the swallows seem to dance to its music. But the swallows, says the narrator, may be martins, 'temple-haunting martins' (182), and immediately one thinks of the deceptiveness of the natural scene in *Macbeth*, which the doomed Banquo misreads as a sign of gentleness. Woolf reminds the reader of regicide by going on to quote a line from Macbeth's soliloquy uttered directly before he does the deed: 'Is this a dagger which I see before me?' (185). It is therefore difficult to believe in the hope offered by the King in his counting house.

Nor can the audience face the future with any illusions about its own powers. When the actors hold the mirrors up to them, as Hamlet insists all actors do, they are shown to be broken people. A voice asks '. . . *how's this wall, the great wall, which we call, perhaps miscall, civilization, to be built by* (here the mirrors flicked and flashed) *orts, scraps and fragments like ourselves?*' (188). The words are taken from another of Shakespeare's plays which reveals the moral collapse of people under pressure—this time *Troilus and Cressida*. After eavesdropping on Cressida when she decides to betray him and capitulate to the importunate Diomede, Troilus complains to Ulysses that

> The fractions of her faith, orts of her love,
> The fragments, scraps, the bits and greasy relics
> Of her o'er-eaten faith, are given to Diomed.

The repulsive metaphor served Woolf as it did the idealistic Troilus because she too feared that few decent impulses would survive the war.

In a series of allusions to *King Lear* Woolf most eloquently voices that fear. She does not select those lines that emphasize man's potential for greatness, but rather alludes to words of insanity or feigned insanity.

Twice she recalls Edgar's decription to his blinded father of one of his five fiends' grimaces, Flibbertigibbet's 'mopping and mowing' (86, 184). She alludes to Lear's 'Look, look, a mouse', said in his madness in the presence of Poor Tom and the blinded Gloucester—in *Between the Acts* taking the form of 'And see! There's a mouse', one of the lines of Albert, the village idiot (87). Twice Woolf quotes the king's statement to Cordelia, from a scene she considered one of the greatest in literature, after he comes out of the worst of the madness: 'I fear I am not in my perfect mind' (85, 185), language she once called 'simple as a child's', and full of pathos. Another line singled out in her earliest recorded reading of the play is recalled in the novel. The description of the Revd Mr Streatfield as 'an irrelevant forked stake in the flow and majesty of the summer silent world' (191) owes something to the mad Lear's description of Edgar, nearly naked and feigning madness: 'unaccommodated man is no more but such a poor, bare, fork'd animal.'

The bleak tone created by all of these allusions to insanity in *King Lear* is sustained by several references to the deaths of major characters in the same play. Isa with her habitual morbidity thinks of two of these, one when she hears a butterfly beating on the window pane, 'repeating that if no human being came, never, never, never,' it would die (17)—Lear when he realizes that his beloved Cordelia will never come back to life, never. And again, at the 'Elizabethan' play, when Carinthia and Ferdinando are united, Isa says, 'It was enough. Enough. Enough' (91). This repeated word always struck Woolf as Shakespearian (*L.* 2003, 17 Feb. 1929; *L.* 2254, 16 Oct. 1930), so vividly did she recall Gloucester's assurance that he would 'bear affliction till it do cry out itself enough enough and die'. And like Gloucester, in *Between the Acts* the aged crone, 'because that was enough, had sunk back on her chair,' lifeless (92–3). The disembodied narrative voice comments on the action, 'Peace, let her pass' (93), echoing Kent's words on the death of Lear.

In *Between the Acts* Woolf alludes to some fifteen plays by Shakespeare, some in passing, some, like *Hamlet* and especially *King Lear*, insistently. By the end of her life she had read and re-read the plays, had referred to them with increasing familiarity in both fiction and non-fiction, and was able to reach out for the apposite allusion without strain. From the start, in *The Voyage Out* and even earlier, *The Tempest* had been a particularly rich source of ideas and images, and it too would be invoked in *Between the Acts*. Woolf sensed 'what a rage and storm of thought' had passed over Shakespeare's mind as he wrote the play (*D.* 9

May 1934), and she believed that the setting of a desert island lent itself to reflections on 'society and the soul' ('Robinson Crusoe'). Allusions to the play would do the same, as those in *The Voyage Out* and *The Years* do. In addition, two passages from *The Tempest* that were often in Woolf's mind stimulated her over the years to ever more complex uses. One was Ariel's song to Ferdinand, 'Full fathom five thy father lies'; the other was Prospero's words to Ferdinand and Miranda after the masque of the three goddesses:

> Our revels now are ended. These our actors
> (As I foretold you) were all spirits, and
> Are melted into air, into thin air,
> And like the baseless fabric of this vision,
> The cloud-capp'd tow'rs, the gorgeous palaces,
> The solemn temples, the great globe itself,
> Yea, all which it inherit, shall dissolve,
> And like this insubstantial pageant faded
> Leave not a rack behind. We are such stuff
> As dreams are made on; and our little life
> Is rounded with a sleep.

The reasons for her fascination with Prospero's speech are evident: the vividness of its images of cloud-capped towers and gorgeous palaces, and the eloquence of its expression of 'the profound melancholy of death. When we think of English literature of the Renaissance, she said, 'we think not only of a pageant, but of the sleep that rounds it' ('Venice' 6).

It is fitting that Woolf used a pageant in a novel dealing with the threatened end of civilization, and that the language from time to time recalls Prospero's words. Wyatt ('Art' 99) points out that Woolf uses Prospero's language for 'the finished pageant of Miss La Trobe too: "a cloud that melted into the other clouds on the horizon . . . the triumph faded" '; and that 'finally pageant and world become identified in their transcendence: "Sitting in the shell of the room she watched the pageant fade. The flowers flashed before they faded." ' With England constantly under the threat of invasion while Woolf was completing the novel, and the bombing already begun, the world seemed as transient as a pageant.

In the last year of her life Woolf's sense of an ending became intimately tied up with Shakespeare. She thought often of *King Lear*, and remembered the last scene in which the Fool appeared. He tried to calm the deranged king, saw the blinded Gloucester, heard the wild words of the disguised Edgar, endured the mock trial of Goneril and Regan. Finally, when the mad Lear says, 'We'll go to supper i' th' morning,' the Fool leaves, never to appear again, but, clever to the end, answers, 'And I'll go to bed at noon.' Those words were in her mind when she thought about the possibility of Hitler's invading England, and the plan she and Leonard had made for suicide, gasoline stored in the garage for that purpose. 'I don't want to go to bed at midday: this refers to the garage' (*D*. 9 June 1940). The important thing was to try to become absorbed by something she loved to do: 'I would like to find one book and stick to it. But can't. I feel, if this is my last lap, oughtn't I to read Shakespeare? But can't. I feel, oughtn't I to finish off [*Between the Acts*]: oughtn't I to finish something by way of an end?' (*D*. 22 June 1940).

She did finish *Between the Acts*, and she did read Shakespeare. As the bombs dropped on London she realized how privileged she had been in contrast to the working classes, for 'we, after all, have at least been to Italy and read Shakespeare' (*L*. 3644, 11–12 Sept. 1940). The reading was a joy, and Woolf venerated the man as others might worship God. Once she had to resist the temptation of capitalizing the personal pronoun: 'I almost put a capital H, and that is rather my feeling' (*L*. 3055, 1 Aug. 1935). When, finally, she was 'reading the whole of English literature through', contemplating a third book of critical essays should the war allow her to finish, she was grateful that she had a 'taste for reading'. At the moment she was 'in the 16th Century', and she could imagine with some equanimity that 'by the time I've reached Shakespeare the bombs will be falling. So I've arranged a very nice last scene: reading Shakespeare, having forgotten my gas mask . . .' (*L*. 3685, 1 Feb. 1941). Like Othello, like her own Clarissa Dalloway, if it were then to die, 'twere then to be most happy. In her last lap she would be reading Shakespeare, thereby holding in her mind, as she had held in every one of her novels, the best of England.

Elizabeth and the Renaissance

WHILE Woolf read Shakespeare and the other Renaissance writers to the end of her life, her knowledge of the time that produced them was uneven, gleaned more from the literature itself than from a study of political, social, or cultural history. Her aim was the enhancement of her ability to read the literature 'as currently and certainly' as she read contemporary works, and to write about it with some accuracy. She knew that without some background she was likely to be 'sham Elizabethan' (XI. 20), to create a 'fancy picture' of Renaissance life bearing little resemblance to the reality (*CE* iii. 32), thereby distorting her evocations of the times in both her criticism and her fiction.

Although every one of her novels alludes to Renaissance literature, only one—*Orlando*—is actually set, in its earlier pages, in Elizabethan times, and only one—*The Voyage Out*—harks back to those times, and that quite briefly. The Elizabethan setting of one part of *The Voyage Out* gained its authenticity by Woolf's reading of a primary source, Sir Walter Raleigh's 'The Discoverie of . . . Guiana'.

A different problem arose in the writing of *Orlando*, whose hero is a young man during the actual reigns of Elizabeth and James. Many details about the time came from Vita Sackville-West's history of Knole. But Woolf needed more than a credible architecture: she needed a picture of real Jacobean life into which she could place Orlando. As was true of her procedure in getting necessary background for *The Voyage Out*, she turned to a text written at the time, one she also knew very well from earlier reading. The work was Thomas Dekker's rare pamphlet about the terrible winter of 1608, a tract virtually unknown before its publication in one of Woolf's favourite anthologies, Edward Arber's *An English Garner*. So frequently did Woolf read these volumes that she eventually had to repair and rebind the set, and she even prepared her own index to works she especially enjoyed (MHP/B2g). One entry is to 'Frost, great. 1608.' Dekker describes the frozen

Thames and also devotes a couple of pages to the effects of the extreme cold in the north of England.

Woolf found many details in Dekker, the elaboration of which makes the Jacobean segment of *Orlando* especially vivid. She probably took from Dekker the January setting; and perhaps his mention that Russia and Moscovia that year were 'more extremely and more extraordinarily afflicted than usually they have been' (97). Woolf's northern scene back in England, with its heavy 'mortality among sheep and cattle' and its concern for shepherds and 'ploughmen' (33–4), can be documented in Dekker; but she overgoes her source in her account of the 'bird-scaring boys all struck stark in the act of the moment, one with his hand to his nose, another with the bottle to his lips, a third with a stone raised to throw at the raven who sat, as if stuffed, upon the hedge within a yard of him' (34). Dekker's account of 'a couple of friends shooting on the Thames with birding pieces [who] . . . struck a sea-pie or some other fowl' (Arber i. 86), vivid though it is, lacks Woolf's panache. She ends her account of the northern scene with an amusing yarn of 'the solidification of unfortunate wayfarers who had been turned literally to stone where they stood'. 'Factual' to the end, she thereby accounts for the large number of rocks in the Peak District (34).

Woolf's King James orders 'a park or pleasure ground' to be set up on the frozen Thames. In Dekker the citizens of London enjoy various sports on the frozen river, buy drinks and fruits, and in general turn 'the goodliest river in the whole kingdom into the broadest street to walk in' (85). The Thames 'is a very pavement of glass, but that it is more strong' (82); in *Orlando* 'though of singular transparency, [the ice] was yet of the hardness of steel' (35). And the same difficulties that one finds in Dekker persist in *Orlando*. Dekker shows concern for the poor because of the fuel shortage (87), and Woolf sends an old country woman out to gather 'what sticks or dead leaves she could find for firing' (44); in Dekker, London is 'cut off from all commerce' (86), and in Woolf 'the trade of the country was at a standstill' (34); Dekker pities the poor fish 'when their houses are taken over their heads' (82), and Woolf fixes her fish in the ice, 'motionless in a trance' (36).

But the details she found in Dekker of which she made best use were these: that 'costermongers' sold their wares to those who wanted to dine on the Thames, and that some people sank to the bottom of the river, 'that never rose again to the top (85–6). Woolf combined these two facts, unrelated in Dekker, to produce this little gem:

Near London Bridge, where the river had frozen to a depth of some twenty fathoms, a wrecked wherry boat was plainly visible, lying on the bed of the river where it had sunk last autumn, overladen with apples. The old bumboat woman, who was carrying her fruit to market on the Surrey side, sat there in her plaids and farthingales with her lap full of apples, for all the world as if she were about to serve a customer, though a certain blueness about the lips hinted the truth. (36)

Some details of the happenings on Woolf's frozen Thames are of course her own, as for example the gorgeous sunset silhouetting the London skyline. The entire description of the courtiers is non-Dekkerian; from Woolf's imagination, fed by a variety of books over the years, come the statesmen in beards and ruffs, the soldiers planning 'the conquest of the Moor and the downfall of the Turk', the admirals straight out of Hakluyt 'telling stories of the north-west passage and the Spanish Armada'. Life on the frozen Thames takes on the brilliance of a painting:

Lovers dallied upon divans spread with sables. Frozen roses fell in showers when the Queen and her ladies walked abroad. Coloured balloons hovered motionless in the air. Here and there burnt vast bonfires of cedar and oak wood, lavishly salted, so that the flames were of green, orange, and purple fire. (35)

The combination of the most obvious fantasy with material the reader can sense to be true conveys the unique pleasure of the earlier parts of this book. Rarely does Woolf make a factual mistake (her Jacobeans should not be dancing a quadrille (43)), and when she creates the fabulous it is as a superimposition upon something 'real' learned from her long acquaintance with the literature in general.

But again and again behind Woolf's Great Frost is Dekker's. The night of Orlando's intended flight with Sasha owes much of its credibility to Dekker's discussion of the effects of a 'sudden thaw [overcoming] this sharp frost' (90). He ends his pamphlet with a wonderful account of a 'merry' accident that occurred just as the thaw was beginning. A man and his two dogs were stranded on a 'floating island' when 'the flake of ice [i.e. iceberg] upon which he stood was in a moment sundered from the main body of the frozen Thames': 'The poor man, perceiving that his ground failed under him, began to faint in his heart [and] . . . was afraid to stir. and yet unless he did lustily stir for life, he was sure there was no way but one, and that was to be drowned.' But he could not leap on to other passing icebergs for

to have done so, had been to have slipped out of one peril into another. Nothing was before his eyes but water mingled with huge cakes of ice. On every side of him was danger and death . . . Being therefore thus round beset with the horrors of so present a wreck, he fell down on his knees, uttering such cold prayers as in this fear a man could deliver.

With his dogs romping around him, the man prayed until he was driven right up to London Bridge, where both he and his dogs found safety (98–9).

Woolf sets up her description of the thaw with Dekker's in mind. As in Dekker the thaw is sudden—overnight—and the river strewn with icebergs that travel quickly downstream. As in Dekker, Woolf's narrator comments that

what was the most awful and inspiring of terror was the sight of the human creatures who had been trapped in the night and now paced their twisting and precarious islands in the utmost agony of spirit. Whether they jumped into the flood or stayed on the ice their doom was certain.

Some are trapped in clusters, or, worse, 'a solitary wretch would stride his narrow tenement alone'. Some fall on their knees to pray, 'crying vainly for help, making wild promises to amend their ways, confessing their sins and vowing altars and wealth if God would hear their prayers' (62–3). Woolf spells out what Dekker had hinted in more general terms, as she does throughout this section. She contrives a spirited effect, employing some verbal echoes (iceberg as 'island', for example) to achieve something of Dekker's amused tone.

In an obscure pamphlet by Thomas Dekker, then, Woolf found the inspiration for some of her liveliest writing in *Orlando*. Although it is true that Hakluyt, Browne, Bacon, and Raleigh tower over the other writers of Renaissance prose in Woolf's estimation, throughout her life she made briefer excursions into the works of a surprisingly varied company, and Dekker was among them (she would go on to quote a passage from *The Wonderful Year* in her essay on Donne in the second *Common Reader*). The giant figure of Shakespeare was always at the centre of the age, but not to the exclusion of Spenser or Marvell or Herrick or Herbert, of Marlowe or Jonson or Webster or Ford. The variety and magnificence of the literature convinced Woolf that the Renaissance was an age of unlimited possibilities, for both action and expression.

Frequently she speculated about the reasons behind such a flowering, once advancing the theory that 'a sense of the presence of the Gods' provided Elizabethan writers with a firm basis for their lives. While religious literature did not rank high in Woolf's priorities, she was at least conversant with some of the sermons of the period, and with both the King James version of the Bible and the *Book of Common Prayer* (from which she quotes in *The Years* 85, 229). Thus it was that she understood what she kept encountering in the plays: she became convinced that, despite the enormous differences in the varied dramatic output of the age, there was a common contempt for the world and a belief in the certainty of eternal rest with God. She said that it would be ridiculous to discount the importance of these attitudes and to assume 'that a whole literature with common characteristics is a mere evaporation of high spirits, a money-making enterprise, a fluke of the mind which, owing to favourable circumstances, came off successfully' (*CE* i. 60). Even Woolf's parodies of the period's 'melancholy obsessions with Death, Fame, and the *vita brevis* are in effect a tribute to the abundant belief of an age in which men pursued values from which . . . we are detached' (Graham, 'Caricature' 356).

So their religion was an obvious asset to writers of the sixteenth and seventeenth centuries. But another asset which Woolf mentions more frequently when trying to understand the Renaissance in England is the age of the English language at that time, for it was still in its youth. Pomeroy has noticed Woolf's frequent use, in descriptions of Elizabethan literature, of the 'organic metaphors' of garden and wilderness, which 'convey her sense of language then in its green time, in its youth and fertility' (500). Modern English had just emerged and writers felt the boon of its boundless possibilities. Woolf imagined them reaching for new words as one pulls up riches from the sea (*CE* i. 50, 60). In that respect the Elizabethans resembled to Woolf's thinking present-day Americans, coining words as the need arose, and finding in already-existing words a newness undimmed by centuries of use. Woolf asked rhetorically 'Is our Georgian literature a patch on the Elizabethans?' and contended that the freshness of their language put the Elizabethans at an advantage (*CE* i. 21; ii.120, 249). The literally thousands of quotations in her reading notebooks attest to the vitality of language she found in these writers.

They were able to tap an enormous potential, and were capable of great eloquence, unlike twentieth-century writers, who 'cant attempt the Elizabethan grandiloquence because we haven't their scurrility & plain speech to match it' (xi. 20). Woolf was always jotting into her notebooks examples of the 'outspoken vigour of the abuse' found wherever she looked, in the plays (*Bartholomew Fair* provided several, as did Webster and Marlowe), in Harvey, in Donne, even in an Elizabethan textbook for the study of French (a draft review of

Hollyband and Erondell's *The Elizabethan Home* (see AEFR i. 95)). And her essays are full of examples of Elizabethan 'grandiloquence', which derive just as much as eloquence of abuse does from the pleasure writers took in their language. Everything was open to them.

The flowering of literature also became possible, Woolf believed, because the country itself was young. It was still undeveloped, the towns small and the distances between them large, so that books and the theatre answered a genuine need. Writers like Spenser and his friends discussed the possibilities of English as a literary language precisely because of 'the sense that broods over them of what is about to happen, of an undiscovered land on which they are about to set foot . . .' (*CE* iii. 37). That 'undiscovered land' was both metaphor and reality. She conceived of the mind of a sixteenth-century Englishman as virgin territory, a *tabula rasa* waiting to be 'written over', and this was one of the attractions she felt for the voyagers: 'It is their youth; it is their immense fund of credulity; their minds still unwritten over and capable of such enormous designs as the American forests cast upon them, or the Spanish ships, or the savages, or the soul of man . . .' (*CE* ii. 17). Given their extraordinary capabilities, the 'designs' traced upon their minds appealed to Woolf in their freshness and forcefulness.

Woolf had no illusions about the times. She knew that credulity was born of ignorance, and she knew about such things as the inadequacies of sanitation and personal hygiene, and the crowded conditions in London (*Orl.* 166). She took the plays at their word, and saw everywhere in Elizabethan life their danger, lust, brawlings, and violence (*Orl.* 224–5). But she could accept the negative side of the times because the good exceeded the bad by a considerable margin. It was a time, she said (slightly misquoting Tennyson, of 'free spacious days' (*L.* 3042, 7 July 1935), an age propitious to the full development of the extraordinary individual. When Woolf first read Fulke Greville's biography of Sir Philip Sidney, with its testimony to his playing roles of poet, soldier, statesman, and patron, his being a model for the good and great 'in life and action', she knew where much of the credit belonged: '. . . it is the virtue of the Elizabethan age, unless imagination is too partial, that such heroes should have space to expand there to their natural circumference, and men can stand back and gaze at them'. ('Philip Sidney'). And if this was true of Sidney, whose achievements were crowded into less than thirty years of life, how much more true was it of Sir Walter Raleigh, to Woolf's mind most representative of the age. Raleigh sailed to the new world, fought the Armada, was the friend of the best writers of his time, and himself wrote some of its best prose:

> Merely to read over the list of his pursuits gives one a sense of the space and opportunity of the Elizabethan age; courtier and admiral, soldier and explorer, member of Parliament and poet, musician and historian—he was all those things, and still kept such a curiosity alive in him that he must practise chemistry in his cabin when he had leisure at sea, or beg an old henhouse from the Governor of the Tower in which to pursue his search for 'the Great Elixir.' (*CE* iii. 27–8)

While Raleigh was the most representative figure of the Elizabethan age, Shakespeare obviously was its finest writer. He was one of the great facts of life, the 'light' of English literature; Woolf considered him 'the most completely articulate of men', the writer who could say everything through his characters (*Mrs. D.* Frag. 183; 'Anon.' 431). She attributed Shakespeare's skill in entering the minds of his characters to his androgyny: as is true of everyone, two powers presided in his brain; but in Shakespeare the two powers fused, and the result was a 'fully fertilised' mind which 'uses all its faculties' (*Room* 170–1). But in finding Shakespeare 'the type of the androgynous', she simply placed him at the pinnacle of an age which encouraged the full development of the 'womanly' side of the male brain. Of course in some writers the development was less impressive than in others (Donne's brain and Ben Jonson's leaned too much to the male side (99, 180)). But Woolf once asserted that Renaissance dramatists never 'make us feel that they are afraid or self-conscious, or that there is anything hindering, hampering, inhibiting the full current of their minds' (*CE* ii. 221). Once again, there was something about the age which nurtured the talents of its artists.

That Woolf recognized the failure of the age to nurture the talents of women is well known (Silver 8–9). In spite of the advantages of religious conviction and a fresh language available to all, some paths were simply closed to women (voyaging, for example, or education, or employment). Woolf contrasted Shakespeare's education and opportunities for development with those of a hypothetical sister, Judith, who did not go to the grammar school, and whose parallel flight to London ended in disaster (*Room* 83–4). Shakespeare himself, soon after arriving in London, 'got work in the theatre, became a successful actor, and lived at the hub of the universe, meeting everybody, knowing everybody, practising his art on the boards, exercising his wits in the streets, and even getting access to the palace of the queen' (81). These were the circumstances that, combined with 'the state of mind most favourable to poetry that there has ever existed' (88), made for the greatness of Shakespeare. These were also the circumstances that made it possible for the general run of the population to be 'capable of song or sonnet' (71).

Two points in Woolf's vision of Shakespeare in London deserve some attention, the first being that he knew everybody, that he practised his art on the boards, and exercised his wits in the streets. Woolf had first articulated the idea in a letter to the *New Statesman* in 1920 in response to Desmond MacCarthy's insistence on women's intellectual and creative inferiority. She asserted that, in contrast to Elizabethan women, Shakespeare was decently enough educated to enjoy the conditions necessary for the production of art, that is, being part of a group 'where art is freely discussed and practised', and having 'the utmost freedom of action and experience' ('The Intellectual Status of Women'). In the London taverns frequented by young writers she imagined that 'the talk would have been of the theatre, of the American voyages, & the possibilities of English literature, & how to import into it the music & splendour of Italy & Greece' (AEFR v. 11 (10 Sept. 1931)). Writers would have encouraged each other (as Marlowe does Shakespeare in *Orlando* (89)) or just engaged in stimulating shop talk (as she frequently imagined Ben Jonson and Shakespeare to have done (*CE* ii. 204; *3Gs* 150)). What critics there were were themselves writers, and shared the problems of others in a relaxed atmosphere removed from public glare and commercialism. Although the professional literary critic was just over the horizon (witness her Nick Greene, modelled in part on Robert Greene, in *Orlando*), the occasional quip of a Greene was as nothing compared with the daily opportunities for conversation with the best playwrights of the time.

The second part of Woolf's vision of Shakespeare in London was that it was possible to gain access to 'the palace of the queen'. It was very much the age of Queen Elizabeth, a figure for whom Woolf felt a fascination compounded of her love for the literature written during the reign or associated with it, and her admiration for (perhaps even identification with) another remarkable woman. Woolf was aware of the religious controversies of the time, and of Elizabeth's policies towards Scotland, Spain and Ireland. Even as a young woman Woolf had shown some interest in the era, and at fifteen she read Mandel Creighton's *Queen Elizabeth* (De Salvo in Marcus, *Virginia* 88). Later Greville's *Life* of Sidney provided a contemporary's account of Elizabeth's handling of parliament, the navy, the universities, and a variety of individuals and groups, and of her excellence in foreign affairs and trade.

Woolf's first published essay on the queen was a review (*TLS* 30 Dec. 1909, 516; repr. *B&P*) of Frank Mumby's *The Girlhood of Queen Elizabeth*, which gives a full account of the subject and prints original documents to tell the story. She also read at this time the account of Elizabeth in the *DNB* and the last volume of Froude's *History of England* by way of background. The review is of considerable interest because it reveals with clarity Woolf's values at the start of her own career. In a sense those values were tested and clarified by the differences between the evaluations of Elizabeth offered by her three sources: each took a different view of the earlier career of a woman whose later achievements were of course tied up in Woolf's mind with the most glorious period of English literary history.

The *DNB* account of Elizabeth, written by the headmaster and antiquarian Augustus Jessopp, meets the high standards set by his editor, Leslie Stephen. But Jessopp sought a female heart and was disappointed to find 'nothing, absolutely nothing, to show that Elizabeth had a heart, nothing to indicate that she ever for a moment knew the thrill of sentiment, the storms of passion, or the throbs of tenderness'. Such prose, and the underlying attitudes it betrays, was less satisfactory than Mumby's. Woolf was set on understanding Elizabeth's temperament since the queen's 'whims and qualities lay at the centre of the vast expansion of the Elizabethan age' (*B&P* 174). Woolf was especially impressed by his inclusion of the Bedingfield papers, which dealt with the imprisonment at Woodstock, whence she was moved after a couple of months in the Tower in 1554. She devoted a long paragraph to Elizabeth's behaviour at that time, and concluded that the 'cold and harsh feelings' universally ascribed to the queen were a necessary armour given the violence of the political machinations in which she was involved for the first twenty-five years of her life (176).

Elsewhere in the review Woolf continues to see Elizabeth from her own angle. Two points that emerge strongly from Mumby's treatment of the princess are her learnedness and her deliberate 'policy, if not her inclination, to cultivate a taste and reputation for piety and sedateness' (63). Although Woolf does not utterly fail to mention Elizabeth's piety, she soft-pedals it. She mentions that in Ascham's account of the sixteen-year-old Elizabeth there is evidence of the princess's enormous range of foreign languages (174–5), but fails to mention that Ascham also praised Elizabeth's achievements in 'religious instruction' (71). And in reporting Elizabeth's mention to Catherine Parr of 'godly learning', Woolf changes the word to 'goodly' (174). The small error probably sprang from the agnostic Woolf's natural sympathy for Elizabeth.

The tone of the review is indeed entirely sympathetic. Woolf skilfully draws on Froude to show that Elizabeth's months in the Tower during her sister Mary's reign made for a warmer Elizabeth: '. . . the memory of her unhappiness was bitter enough also to rouse in her the one "sustained and generous feeling" of her life; she showed, Mr Froude thinks, true pity for the Queen of Scots when, years afterwards, she too lay in prison' (Froude, *History* xii. 586; *B&P* 175). And so it goes throughout the review: Woolf is fair to Elizabeth, despite the princess's overbearing and argumentative qualities, and yet she does not in any major way distort Mumby's book. It was a source of information such as Woolf always valued, letters by and about a woman, and she read it in its entirety. The letters are often long-winded, yet she extracted from them the kernels of fact that she needed for an informed view of a lesser-known part of Elizabeth's life.

Material from Mumby's book and from other works Woolf read about Elizabeth during the early days of reviewing was to remain with her throughout her life. And issues raised in Mumby were to be called to the forefront again some twenty years later.

. . . her crowning virtuosity was her command over the resources of words. When she wished, she could drive in her meaning up to the hilt with hammer blows of speech . . . In private talk she could win a heart by some quick felicitous *brusquerie*; but her greatest moments came when, in public . . . the splendid sentences, following one another in a steady volubility, proclaimed the curious workings of her intellect with enthralling force . . . The tall and bony frame was subject to strange weaknesses. . . . intolerable headaches laid her prone in agony . . . Though her serious illnesses were few, a long succession of minor maladies, a host of morbid symptoms, held her contemporaries in alarmed suspense and have led some modern searchers to suspect that she received from her father an hereditary taint. Our knowledge, both of the laws of medicine and of the actual details of her disorders, is too limited to allow a definite conclusion, but at least it seems certain that, in spite of her prolonged and varied sufferings, [she] was fundamentally strong . . . she took a particular pleasure in standing up . . . most of her ailments were [probably] of an hysterical origin. That iron structure was prey to nerves. The hazards and anxieties in which she passed her life would have been enough in themselves to shake the health of the most vigorous; but it so happened that . . . there was a special cause for a neurotic condition: her sexual organisation was seriously warped.

This account, which includes the 'excitement, terror, and tragedy' of its subject's early childhood, goes on to mention the behaviour of a man in his early thirties, a senior family member, who tickled and fondled his fourteen-year-old relative, producing in her 'a deeply seated repugnance to the crucial act of intercourse . . .'.

Is this an analysis, oversimplified and overheated, of Virginia Stephen Woolf? No, despite the great similarities to her life, the description is taken from Lytton Strachey's account of Queen Elizabeth in his *Elizabeth and Essex* (18, 19–20, 21, 24). The similarities would not have been lost on Woolf, nor would the tawdriness of treatment have pleased her. In fact, for a number of reasons the book alienated her: 'I disliked Lytton for writing Q. Eth. I remember' (*D.* 16 Nov. 1931). Certainly his steamy account of Elizabeth and Seymour was repugnant. It was at one extreme, the *DNB*'s at another, an eminently Victorian view of Seymour, whose familiarities were 'wholly inexcusable towards a young lady whom he had actually offered to make his wife . . .'. Although Elizabeth was 'in some way implicated', her servants' confessions were 'hearsay stories, backstairs gossip, and all the vulgar tattle of waiting-maids and lackeys', and she exonerated herself handily, icily above the 'delight' that Lytton Strachey imagined. In Mumby's book Woolf found yet another view of the matter, midway between the others and probably the closest of the three to the truth: that Seymour had taken liberties, though probably 'nothing worse than unseemly romping', and that he 'seems to have kindled a spark of real affection' in Elizabeth because of her 'parentage and precociousness' (37–8).

When Woolf had reviewed Mumby's book she mentioned Elizabeth's 'serious flirtation' with Seymour, but was not really concerned about it one way or the other. Far from belabouring what she called Elizabeth's 'precocious love-making' Woolf found matter for sympathy in an area on which Mumby had not thought to comment: 'Yet, though Elizabeth was forward enough according to her governess, it seems pitiable that a girl of that age should have her feelings made the subject of inquisition by a council of noblemen' (174). Years later, when Strachey elaborated on the bedroom scenes with details of his own invention, and decided that Elizabeth had been 'delighted', it must surely have struck Woolf as another sitting of that council.

Strachey's tendency to dwell on the parts of Elizabeth's life and character which bear some similarity to Woolf's, coupled with his facile attempts at psychology, certainly would have estranged her. Once over lunch Strachey had quoted Elizabeth's letter to an ambassador: ' "Had I been crested and not cloven you would not have dared to write to me thus." "Thats style!" I cried. "It refers to the male and female parts" he said' (*L*. 1621, 17 Feb. 1926). After such a warning, and such condescension, Woolf expected something cheap, and not a careful consideration of the feminist implications of the queen's spirited statement. She was not wrong. Here is a sample of Strachey in *praise* of Elizabeth:

Only a woman could have shuffled so shamelessly, only a woman could have abandoned with such unscrupulous completeness the last shreds not only of consistency, but of dignity, honour, and common decency, in order to escape the appalling necessity of having, really and truly, to make up her mind. Yet it is true that a woman's evasiveness was not enough; male courage, male energy were needed . . . (13)

It is difficult tb discover beneath this cliché-ridden and antifeminist description the fact of Elizabeth's brilliant management of public affairs. Woolf felt that Strachey had 'palmed off' on the world a 'lively superficial meretricious book' (*D*. 28 Nov. 1928), and could not even broach the subject with him, for 'the spectre of Queen Elizabeth stands between us' (*L*. 2002, 15 Feb. 1929).

It is clear that Woolf believed Elizabeth to be worth more than cheap effects. As she said when reviewing Mumby's book, the qualities of this woman 'lay at the centre of the vast expansion of the Elizabethan age'. Also in 1928, but before Strachey's book, Woolf published 'Waxworks at the Abbey', about the wax effigy of Elizabeth at Westminster Abbey, commissioned by the chapter to mark the bicentenary of the queen's grant of a charter to found the Collegiate Church at Westminster. By showing how the effigy dominates the Islip Chapel, Woolf emphasizes the political clout of the woman who 'once dominated England' (*CE* iv. 205); and by means of well-chosen details she reveals her driving force of character:

It is a drawn, anguished figure, with the pursed look of someone who goes in perpetual dread of poison or of trap; yet forever braces herself to meet the terror unflinchingly. Her eyes are wide and vigilant; her nose thin as the beak of a hawk; her lips shut tight; her eyebrows arched; only the jowl gives the fine-drawn face its massiveness. The orb and sceptre are held in the long thin hands of an artist, as if the fingers thrilled at the touch of them. She is immensely intellectual, suffering, and tyrannical. She will not allow one to look elsewhere.

The waxwork of Elizabeth takes on the status of art, for it is a 'presence' which seems to control the Abbey's 'incoherence' (206). Two things are noteworthy about Woolf's description of the effigy: the first is the remarkable amount of drama compressed in few words, and the second is that Woolf hints at an androgynous quality in the queen, physically represented in the waxwork by 'fine-drawn' features and a massive jowl.

Woolf had long conceived of Elizabeth in this way. In an essay written in 1919 she contrasted the stiffness and fragility of the queen, imagined she thought from 'some tinted waxwork', with the 'masculine and rather repulsive vigour' of her rapping out her favourite oath, 'God's Death'. She thought that the masculine side might predominate: 'Perhaps, under all that stiff brocade, she has not washed her shrivelled old body? She breakfasts off beer and meat and handles the bones with fingers rough with rubies' (*CE* ii. 17). This is the same 'rather repulsive' figure Woolf conjured up a year later, the queen not only 'a model of vigour', but also 'a dirty old woman, dabbling her fingers in the gravy, and amenable, one supposes, to pains and pleasures only of the most direct kind' (*CW* 113). Woolf's gaze was unflinching, but it is clear that, whether or not she saw the 'masculine' side of the queen as repulsive (and by the time of the waxworks essay she did not), it was a necessary balance to the 'feminine' side. The combination produced just enough of a hint of androgyny to suggest a kinship with the great writers of the age.

Orlando, written with the same *jeu d'esprit* (and in the same year) as 'Waxworks at the Abbey' draws on the same vision of the queen. Orlando sees the 'memorable hand' of Queen Elizabeth,

a thin hand with long fingers always curling as if round orb or sceptre; a nervous, crabbed, sickly hand; a commanding hand; a hand that had only to raise itself for a head to fall; a hand, he guessed, attached to an old body that smelt like a cupboard in which furs are kept in camphor; which body was yet caparisoned in all sorts of brocades and gems; and held itself very upright though perhaps in pain from sciatica; and never flinched though strung together by a thousand fears; and the Queen's eyes were light yellow. (22)

There may be a bit of mustiness attached to this version of the queen, but she has the same power, opulence, and courage that make up her portrait in the essay. Elizabeth looks down at Orlando with eyes that 'were always, if the waxworks at the Abbey are to be trusted, wide open' (23), a sign of vigilance and endurance. The waxwork of the queen seemed truer to Woolf when she wrote both essay and novel than Strachey's overwrought, imbalanced, often inaccurate and superficial portrait.

Yet Woolf continued over the years to work out the problem of her friend's failure in *Elizabeth and Essex*, for her opinion of him actually rose when she read biographies by others (letter 3146a in Banks 190–1). In 'The Art of Biography', which Woolf wrote seven years after Lytton Strachey's death, she suggested that the insufficiency of *Elizabeth and Essex* could be ascribed more to the nature of biography itself than to the nature of the biographer. 'Strachey's quest for a 'tragic history' in the story of Elizabeth and Essex was bound to be frustrated since too little was known about that aspect of Elizabeth's life for a 'straight' biography, while at the same time too much was known for a purely imagined one (*CE* iv. 224–5). Moreover, such an emphasis must necessarily distort the portrait, for, as Woolf maintained in another context, it is odd for women to be seen 'only in relation to the other sex. And how small a part of a woman's life is that; and how little can a man know even of that when he observes it through the black or rosy spectacles which sex puts upon his nose' (*Room* 143). In *Orlando* Woolf sketched a picture of Elizabeth as both lover and head of her country, for to omit the latter would be to neglect the most important thing that could be said about the queen.

When Woolf does treat Elizabeth 'in relation to the other sex', the man is not Essex but Orlando, a reflection of whose Sackville 'ancestry' allows Woolf to suggest that love was used in the service of the state. On a progress, for example, Elizabeth cements her ties with Orlando's family, giving the estate to Orlando, and winning in return his services some time after 'on a sad embassy' to Mary Queen of Scots (25). The narrator of *Orlando* is satirized for believing (with unnamed others) that in a woman's biography we may 'waive our demand for action, and substitute love instead' (268). The queen in *Orlando* is at the heart of the action, always aware of 'the sound of cannon . . . the glistening poison drop and the long stiletto . . . the guns in the Channel', all of which form 'the dark background' against which Orlando's 'innocence [and] simplicity' shine (23). All the offices, honours, lands, and houses that Elizabeth lavishes on Orlando—the gifts of an enamoured woman—also ensure his willingness to serve the crown in a variety of capacities, as he does from her reign through that of Charles II.

Elizabeth's brilliance in winning the loyalty of her courtiers was matched in Woolf's mind by her active role in the voyages of discovery. Woolf had been reading about it since she was a child, and, with reviews in mind, taking notes from as early as the first decade of the century. She gathered a great deal of material on the voyagers of the sixteenth century, and on Elizabeth as the monarch whose men went down to the sea in ships, some to be captured, some to die, some to return home laden with stories and treasure, both of which they shared with the queen. The material redounded to the queen's credit, showing both her political astuteness and the kind of loyalty she inspired. Pirates were unacknowledged by the queen if they were captured, but, if they returned with loot, 'the crown would gladly accept a share in the spoil . . . It is surely a high tribute to Elizabeth, and to the trust and love she inspired in her subjects, that they accepted these conditions without a murmur' (Raleigh 66; MHP/Bla, 146). This sort of positive association of the queen with the voyagers sounds in Woolf's essay on the Elizabethan Sir Walter Raleigh.

Such links between Elizabeth and the voyagers were thus firm from the start. But one, forged very possibly as early as Woolf's first reading of Hakluyt's *Voyages*, in 1897, but demonstrably no later than the re-reading of 1918, remained in Woolf's mind with a peculiar tenacity thereafter, to the end of her days, like one of her 'moments of vision'. It is from Frobisher's first voyage to the Northwest, in 1576, which begins thus:

The 8. day being Friday, about 12 of the clocke we wayed at Detford, and set saile all three of us, and bare downe by the Court, where we shotte off our ordinance and made the best shew we could: Her Majestie beholding the same, commended it, and bade us farewell, with shaking her hand at us out of the window. (iii. 52–3; MHP/B2d, 28)

The scene would recur in Woolf's imagination over the years. In a draft of 'The Elizabethan Lumber Room' written in January of 1925 it appears in the opening paragraph, where Woolf says that to read the volumes of Hakluyt 'is to set out in one of those little ships which were no bigger than a nobleman's yacht', in the company of 'men who might have seen Shakespeare, who had seen Elizabeth waving her hand when they raised anchor at Greenwich . . .' (*Mrs. D. Corr.* 107). That was how Woolf most remembered the queen, waving to the voyagers as they set out on their travels. She believed that Elizabeth, 'of all our kings and queens, seems most fit for that gesture which bids the great sailors farewell, or welcomes them home to her presence again'. More than any other British monarch, Elizabeth, 'lusting for the strange tales' of the voyagers, was young in imagination (*CE* ii. 17), like her own subjects and of course like Woolf herself.

When Woolf envisaged Elizabeth 'at the centre of the vast expansion of the Elizabethan age', she pictured someone who not only inspired others, but also set the pace for them. As Froude acknowledged in the *History*, in a passage from which Woolf had extracted another quotation early in her career, Elizabeth 'had a proper contempt . . . for idle luxury and indulgence. She lived simply, worked hard' (583), at uniting a country torn by religious conflict, at establishing an advantageous position for her country, politically and financially, among the nations of Europe. She exemplified Woolf's belief that queens enjoyed a special kind of happiness, made up of 'work and independence' (*3Gs* 204), power and wealth, and the attitudes and activities they make possible. In *Orlando* she drew on an historically accurate anecdote to illustrate the meeting of all these traits in Queen Elizabeth, who once stood in the library of Orlando's house

astride the fireplace with a flagon of beer in her hand, which she suddenly dashed on the table when Lord Burghley tactlessly used the imperative instead of the subjunctive. 'Little man, little man . . . is "must" a word to be addressed to princes?' And down came the flagon on the table . . . (235)

(Woolf once cast herself in the role of Queen Elizabeth in this scene, to Nelly Boxall's Burghley (*D*. 3 Jan. 1924).) The scene embodies many traits that she found in the queen, not just her independence, but also her imperiousness, the expression in bearing and habits of her androgynous mind, and her dedication to work—here discussing important matters with her secretary of state while on one of the many progresses by which she bound to herself the nobles and commoners of England.

The pageant in *Between the Acts* calls forth many of the same characteristics of the queen that are evident in *Orlando*. Both emphasize the hard-working aspect of Elizabeth. In *Between the Acts* the point is made by the queen's being portrayed by a muscular working woman, Eliza Clark, 'licensed to sell tobacco' (a commodity introduced into England during Elizabeth's reign). As in *Orlando*, there is about the queen a masculine vigour: Eliza 'could reach a flitch of bacon or haul a tub of oil with one sweep of her arm in the shop'. As in *Orlando*, there is a sense of Elizabeth as head of state, '*the Queen of this great land*', '*Mistress of pinnacles, spires and palaces*'. She is surrounded by an aura of power: like the picture of the queen fronting Raleigh's *English Voyages of the Sixteenth Century*, Mrs Clark's Elizabeth looks gigantic as she stands, 'eminent, dominant . . . with the blue and sailing clouds behind her' (83). And like the picture of Elizabeth always in Woolf's mind, the queen is associated with the voyagers:

> Mistress of ships and bearded men
> Hawkins, Frobisher, Drake,
> Tumbling their oranges, ingots of silver,
> Cargoes of diamonds, ducats of gold,
> Down on the jetty, there in the west land—

All the accounts in Hakluyt inform this passage and validate the 'contentment' Woolf envisages at its end, *'As home from the Isles came | The sea faring men . . . '* (84–5).

On a sheet among the papers written during Woolf's last year of life (TS hol. fragment of 'Anon.' 8ᵛ) is this heading: 'People one would have liked to have met'. But there is only one entry. I shall quote it in its entirety:

Queen Elizabeth. Not face to face; but with a pane of glass between us. [Not in her palace; but] At Greenwich: [pacing up & d] The first word wd be awkward About the Tower perhaps. The 2nd

It is not difficult to complete the thought, for the location, at Greenwich, brings to mind Woolf's moment of vision. Her conversation with the queen—after some discussion of Elizabeth's use of power—would be about the voyagers. The queen, part patron, part audience, part muse, had listened to the stories of the seafaring men.

Elizabeth's speech introducing her part of the pageant also points to her connection with *'warrior and lover, | The fighter, the singer'* (84), for she was their patron/audience/muse as well. But apart from the Armada, Woolf herself never showed any great interest in 'warriors'. She has Queen Elizabeth keep Orlando from battle, 'for how could she bear to think of that tender flesh torn and that curly head rolled in the dust?' (25). Woolf preferred the allegorical battles in the *Faerie Queene* to the real thing, and even they became tiresome after she had read for a while. William Browne's 'Sirens' Song', with its vision of love and rest after battles and wanderings, suited Mrs Ramsay, just as Woolf opted to discuss Sir Walter Raleigh's meditations upon life and death rather than his account of a battle.

Such meditations were the staple of Elizabethan literature. The following typical stanza is from a poem Woolf prized:

> His golden locks time hath to silver turned:
>   Oh, time too swift, oh, swiftness never ceasing!
> His youth 'gainst time and age hath ever spurned,
>   But spurned in vain; youth waneth by increasing.
> Beauty, strength, youth, are flowers but fading seen;
> Duty, faith, love, are roots, and ever green.

Woolf used the conventional Elizabethan image of a fading flower for the passage of time in *Between the Acts* (95), and when she needed an image for the transition to the peace and reason of the eighteenth century, she found exactly what she wanted in the poem whose first stanza I have just quoted, which is taken from George Peele's *Polyhymnia*. Peele's poem describes a tournament held in honour of Queen Elizabeth's birthday, its best-known segment the song about Sir Henry Lee, who at sixty was too old to take part in the tournament. Popularized in Thackeray's *The Newcomes* and often anthologized, it would have appealed to Woolf both because its opening stanza is a meditation on time and because the beautiful images of its second stanza glorify peace:

> His helmet now shall make a hive for bees,
>   And lover's sonnets turned to holy psalms,
> A man-at-arms must now serve on his knees,
>   And feed on prayers, which are age his alms
> But though from court to cottage he depart,
> His saint is sure of his unspotted heart.

As Sir Henry aged, the regalia of battle became instruments of peace and holiness. The opening line captures the idea perfectly (Woolf once quoted it to describe the tomb of Agamemnon (*L.* 2579, 4 May 1932)), and she evoked the first two stanzas of the song in the pageant of *Between the Acts*: as the centuries pass, and Queen Anne assumes the throne,

Time, leaning on his sickle, stands amazed . . . the armed warrior lays his shield aside; the heathen leaves the Altar steaming with unholy sacrifice. The violet and the eglantine over the riven earth their flowers entwine . . . And in the helmet, yellow bees their honey make. (123)

The lush passage, describing the reign of Queen Anne, takes its richness from an Elizabethan poem which was in fact dedicated to Queen Elizabeth (the 'saint' in the final line of poetry quoted above). Woolf may have been especially receptive to this poem because it showed the best side of Elizabeth, who, though queen of 'warrior and lover, | The fighter, the singer', was just as celebrated when the trappings of battle were laid aside. For participants and non-participants alike, Elizabeth was both audience and muse of the tournaments in her honour, and she took on the same functions for the poets who marked the occasion.

Elizabeth adopted these roles to some extent with all the writers of her time. But in the queen's speech that opens the 'Elizabethan' part of the pageant in *Between the Acts*, Woolf singles out just one: '*For me Shakespeare sang*' (84). This was the crucial fact about the queen. It was probably of less consequence to Woolf that she had ruled ably for close on to fifty years, directing affairs of state at home and abroad with a sure hand, commanding the loyalty of advisers, courtiers, nobles, and commoners. It was probably of less consequence that Elizabeth's courage, intelligence, imaginativeness, dedication, and capacity for hard work brought stability to her country. Elizabeth would be remembered most vividly and with the greatest affection because these conditions made it possible for Shakespeare to have flourished in her time.

Woolf forges the link between Elizabeth and Shakespeare most obviously in *Orlando*. When the great queen visits Orlando's magnificent home, and he is walking through its many corridors on his way to meeting her, he passes a poet sitting in the servants' quarters, in the throes of composition. This 'rather fat, rather shabby man, whose ruff was a thought dirty, and whose clothes were of hodden brown', is of course Shakespeare. Orlando assumes that Shakespeare's eyes are fixed on 'ogres, satyrs, perhaps the depths of the sea' (21), and years later it is the similarity of his own metaphors to such visions that persuades Orlando to write to please himself (101–3). Shakespeare is often in his/her mind, the 'earliest, most persistent memory' (163–4), and that memory is linked with 'old Queen Bess' (79), as it was from the start. The link persists to the present, when the Lady Orlando remembers the wonderful smells and rich booty of the ships in the time of Elizabeth (300–1), and is haunted by the vision of 'Sh—p—re (for when we speak names we deeply reverence to ourselves we never speak them whole)' (313).

As Elizabeth was Shakespeare's muse, so Shakespeare was Orlando's. The poem that Orlando wrote over the centuries was begun around the time of Shakespeare's visit, and grew and changed under his eyes. Now in 1928 the Lady Orlando is a prize-winning poet, having been shaped by all of her experiences and the deposit they laid in her mind, 'now Shakespeare, now a girl in Russian trousers, now a toy boat on the Serpentine, and then the Atlantic itself, where it storms in great waves past Cape Horn' (327). Close to midnight, and to Shelmerdine's arrival home, she sees 'a phantom castle upon earth', her ancestral home as it had been in Elizabeth's time: 'All was lit as for the coming of a dead Queen', and Elizabeth steps from her carriage, to be welcomed by Orlando (328).

Shakespeare and Elizabeth enter the twentieth century, then, in the person of the Lady Orlando. Miss La Trobe accomplishes the same feat in *Between the Acts*. Not only does Queen Elizabeth introduce the Elizabethan pageant, but that entire segment—play and audience—contains a number of allusions to Shakespeare. It was Woolf's way of 'boasting of the English descent from Shakespeare' (*CW* 135). In her own person she thus joins Miss La Trobe in bringing Shakespeare into the present, and in fact does so throughout the novel. The queen, the Elizabethan age, and its greatest exemplar are the heritage that was Woolf's and that she in turn handed over to her readers.

Bookworm that she was, she read all sorts of things, many of them works that others might miss. And mad about the Renaissance as she was, the poetry and prose and plays that she read were often drawn from the period. She had a good eye for material that she might use in her essays and fiction. Dekker's 'The Great Frost' comes to mind, a tract that Woolf had known for some time until, needing an authentic Jacobean scene, she had the good sense to use it in *Orlando*. And so the story goes, all of the novels enriched by her allusions to Renaissance literature. She was comfortable with these materials in her fiction, and over the years gained confidence in speaking of them in critical essays as well. Criticism had seemed a male prerogative, Elizabethan literature a male preserve, and Woolf was reticent about making forays into that area. But all of the forces that I have mentioned (chief among them her love of the literature and her need to 'prove her credentials') conspired to call forth a considerable body of criticism. Despite the fact that the bookworm never had the sun of Oxford and Cambridge, it turned into a granite-based butterfly.

BIBLIOGRAPHY

WORKS BY VIRGINIA WOOLF REFERRED TO IN THE TEXT

' "Anon" and "The Reader": Virginia Woolf's Last Essays', ed. Brenda Silver, *Twentieth Century Literature*, 25 (1979), 356–441.

Articles, essays, fiction, and reviews (Berg).

Between the Acts (New York: Harcourt-Harvest, 1941).

Between the Acts, typescript dated 2 Apr. 1938–30 July 1939.

Books and Portraits: Some Further Selections from the Literary and Biographical writings of Virginia Woolf, ed. Mary Lyon (London: Hogarth, 1977).

'Byron and Mr. Briggs', ed Edward A. Hungerford, *Yale Review*, 68 (1979), 321–49.

'Charlotte Bronte', *Times Literary Supplement*, 13 Apr. 1916, 169–70.

Collected Essays, ed. Leonard Woolf (4 vols.; New York: Harcourt, 1967).

Contemporary Writers, ed. Jean Guiguet (New York: Harcourt-Harvest, 1965).

The Diary of Virginia Woolf, ed. Anne Olivier Bell (5 vols.; New York: Harcourt, 1977–84).

'Dickens by a Disciple', *Times Literary Supplement*, 27 Mar. 1919, 163.

Early Notebooks: various holograph notebooks, dated 1897 and later (Berg).

'Experiences of a Pater-familias' in *A Cockney's Farming Experiences*, ed. Suzanne Henig (San Diego: San Diego State University Press, 1972).

'Friendships Gallery', ed. Ellen Hawkes, *Twentieth Century Literature*, 25 (1979), 270–302.

Holograph drafts (all at Berg except *Mrs. D.* and *Orlando*).

Holograph reading notebooks (Berg).

Holograph reading notes, Jan. 1909–Mar. 1911; at back of *Night and Day*, Chaps. 11–17, holograph draft.

'How it strikes a contemporary', *Times Literary Supplement*, 5 Apr. 1923, 221–2.

'How Should One Read a Book?' holograph, unsigned and undated.

'How Should One Read a Book?' [original version] *Yale Review*, 16 (Oct. 1926), 32–44.

'The Intellectual Status of Women', *New Statesman*, 16 Oct. 1920, 45–6.

Jacob's Room (New York: Harcourt-Harvest, 1923).

'Lady Fanshawe's Memoirs', *Times Literary Supplement*, 26 July 1907, 234.

The Letters of Virginia Woolf, ed Nigel Nicolson and Joanne Trautmann (6 vols.; New York: Harcourt, 1975–80).

Melymbrosia: An Early Version of The Voyage Out, ed. Louise De Salvo (New York: New York Public Library, 1982).

Moments of Being: Unpublished Autobiographical Writings, ed. Jeanne Schulkind (New York: Harcourt, 1976).

Monday or Tuesday (New York: Harcourt, 1921).

Monk's House Papers (Sussex).

Mrs. Dalloway (New York: Harcourt, 1925).

Mrs. Dalloway (corrections). Holograph, in notebook dated 22 Nov. 1924 (Berg).

Mrs. Dalloway. Fragments (Berg).

Mrs. Dalloway, holograph, British Library Additional MS 51,044.

Mrs. Dalloway, holograph, British Library Additional MS. 51,046.

Night and Day (New York: Harcourt-Harvest/HBJ, 1920).

'On Being Ill' [original version], *New Criterion*, 4 (Jan. 1926), 32–45.

Orlando: A Biography (New York: Harcourt-Harvest/HBJ, 1928).

'The Pargiters' (8 vols.; holograph draft (Berg)).

'Philip Sidney', *Times Literary Supplement*, 31 May 1907, 173–4.

'Pure English', *Times Literary Supplement*, 15 July 1920, 453.

'Robinson Crusoe', *Nation and Athenaeum*, 6 Feb. 1926, 642.

'Romance', *Times Literary Supplement*, 18 Jan. 1917, 31.

A Room of One's Own (New York: Harcourt, 1929).

'Sir Thomas Browne', *Times Literary Supplement*, 28 June 1923, 436.

'Sir Walter Raleigh', *Times Literary Supplement*, 15 Mar. 1917, 127.

'Small Talk about Meredith', *Times Literary Supplement*, 13 Feb. 1919, 81.

Three Guineas (New York: Harcourt, 1938.

To the Lighthouse (New York: Harcourt, 1927).

'Trafficks and Discoveries', *The Speaker*, 11 Aug. 1906, 440–1.

'Trafficks and Discoveries', *Times Literary Supplement*, 12 Dec. 1918, 618.

'Venice', *Times Literary Supplement*, 7 Jan. 1909, 5–6.

The Voyage Out (New York: Doran, 1920; New York: Harcourt-Harvest, 1948).

The Waves (New York: Harcourt-Harvest/HBJ, 1931).

The Waves: The Two Holograph Drafts, ed. J.W. Graham (Toronto: University of Toronto Press, 1976).

Women and Writing, ed. Michele Barrett (New York: Harcourt-Harvest/HBJ, 1979).

The Years (New York: Harcourt-Harvest/HBJ, 1937).

OTHER WORKS CITED

ALBRIGHT, DANIEL, *Personality and Impersonality: Lawrence, Woolf and Mann* (Chicago: University of Chicago Press, 1978).

ARBER, EDWARD (ed.), *An English Garner* (8 vols.; London: E. Arber, 1877–96).

BALDANZA, FRANK, 'Orlando and the Sackvilles', *PMLA*, 70 (1955), 274–9.

BANKS, JOANNE TRAUTMANN (ed.), 'Some New Woolf Letters', *Modern Fiction Studies*, 30 (1984), 175–202.

BAZIN, NANCY TOPPING, *Virginia Woolf and the Androgynous Vision* (New Brunswick: Rutgers University Press, 1973).

BELL, BARBARA CURRIER, and CAROL OHMANN, 'Virginia Woolf's Criticism: A Polemical Preface', *Critical Inquiry*, 1 (1974–5), 361–71.

BELL, QUENTIN, *Virginia Woolf: A Biography* (2 vols.; New York: Harcourt-Harvest, 1972).

BOYD, ELIZABETH FRENCH, *Bloomsbury Heritage: Their Mothers and their Aunts* (New York: Taplinger, 1976).

BRANDES, GEORGE, *William Shakespeare: A Critical Study* (2 vols.; London: Heinemann, 1898).

COLERIDGE, S.T., *Coleridge's Shakespearean Criticism*, ed. Thomas Middleton Raysor (2 vols.; Cambridge: Harvard University Press, 1930).

COMSTOCK, MARGARET, ' "The current answers don't do": The Comic Form of *Night and Day*', *Women's Studies*, 4 (1977), 153–71.

DE SALVO, LOUISE A., 'Sorting, Sequencing, and Dating the Drafts of Virginia Woolf's *The Voyage Out*', *Bulletin of Research in the Humanities*, 82 (1979), 271–93.

_____'Virginia Woolf's Revisions for the 1920 American and English Editions of *The Voyage Out*', *Bulletin of Research in the Humanities*, 82 (1979), 338–66.

DIBATTISTA, MARIA, *Virginia Woolf's Major Novels: The Fables of Anon* (New Haven: Yale University Press, 1980).

FAREWELL, MARILYN R., 'Virginia Woolf and Androgyny', *Contemporary Literature*, 16 (1975), 433–51.

FLEISHMAN, AVROM, *Virginia Woolf: A Critical Reading* (Baltimore: Johns Hopkins University Press, 1975).

FOX, ALICE, 'Literary Allusion as Feminist Criticism in *A Room of One's Own*', *Philological Quarterly*, 63 (1984), 145–61.

FROUDE, JAMES ANTHONY, *English Seamen in the Sixteenth Century* (London: Longmans, 1918).

_____ *History of England from the Fall of Wolsey to the Defeat of the Spanish Armada* (12 vols.; New York: Scribner's, 1890), vol. xii.

GOLDMAN, MARK, 'Virginia Woolf and the Critic as Reader', *PMLA*, 80 (1965), 275–84.

GORDON, LYNDALL, *Virginia Woolf: A Writer's Life* (Oxford: Oxford University Press, 1984).

GRAHAM, JOHN, 'The "Caricature Value" of Parody and Fantasy in *Orlando*', *University of Toronto Quarterly*, 30 (1961), 345–66.

_____'Manuscript Revision and the Heroic Theme of *The Waves*', *Twentieth Century Literature*, 29 (1983), 312–32.

HAKLUYT, RICHARD, *Hakluyt's Collection of the Early Voyages, Travels, and Discoveries of the English Nation* (5 vols.; London: R. H. Evans, 1809–12).

HARVEY, GABRIEL, *The Works of Gabriel Harvey*, ed. Alexander Grosart (3 vols.; London: Huth, 1884).

HILL, KATHERINE C., 'Virginia Woolf and Leslie Stephen: History and Literary Revolution', *PMLA*, 96 (1981), 351–62.

HOFFMANN, CHARLES G., 'Fact and Fantasy in *Orlando*: Virginia Woolf's Manuscript Revisions', *Texas Studies in Language and Literature*, 10 (1968), 435–44.

HOLROYD, MICHAEL, *Lytton Strachey* (2 vols.; London: Heinemann, 1968).

_____ *Lytton Strachey: A Critical Biography* (2 vols.; London: Heinemann, 1967).

HOLTBY, WINIFRED, *Virginia Woolf: A Critical Memoir* (1932; Chicago: Academy-Cassandra, 1978).

HYMAN, VIRGINIA R., 'Late Victorian and Early Modern: Continuities in the Criticism of Leslie Stephen and Virginia Woolf', *English Literature in Transition (1880–1920)*, 23 (1980), 144–54.

LAING, DONALD A., 'Virginia Woolf's Account of Roger Fry's Early Career as a Writer', *Virginia Woolf Miscellany*, 14 (1980), 2.

LEASKA, MITCHELL (ed.), *The Pargiters: The Novel–Essay Portion of* The Years (New York: New York Public Library and Readex, 1977).

_____'Virginia Woolf, the Pargeter: A Reading of *The Years*', *Bulletin of the New York Public Library*, 80 (1977), 172–210.

LENZ, CAROLYN R. S., Gayle Greene, and Carol Thomas Neely (eds.), Introduction, in *The Woman's Part: Feminist Criticism of Shakespeare* (Urbana: University of Illinois Press, 1980).

MAITLAND, FREDERIC WILLIAM, *The Life and Letters of Leslie Stephen* (London: Duckworth, 1907).

MARCUS, JANE (ed.), *New Feminist Essays on Virginia Woolf* (Lincoln: University of Nebraska Press, 1981).

_____ *Virginia Woolf: A Feminist Slant* (Lincoln: University of Nebraska Press, 1983).

McLAURIN, ALLEN, *Virginia Woolf: The Echoes Enslaved* (Cambridge: Cambridge University Press, 1973).

MEISEL, PERRY, *The Absent Father: Virginia Woolf and Walter Pater* (New Haven: Yale University Press, 1980).

MUMBY, FRANK, *The Girlhood of Queen Elizabeth: A Narrative in Contemporary Letters* (London: Constable, 1909).

NASHASHIBI, PAULINE R., 'Alive and There: Virginia Woolf's Presentation of Reality', *Dutch Quarterly Review*, 7 (1977), 184–99.

PACEY, DESMOND, 'Virginia Woolf as a Literary Critic', *University of Toronto Quarterly*, 17 (1947–8), 234–44.

PATRIDES, C. A., 'The Achievement of Edmund Spenser', *Yale Review*, 69 (1980), 427–43.

POMEROY, ELIZABETH W., 'Garden and Wilderness: Virginia Woolf Reads the Elizabethans', *Modern Fiction Studies*, 24 (1978–9), 497–508.

QUINN, D. B., 'Hakluyt's reputation', in *The Hakluyt Handbook*, ed. D. B. Quinn (2 vols.; London: Hakluyt Society, 1974), vol. i.

RADIN, GRACE, *Virginia Woolf's* The Years: *The Evolution of a Novel* (Knoxville: University of Tennessee Press, 1981).

RALEIGH, WALTER, *The English Voyages of the Sixteenth Century* (Glasgow: MacLehose, 1906).

ROSENBAUM, S. P., 'An Educated Man's Daughter: Leslie Stephen, Virginia Woolf and the Bloomsbury Group', in Patricia Clements and Isobel Grundy (eds.), *Virginia Woolf: New Critical Essays* (London: Vision and Barnes and Noble, 1983), 32–56.

RUBENSTEIN, ROBERTA, 'Orlando: Virginia Woolf's Improvisations on a Russian Theme', *Forum for Modern Language Studies* (St Andrews, Scotland), 9 (1973), 166–9.

SANDERS, CHARLES RICHARD, *Lytton Strachey: His Mind and Art* (New Haven: Yale University Press, 1957).

SCHAEFER, JOSEPHINE O'BRIEN, *The Three-fold Nature of Reality in the Novels of Virginia Woolf* (The Hague: Mouton, 1965).

SCHLACK, BEVERLY ANN, *Continuing Presences: Virginia Woolf's Use of Literary Allusion* (University Park: Pennsylvania State University Press, 1979).

——'The Novelist's Voyage from Manuscripts to Text: Revisions of Literary Allusions in *The Voyage Out*', *Bulletin of Research in the Humanities*, 82 (1979), 317–27.

SILVER, BRENDA R., *Virginia Woolf's Reading Notebooks* (Princeton: Princeton University Press, 1983).

STEPHEN, LESLIE, *Studies of a Biographer* (4 vols.; London: Duckworth, 1902).

STRACHEY, JAMES (ed.), *Spectatorial Essays* (New York: Harcourt, 1965).

STRACHEY, LYTTON, *Elizabeth and Essex: A Tragic History* (New York: Harcourt, 1928).

——'A Poet on Poets', *Spectator*, 3 Oct. 1908, 502.

ULLMANN, S. O. A. (ed.), *Men, Books, and Mountains* (Minneapolis: University of Minnesota Press, 1956).

WELLEK, RENE, 'Virginia Woolf as Critic', *Southern Review*, 13 (1977), 419–37.

WOOLF, LEONARD, Introduction, *Hours in a Library* (New York: Harcourt, 1957.

—— *Sowing* (London: Hogarth, 1960).

—— and James Strachey (eds.), *Virginia Woolf and Lytton Strachey Letters* (New York: Harcourt, 1956).

WYATT, JEAN, 'Art and Allusion in *Between the Acts*', *Mosaic*, 11 (1978), 91–100.

——'The Celebration of Eros: Greek Concepts of Love and Beauty in *To the Lighthouse*', *Philosophy and Literature*, 2 (1978), 160–75.

—— *Mrs. Dalloway*: Literary Allusion as Structural Metaphor', *PMLA* 88 (1973), 440–51.

ZWERDLING, ALEX, *Virginia Woolf and the Real World* (Berkeley: University of California Press, 1986).

INDEX

Works studied and cited will be found under their titles.